Résumés Don't Get Jobs

The Realities and Myths of Job Hunting

Bob Weinstein

McGraw-Hill, Inc.

New York   San Francisco   Washington, D.C.   Auckland   Bogotá
Caracas   Lisbon   London   Madrid   Mexico City   Milan
Montreal   New Delhi   San Juan   Singapore
Sydney   Tokyo   Toronto

About the Author

Bob Weinstein is a nationally known and respected journalist and trendwatcher in the career field. He is the author of eight highly acclaimed books on careers, including *Jobs for the 21st Century, 20 Ways to Be More Creative in Your Job, How to Get a Job in Hard Times,* and *How to Switch Careers.*

Library of Congress Cataloging-in-Publication Data

Weinstein, Bob.
    Résumés don't get jobs : the realities and myths of job hunting /
Bob Weinstein.
        p.   cm.
    Includes index.
    ISBN 0-07-069143-6 (hard : acid-free paper).—ISBN 0-07-069144-4
(pbk. : acid-free paper)
    1. Job hunting.   I. Title.
HF5382.7.W443   1993
650.14—dc20   93-17340
                                                                    CIP

    4 5 6 7 8 9 0   DOC/DOC   9 9 8 7 6 5

ISBN 0-07-069143-6 (HC)
ISBN 0-07-069144-4 (PBK)

The sponsoring editor for this book was James Bessent, the editing supervisor was Jane Palmieri, and the production supervisor was Pamela A. Pelton. It was set in Palatino by McGraw-Hill's Professional Book Group composition unit.

Printed and bound by R. R. Donnelley & Sons Company.

Contents

Acknowledgments

There were hundreds of valuable sources who helped me put this project together. Unfortunately, I don't have the space to name them all, but I will single out a few deserving special attention: My editor, Jim Bessent, for fine-tuning my concept with constructive criticism; friend and colleague Tom Popp for tightening the prose and keeping me targeted throughout the long year it took to report and write the book; Victor Lindquist, director of Northwestern University's Placement Center in Evanston, Illinois, for explaining what real networking is all about; my wife, Bonnie, and my children, Jenny and Josh, for always believing in me; and last but by no means least, T. Pete Bonner, my high school buddy and collaborator, for never disappointing me.

Bob Weinstein

"Résumés over there."

For Bonnie

Prologue: *"The Times They Are A-changin'"—Bob Dylan*

Chapter Snapshot

- ☐ Tough Road Ahead
- ☐ Plug Into the Corporate Grapevine
- ☐ Survival of the Fittest
- ☐ The "Organization Man" Is Dead
- ☐ The Pain of Starting Over
- ☐ Profits Are More Important Than People
- ☐ Return of the Frontier Work Ethic
- ☐ Welcome to the Real World
- ☐ Job Hunting, Then and Now

❊ ❊ ❊ ❊ ❊ ❊ ❊ ❊

Think of this book as a one-stop job information source. Sort of like the Sears for job-hunting tips. I'm selling job-hunting tips, strategies and a philosophy for the 1990s and beyond. It's a new world calling for a new game plan. Career experts are still preaching the same old tired advice that went out with prop planes. Like everything else, information and advice must be updated. Old paradigms have to be discarded for new ones. Like a business constantly improving its product or service to stay competitive, I have molded my advice to today's market. It's fresh, timely, honest—and it works.

You're facing a scary job market—maybe the toughest ever. There are jobs to be had, but the new twist is there are fewer of them with more competition for each. Finding a job calls for strategy, timing and shrewd maneuvering. According to the U.S. Department of Labor, the average job seeker will spend 20 weeks looking for work, almost 4 weeks more than it took in the early 1990s.

Many of the job-hunting strategies you've been taught are myths. It's high time they were debunked.

1

Tough Road Ahead

Forecasters at Data Research Sources/McGraw-Hill project that payrolls will grow an average of 1.1 percent a year in the 1990s, compared with 1.7 percent in the 1980s. For the past three decades, banks, fast-food restaurants, hospitals, law firms, retail chains and government offices, better known as the service sector, have fueled job growth. During the 1980s, services added a whopping 21 million jobs and employed almost four out of five workers. Americans assumed that demand for service workers would continue well into the 1990s.

The unexpected happened. Except for health care, the service industries are in the throes of a pervasive shake-up very much like the one that racked smokestack manufacturing a decade ago. The concerted drive to squeeze costs and improve profits has resulted in extensive cost cutting, job freezes, layoffs, consolidations and takeovers. Although service companies are likely to generate almost all the remaining jobs outside of health care, they will do so at less than half the rate of the 1980s. Additionally, auto, steel and textile manufacturers, some of the most expansive and competitive parts of the economy, are pruning payrolls as well.

The future? Most economists expect the great U.S. job machine, even after it revs up again, to run at just half speed through the rest of the decade. And job security—the comfortable expectation of being able to settle down somewhere for life, one hopes by middle age—may be gone for good.

Plug Into the Corporate Grapevine

What does it take to get a job today? Shrewd maneuvering along with a new attitude about career and self. Corporate America is no longer the bastion of security it was in the past. Hence, job seekers have to be tough, resilient, flexible—even entrepreneurial. Hardly more than a decade ago, you could practically crawl into a womblike corporate cubicle and hide out from 9 to 5, doing the same job year after year. Now, hiding out is not only practically impossible, it's also dangerous. It's only a matter of time before you're deemed a useless organizational sponge and are given the proverbial boot.

Getting a job is tough enough, holding onto it is equally challenging. One thing is certain: Once a job is conquered, you can't sit back and let the organization take care of you. If you're smart, plug into the information power lines as soon as you're part of the computer network. Find out how the system works, who to trust and who is potentially dangerous. Work toward being an information reservoir. Find out who wields power and how the decision-making process works; separate the fast-trackers from the slackers.

Survival of the Fittest

Corporations are societies in microcosm. They're made up of cliques, groups, subgroups and power groups; they have their own bylaws and customs. In a word, they're complex, with a sea of difference separating appearance and reality. You can't be lazy or indifferent to your corporate culture. Complacency is a precursor of corporate atrophy.

Don't naively think you can blindly throw yourself into your work and turn off everything else. With corporate America reshaping itself around you, this behavior could mark the beginning of your end. The system could crumble beneath you and you'll be the last to know about it. It's survival of the fittest. If you're wired to the grapevine, you stand a fighting chance of jumping ship before it sinks, taking everyone with it. In short, know more than your job.

The "Organization Man" Is Dead

What does it take to find that great job and board the roller coaster bounding toward a fulfilling career? Strength, resilience and hard work. It requires a street-fighter mentality. Start the job hunt knowing no organization will take care of you. The "Organization Man" is officially dead. Organizational security is a thing of the past. In the '40s, '50s, '60s and '70s, workers prided themselves on organizational loyalty. Their identities merged with their companies. For good reason. Most companies took good care of their people, offering secure futures and pleasant lifestyles all rolled into one. Lifetime security was taken for granted. Workers repaid their companies with hard work and blind faith.

The Myth of Lifetime Security

By the mid-1980s, fantasies of climbing organizational ladders shattered. The world had changed. The economy took a nose dive as new overseas markets emerged. With the official launching of the European common market in 1992, plus the privatization of several Eastern European and Latin American companies, competition for world markets intensified. At home, the U.S. corporation was already under siege. Bloated from dead weight and suffering from overcapacity and competition from cheap imports, profits steadily plummeted.

For the first time, corporations faced big trouble. The only solution: either shed unnecessary fat or perish. So much for corporate loyalty. To lighten its payrolls, Corporate America invented a frightening new word—*downsize*. So began a new era, the downsizing of corporate America. Millions of loyal workers' dreams of lifetime security were shattered as corporations changed their game plans. The speedy dismemberment of the U.S. corporation signalled the dawn of a new era.

A Superstar Casualty List

When IBM exiled thousands of workers to early retirement in the early '90s, it marked the official start of a new corporate age. Big Blue's "no fire" policy had been a bulwark of corporate paternalism. The number of U.S. corporations that followed IBM's lead by cleansing their ranks reads like a blue chip list of top U.S. corporations. Cut, slash, chop! Eastman Kodak, Xerox, TRW, General Motors, American Express, and Digital Equipment Corporation, to name only a few, have lightened their payrolls by hefty percentages. And within a space of a couple of years, retail giants the likes of R.H. Macy & Co. (251 stores), Federated Department Stores (140 stores), Allied Stores (82 stores), Carter Hawley Hale Stores (88 stores), Revco D.S. (1,141 unit drugstore chain), Ames Department stores (371 stores), and Hills Department Stores (154 stores) filed for bankruptcy protection. And white-collar jobs were being eliminated at the rate of 2,600 per day, according to some economists.

Suddenly, shocked and unprepared workers found themselves in the cold, ill-equipped to fend for themselves. Many deluded themselves into thinking the layoffs were temporary. It was like a bad dream—but worse. The former employers never intended to rehire those laid off. These cuts were permanent; workers' lives were abruptly forced to take a new turn. Like a ship tossing heavy cargo overboard so it could complete a dangerous voyage on little fuel, companies are similarly discarding excess human baggage to survive. And they are doing it with machinelike precision in every city in the nation.

The Pain of Starting Over

No longer could workers amble through careers as one-dimensional specialists, cogs in cumbersome corporate machinery. Survival depended upon learning how the whole engine worked. Workers were forced to adopt a new mindset and start over. For the first time, they had to see themselves as self-sufficient, mobile commodities capable of maneuvering in a tough world with new rules. American workers had to toughen up, learn new skills, broaden their horizons, and see beyond the moment. Sadly, most were unprepared. As corporations aggressively cut staffs throughout the '80s and early '90s, most workers found themselves floundering in an uncertain sea.

Naturally, many Americans were less than bullish about the future. Blinded by loss and fear, displaced employees couldn't see beyond their pain; they couldn't visualize better things ahead. They didn't realize they were standing at the foothills of a new age, unprepared for change. After being coddled and mothered by smothering corporations, they lacked basic coping skills. Many didn't even have a résumé, much less know the first thing about job hunting.

Profits Are More Important Than People

Bewildered and confused, displaced employees couldn't understand how their surrogate corporate parents could abandon them. Adrift on unfamiliar seas, most didn't know the first thing about charting a new course. But let's be practical. Real life doesn't read like a TV sitcom episode of "Father Knows Best" or "Family Ties." This is business, and *profits are more important than people.*

Out of guilt, fear of bad press and a tinge of loyalty to its severed workers, corporations retained outplacement firms to teach former employees job-finding skills. It's no small wonder the outplacement business bolted to more than a $640 million niche industry in almost three decades. Outplacement firms hired human resource professionals and industrial psychologists, some with Ph.D.s affixed to their names, to teach rudimentary career basics to people who had forgotten how to look for a job. Advice ranged from strategic job market insights to high-priced hand-holding.

Return of the Frontier Work Ethic

As Corporate America redefines and realigns itself, we've returned to a "frontier" work ethic. Like it or not, Americans have no choice but to tap their survival skills and test the elements. The job-finding tactics used by our parents and grandparents no longer work. The same goes for most of the career advice dished out by college career advisors. Safe and secure behind the tenured walls of academia, what do most college advisors know about pounding the pavement, the subtleties of networking and the secrets of scoring points on interviews? They're still teaching students how to write chronological résumés, an exercise in futility. That's just one of many tired career myths I will debunk. Plain and simple, *résumés no longer work*. They were effective a decade ago, but not today.

College Degrees Are No Longer Meal Tickets

What worked for our predecessors no longer applies. I wrote this book to fill a void. The hundreds of dull, constipated books dishing out generic career platitudes are outdated. Even Richard Bolles's *What Color Is Your Parachute?* does not cut it any longer. That revolutionary career book, which debuted in 1970, is updated yearly, yet it still rambles on about helping job seekers find their true calling *without* imparting hard-nose street smarts about the current market.

Until the 1993 edition, Bolles made only slight changes every year. But even the heavily rewritten 1993 edition failed to capture the drama and tension of the present stormy market. Job seekers don't need long-winded and gimmicky maps, diagrams and artsy graphics. Entry-level or experienced, job hunters are not skipping off to a merry-go-round ride; they're revving up for the equivalent of an athletic event, a competitive joust with thousands of other highly qualified applicants. Bolles's singsong poetic style doesn't parallel the human drama being played daily on America's streets.

Thousands of bright people are graduating college and they're not finding jobs; veteran workers are being laid off and waiting months before latching onto new jobs. After six months of aggressively looking for a job, a 29-year-old man with a Ph.D. in sociology told me in an anguished voice: "I can't get a job in my field!" A month later, he landed a job with Federal Express delivering overnight packages. He was delighted to get it.

Americans Are Working Harder Than Ever

Those employed are working harder than they ever imagined. The U.S. Bureau of Labor Statistics reported that 22.8 percent of the nation's 87.4 million people with full-time jobs spend 49 or more hours a week on the job. A decade ago, only 17.7 percent worked that much. In *The Overworked American: The Unexpected Decline of Leisure*

(Basic Books), Juliet B. Schor, an associate professor of economics at Harvard University, pointed out that the myth of the four-day workweek projected by economists in the '50s has been blown to smithereens as Americans work harder and longer than ever before. Economists thought economic progress would surely result in a better lifestyle and early retirement for most Americans. Not so. A growing number of older workers, especially those fortunate enough to find new jobs after being fired because of a downsizing, are working into their mid-70s. Many Americans are putting in 14- and 16-hour work days just to break even. Forget about the luxurious extras. For the majority, this work translates to 60 to 90 minutes less sleep a night, says Schor, not to mention an increase in stress-related illness. Schor points out that many Americas are working themselves to death. By the time this century winds itself out, the situation could get worse. It's certainly not going to get better.

Welcome to the Real World

What's needed is not hand-holding but hard information and solid advice. Like Marsha Sinetar's *Do What You Love, the Money Will Follow* (Dell), Bolles makes job seekers *feel good* about themselves, but that's not what they need. My job is not to play therapist and tell job seekers everything is okay and that they're sterling people but to impart job-hunting realities and strategies. I am neither a job counselor nor a psychologist, but a career journalist who's observed career trends for two decades. I've written 10 career books and this is the best of the lot.

Unlike Bolles or Sinetar, I am not going to help you discover who you are or what you want to be. Career counselors have that down to a science. I never intended to write another "touchy-feely" '60s-style career-finding tome.

This book contains no cutesy pictures, artsy layouts or fancy type, nor exercises for discovering what fields turn you on or off. Simply, it's a down-and-dirty job-hunting guide. If you recently bought other job-finding books, grab the receipt and bolt to the store immediately to get your money back. Or take a loss and sell them back to the store at a discount. This is the only job-hunting book you'll need.

I've accomplished my goal if this book does nothing more than help you think and ask questions about yourself, the job-getting process and the meaning of a career. It's time to debunk tired career myths and prepare readers for the future. In short, provoke some fresh thinking.

I'm selling hard information—facts, strategies and observations—to help you land a job. No outlandish theory or philosophical observations about life. No recycled Eastern or ESTian formulas or New Age proclamations about success and happiness. I'm not rehashing career platitudes that have been passed down since Adam hacked his way through the forest searching for his first job, nor am I treating job hunting as if it were a visit to a root canal specialist.

Job Hunting, Then and Now

In the '60s and '70s job finding was easy. It was a straightforward process most of us went at casually. Nobody devoted a lot of time to it because we knew we'd get jobs. There were plenty of jobs, and it didn't take much effort to find one. In many fields, demand for people outpaced supply; in others, the economic variables were evenly matched, making job hunting easy.

A month or two after conquering our sheepskin, most of us were gainfully employed. Like throwing a ball in the air and knowing someone will catch it, we knew that by sending out a couple of dozen résumés, we'd get at least one bite. In those good old days, job hunting didn't require a massive time investment. Our goal was to get résumés out quickly, schedule interviews, then goof off the rest of the day.

Those days are over. Adopt my generation's attitude and you're playing Russian Roulette with your career. Today, job hunting requires the cunning of a military strategist and the energy of a professional quarterback.

The Best Game in Town—It's You Against Them

Yet despite hard times, job finding is easy—if you know what you're doing. Unfortunately, most of us put all our energy into preparing for a job. When it's time to look for one, we assume everything will fall into place by itself—like some career guru will descend from the sky and guide us to our dream job. And when the job hunt begins, we go about it as if it were an arcane process governed by axioms passed down from Aristotle himself.

Instead of looking at job finding as a deadly serious exercise governed by unyielding tenets, see the process as a sophisticated game. It's you against them. Play the game well and you stand to reap a great job, steady paycheck and some satisfaction thrown in. Play it brilliantly and you're priming yourself for the fast lane and the

American dream—wealth, power, prestige, respect and a $45,000 Corvette thrown in for good measure.

Creativity Wins—Mastering the Job Seeker's Hustle

Like any good game, there are many ways to play. If you're insightful and creative, you'll discover subtle nuances and new and better ways to get what you want. You'll find that traditional techniques work for some, not for all. The message is creativity wins. Employers are looking for creative job seekers who bring new thinking to the table. We're going to take a fresh look at job hunting, from appraising and negotiating the career maze to interviewing and networking to charting a realistic course.

It's time for a new approach—an open-minded, freewheeling attitude sparked by individuality, creativity and guts. The proof of the pudding will be faster results. Let's drop the jargon and computer-speak and put everything on the table so it's crystal clear.

Start with your feet firmly planted on the ground. Some of us find jobs immediately, but most will have to master the job seeker's hustle before they land one. In our present market, that's no small feat. It's tougher than ever out there, but like my Dad used to tell me, "You get what you put in." Put your minds and back to the task and you'll win.

Let's cut to the chase and find out what it takes to be streetwise.

Introduction: Career Reality 101: Survival Tactics for the '90S (Me Seller, You Buyer)

Chapter Snapshot

- The Myth of the Storybook Life
- Still Clinging to Old Values
- What Do You Mean I'm *"Redundant"*?
- Companies Don't Give a Damn
- Demystifying the Job Hunt—Employers Want Sizzle *and* Steak
- You Are *the* Product
- A High-Stake Game

* * * * * * * *

Three biggest employer lies:

1. You've got a future with us.
2. We're all one big happy family.
3. We take good care of our people.

Think seriously before working for employers who spit out any of the above clichés. Chances are they are lying. Back in the '50s and '60s, if an employer promised you a long and fulfilling career, you'd walk away feeling like you had the world locked up. "Wow! This is the place for me." Compare a company to a home and family and a string of cozy adjectives come to mind—sharing, fair, friendly, secure. Even cynical job seekers fell for the corporate spiel because there was a good chance the employer meant it. After all, they had at least a dozen relatives who would stake their lives on their companies. For them, a job meant more than a weekly paycheck, it was a lifestyle.

The Myth of the Storybook Life

Until the late '70s, the prototypical U.S. company took pride in caring for its people. It offered stock option plans, elaborate benefits packages, liberal vacation leave, promotions, yearly bonuses, as well as a smorgasbord of social gatherings. What more could you ask for? It was like a formula Hollywood movie of the mid-'50s. You left a loving, supportive home and joined a caring, supportive company. For many, it was indeed a storybook life.

Working for a company 30-plus years is not unlike being married. Instead of contending with one person, you deal with a cadre of familiar faces and predictable routines, schedules and demands. Depending on your point of view, it provided either utopia or mental suffocation.

Are You Sure You Want a Gold Watch?

We've all heard stories about family members working umpteen years for a company that repaid them with a retirement package, gold-plated watch and a bargain-counter farewell party replete with budget champagne and cheap beer.

The stories strike familiar chords. Those were the good old days, they say. But were they? Certainly, they were secure, but for many, they were boring as hell. Imagine doing the same thing every day for over 40 years? Those are the best years of your life. And your most productive years to boot. Almost half a century. For what? Company loyalty, peace of mind, a steady paycheck, pension, the proverbial gold watch and a company bash?

If relatives were honest, they'd recast the situation and tell you it wasn't any bed of roses. What about the silly corporate politics they had to endure, not to mention incompetent bureaucrats whose necks were permanently out of alignment from years of looking over their shoulders? They probably repressed the times they considered tossing in the towel and heading to the Adirondacks to run a little business of their own—maybe a restaurant or specialty store. They figured anything was better than reentering that cell of an office and clapping eyes on an office-full of disgruntled, burned-out bureaucrats reeking of Old Spice and Chanel No. 5. The endless days of monotonous work broken with metallic-tasting coffee at 10:30 a.m., a tasteless lunch at 12:30, another coffee at 3:30, Maalox at 4:30 and finally freedom at 5:15. For many, it was a study in endurance. After putting in 15 or more years, they're unwilling to brave the job market wilds and take their chances.

For good reason. They've logged in pension time and earned bonuses often based on seniority and corporate ranking. "Where else am I going to cut a deal like this?" they ask themselves. Maybe they're right. And what about the friends they've made? The company is like a worn, cozy blanket we wrap around ourselves in front of a fire.

"Happy Hour" and Boredom

Maybe I overdramatized it, but the sad fact is the above scenario is still being replayed a million different ways in companies from East Lansing, Michigan, to Durham, North Carolina. No wonder "happy hour" has become an American institution. It signals the completion of—and escape from—another boring day.

An old high school buddy of mine is a case in point. When we were juniors and seniors we talked often about our career goals. I knew I wanted to be a journalist, but I didn't have the foggiest idea how to break into the field. My friend, however, had the world locked up. Like his father and brother, he planned on doing a two-year Army stint and then getting a job in a bank. His father joined a bank when he was 19 and left 47 years later at 66.

My buddy followed in his dad's footsteps except that he got a college degree before enlisting in the Army. Then he enrolled in a bank's executive training program and proceeded to climb the long middle-management ladder one tired rung at a time. A year ago, he was put out to pasture after logging in 23 years with a major Chicago bank. At a paunchy and ashen age of 50, he had the attitude and outlook of a 75-year-old. After earning some $65,000 a year as an assistant branch manager, he left the bank with a more than $200,000 pension plus six months' severance pay. Perfunctorily he talks about finding something else to do, but he is in no hurry. The family balance sheet is solid. He still thinks he has the world locked up.

When pressed, he admits the chances of taking another bank job are rare indeed. He's fed up with terminally boring work routines, aggravated by the frustration of morning and evening rush hour. Now he watches old movies until 3 a.m., wakes up at 11 a.m., shaves every other day, enjoys leisurely breakfasts and looks forward to extended cocktail hours at his favorite watering hole—incentives enough for not returning to his old lifestyle. For now, he's content. It remains to be seen whether vegetating will hold the same allure two years down the road.

My friend and thousands like him are soon to be vestiges of a turning-point work era. "You say your dad held one job his entire career?

Incredible! How did he swing that?" In another decade, you'll be hard pressed to find many workers who logged in even 15 or more years with one company. Alvin Toffler's "mobile society" is here. As corporations consolidate, the days of working for one company for most or all of our careers are fast disappearing.

Still Clinging to Old Values

Job-Hoppers Aren't Derelicts

If veteran workers are disoriented by what's happening, imagine how new entrants are taking it. The irony is that even though the job market has changed more in the past decade than it has in the past century, most of us still cling to old values. On one hand, we extol the rough-and-tumble virtues of the frontier—the uncertainty, individualism, every-man-for-himself ethic—yet we still put security, certainty and conformity on a pedestal. For many, the one-company job remains sacrosanct. Our parents told us it translated to a solid career; we believe it even though Corporate America is aggressively restructuring itself. The new reality is the "rah-rah everything-for-the-company" ethic that we were spoon-fed since we were kids isn't going to keep you permanently employed at one company.

No wonder you're uptight about stepping into this strange job market. No matter how you look at it, this market is like no other.

The U.S. Department of Labor's Bureau of Labor Statistics (BLS) reports that the average job seeker will have three to five jobs throughout his or her career and a significant number will change careers at least twice. And that's a pretty conservative reading. BLS economists are paid to be cautious. Economists at private think tanks offer a more realistic picture. They say the average job holder will change jobs every three years and have as many as 13 jobs throughout a career. And 1 in 10 will change careers four times throughout their lifetimes.

Yet our relatives warned us against job-hopping and career changing. A job-hopper was a few short steps away from a derelict, lacking grounding, stability, loyalty or direction. And career changers asked for trouble by turning their lives upside-down midstream. Responsible people stick with their jobs—even though they hate them. If something was wrong, the individual, not the company, was at fault. That's military thinking—"Do what you're told and don't ask questions."

Today, job-hopping is more than a career-building strategy, it is a survival tactic. The best way to advance your career is by changing jobs.

Security Isn't All It's Cracked Up to Be

The message is loud and clear: Don't put the prior generation's work ethic on a pedestal. Yes, there are clear advantages to certainty, security and long-term employment. But there are limitations as well, uppermost being frustration, lethargy, boredom, atrophy—even premature death. Constant change, on the other hand, keeps you razor sharp. Except for the post-Depression years, no other job market has been marked with so much excitement, tension, challenge—and *opportunity*. Sure it's tough out there, but this environment also brings enormous rewards and satisfaction beyond your wildest imagination—if you make it.

What Do You Mean I'm *"Redundant"*?

What makes this job market different from other job markets? There are no guarantees. Even if a company promises you promotions, perks, travel, take the promises with a grain of salt. The person making the promises may be out tomorrow. The company may suddenly lose market share or profits may plummet. New and better products from foreign competitors may force it to retrench and overhaul its product line; the company may be gobbled up by a larger company, or it may pare operating costs by dumping 30 percent of its staff.

If a dapperly dressed human resource executive (they used to be called personnel directors before they gained respectability) smiles and tells you you've been "excessed," or rendered "redundant" because of massive corporate retrenching and budget realignments, don't mistakenly think you've been given keys to the executive washroom. You've been axed, canned, dumped—you know, fired! You've been asked to empty your desk and take a permanent hike. The telephone number he hands you is not a new client but the outplacement company retained to help you rebuild your career.

Companies Don't Give a Damn

Corporate communications departments, speaking in corporatespeak, tell us companies are "running lean and mean," stripping unnecessary fat and shedding unwieldy middle-management layers in order to fatten their bottom lines. When you translate all that gobbledygook, you're left with the unwritten subtext: Most companies don't really give a damn about you. Their unspoken credo is "profits over people." But when you're hired, you'll hear the proverbial corporate song-and-dance about how people are the company's greatest asset. My favorite line: "We take care of our people." Some companies do because they honestly care. Many others just say so because it's good public relations. But when it comes to eliminating a percentage of a work force, it pays to be careful and ethical or else mighty lawsuits, not to mention nasty press, follow. This is America, and money talks.

Walk into the job market with your feet planted firmly on the ground. Don't expect anyone to take care of you. Learn to fend for yourself and be self-sufficient, or you're doomed to be at other people's mercy. Like it or not, this job market is forcing us to grow up fast. Be selfish. You come first. As the saying goes, there are no free rides.

Demystifying the Job Hunt—Employers Want Sizzle *and* Steak

What are employers looking for? Answer: Perfection. "Ridiculous," you scream. You're right. You don't have to endure a decade of psychoanalysis to know no one is perfect, nor should anyone expect it. Nevertheless, employers want it. No, they demand it. Since they're forking up big dollars in salaries, or so they say, they figure they're entitled to the world. They want blood. Big companies are looking for undying loyalty, the smaller entrepreneurial operations insist upon it. In bizspeak, that's *bottom-line* thinking.

Once you get past the word *perfection,* what are employers really looking for? Answer: Sizzle and steak. Substance and fluff. Technical smarts, selling ability and a nice person all wrapped up in one high-functioning committed humanoid. Back in the '60s, companies routinely hired *wunderkinds,* threw them in cubicles and told them to be brilliant. Whether they were mathematicians, statisticians, computer programmers or electrical engineers, it didn't matter if they didn't clap eyes on another worker for months on end. As long as they did what they were hired to do, no one bothered them. Or they hired high-powered salespeople who could sell ice in Antarctica and asked them to do so until they dropped.

It didn't matter whether they were rootless former aluminum siding salespeople, or tin men, as they were eloquently captured in the 1987 cult film, "Tin Men." Employers couldn't care less if salespeople had eighth-grade educations, as long as they could pound the pavement and move product. The technical staffer didn't care about the salesperson's job, and the salesperson didn't know the battalion of high-IQ gnomes existed. Not any more.

You Are *the* Product

Today, companies demand both technical and sales skills in one neat package. And they're getting it. Think of yourself as a high-performing product, kind of an all-in-one, jack-of-all-trades specialist/generalist who is not uptight about emptying your own trash if need be. You're a super product, someone who is going to solve an employer's marketing problem and still be a great person all rolled into one.

You are the human equivalent of Corn Flakes, a Whopper or a Hershey bar. You must be both well-packaged and have intrinsic value. Neither ebullient personalities nor razor sharp brilliance alone secure great jobs. Together they are a marketable widget ready to compete in the open market. Take Microsoft's brilliant founder Bill Gates, heralded as a founding visionary of the computer industry. He's been called a power-obsessed, reclusive loner. The power part may be right, but reclusive loners don't drive an entire industry. They bring up the rear. Gates works hard at keeping a low profile, but that's to his credit. When it comes to his obsession—Microsoft—he is salesman and technician, strategist and market tactician all in one. He's a high-performing machine that works 18 hours a day—often seven days a week.

You don't have to be another Bill Gates, but you have to be a saleable product with a strong ego and a good self-image. You have to walk into an employer's office knowing what you can do, and equally important, understanding how to drive that point home. If you can't sell you, who will?

A High-Stake Game

Yes, organizations have grown into oppressive bureaucratic monsters. There's nothing new about that. Nevertheless, the hiring process is elementary-school simple. Like any marketplace, the job market is made up of buyers and sellers. The employer who is going to hire you and pay you a salary is the buyer. What could be simpler? If you brilliantly package, market and sell yourself, you've got the world wrapped up.

It only sounds scary. Look at it another way. Instead of being frightened and intimidated, look at the job market as an exciting challenge. Compare it to an athletic event, a high-stake game. Play it smartly and you stand to conquer potentially big rewards. It may not be the dream job you fantasized about, but it may be the coveted key to others. Don't try and put a price tag on that.

$Myth\ 1:$ Job Hunting Is a Logical Process.

Reality: *No matter how much planning goes into it, jub hunting amounts to a random activity, governed more by serendipity than by methodical planning.*

Chapter Snapshot

- ☐ You Only Think You Know How Decisions Are Made
- ☐ There Is Comfort in Order
- ☐ A Day in the Life of a Job Hunter—Make Time Count
- ☐ Secrets of Reaching Busy People
- ☐ Five Phone Rapport Commandments
- ☐ There Are Only Twenty-Four Hours in a Day

❋ ❋ ❋ ❋ ❋ ❋ ❋ ❋

If you believe job hunting is a logical process, you probably think all politicians are working in the public interest and most companies sincerely care about cleaning up the environment. Or that stock market movements are predictable.

Don't expect too much from the process. No matter what you've been taught, the job market is neither logical, coherent, nor orderly.

Believe it or not, companies are run by people like you and me. Some of these leaders are brilliant. Others, although they may be sharp entrepreneurs, are alarmingly dull. Many are fairly normal (whatever that means); some are outright insane. But none of them are logical. No human being is. Some of us try hard to be logical; others don't feel it's worth the effort.

If illogical people run our world, how can an amorphous process like job hunting fall into logical perimeters? The best we can hope for is making our days count by accomplishing as much as possible. We can't control the outside world, but we can attempt to shape our days and deal with unplanned events as they occur.

Some career writers make decent livings telling folks job hunting is a logical process. It's a lot simpler than saying the world is a gigantic test tube of personalities and body types. Create a job-finding system, insist it's logical, shout it from the rafters, and people are bound to believe you. Back in 1492, a lot of intelligent people were convinced the world was flat until Kris Columbus proved them wrong.

You Only Think You Know How Decisions Are Made

Once we understand that no divine system governs either humans or markets—stock, retail or job—do we abandon logic, organization and systems? Absolutely not. The search for logic and order is all the more important. We can't control the process, but we can do everything possible to maximize our time to make things happen.

What makes the job market both scary and exciting is we'll never understand how decisions are made. We only think we do. Yes, organizational psychologists and management consultants tell us how businesses ought to work, the type of atmosphere most conducive to high productivity and how to motivate workers. Sounds great. But when it comes to creating a system for selecting human beings, separating superstars from duds, psychologists and management consultants are doing what their predecessors did 200 years ago. They're guessing. Call it informed judgments based on rational data if it makes you feel better. Better still, a judgment call. More on this important topic later when we explore Myth 10, "Employers Are Autocratic Powerlords Who Know Exactly What They're Looking For: Ergo, They Hold All the Negotiating Cards."

The Hiring Process Is a Throw of the Dice

Trying to get a clear fix on how employers choose an applicant when faced with almost identical qualifications requires accepting that hiring decisions frequently amount to a throw of the dice. Hypnotize a half-dozen employers and you may be shocked when you discover decisions were made for ridiculous reasons. Will anyone admit to hiring someone because they liked the way the person dressed?

Take the interview process. Don't beat yourself up trying to figure out what employers are looking for. When you're rejected after giving what you felt was the most brilliant interview performance of your life, you'll be wrecked. "How could they do that? I was incredible," you say to yourself, before leaping out the first window you find.

"There is just no pleasing some folks," you think, trying to justify the fickleness and unpredictability of interviewers. You'll rehash the events and conclude: "I *just* don't get it." You never will. The head of a New Jersey cookie company put it this way: "If I can't predict my own behavior, how could I even pretend to get a clear reading on someone else's?"

Learn to Cope with a Chaotic World

Even when you are hired, you'll never know for sure why you were chosen over the 100-odd applicants interviewed. Despite what sooth-sayers, astrologists and an army of academics tell us, the world is governed as much by random events as by proven principles. Tack constant technological changes and global business deals on top of the restructuring of U.S. business, and you have a mystifying world that is changing as you read this sentence. Management consultant Tom Peters calls the business climate "chaotic."

Peters advises taking chaos as a given and learning to thrive on it. He insists it's a strategic tool for tomorrow's winners, a razor-sharp sword for gaining market advantage. In sum, rather than seeing it as an unsurpassable moat, chaos ought to be viewed as a ready-made opportunity. It is a key to success.

There Is Comfort in Order

What better way to deal with a topsy-turvy world than by organizing your life? It may be an impossible task, but it's worth a try.

Your days may never work exactly as planned, yet there is a sense of comfort knowing you're guided by a master plan. If nothing else, it gives each day cohesion, even if things are seldom done in chronological order. Create an order and be willing to modify it according to unplanned events and whim. Expect change. Since there is no logic to job hunting, you ought to do everything you can to bring some order to it.

Create a Model

What follows is a model organization plan. Don't feel you have to follow it verbatim. Take what you need, change, add, delete. It's food for thought. The hardest thing for a job seeker is getting up in the morning and staring at the long day ahead. It's 7:30 a.m., and there are nine hours to fill. How will you do it? A scary thought.

You're not alone. It's especially tough for first-time job seekers. Job hunting requires discipline and organization. When employed, another person is creating your schedule. You simply follow it. You're motivated by either the work, the paycheck, or better yet, both. When looking for work, the tables are turned. You're forced to function as a self-motivated lone wolf, a frightening and exciting prospect all at the same time. No one is watching you, you're in charge.

It's as simple as this: The more organized, driven and hard-working you are, the better the odds of finding a job quickly. Those are the realities; now down to basics.

Tools of the Trade

Think of yourself as a business—a one-person job-searching enterprise. Here is what you need:

Home Office. We're not talking corner office, floor-to-ceiling windows, view of the city, intercoms, Dictaphones, fax machines and portable bars. Since you're not going to be entertaining employers or courting clients, your little office can be downright puny. Nevertheless, you need some space so you can maneuver an orderly job search without pulling your hair out every time you have to mail something out.

Avoid makeshift offices. Using a kitchen table or bed for a desk is not recommended. It may be convenient in the beginning, but when you're burdened with paperwork, reading material, plus documents to be filed away for future reference, sorting through the mess could turn into a daily nightmare. There are plenty of alternatives, from an attic or basement room to partitioning off a small corner of a studio apartment. When you feel like your world is unmanageable, there is a comforting sense of security knowing your job search tools are in order—and in reach.

Telephone. Just try and get along without a telephone. Ideally, you ought to have your own line, especially if you're living with others. The idea is not to miss calls. The telephone is your lifeline to the cruel world.

Answering Machine. Cheaper than the telephone but just as essential. Answering machines are the equivalent of bargain-counter automated secretaries. You can buy one for as little as $50, even less at discount electronics chains. And make sure it has a remote call-in feature to retrieve messages when you're away from the office. The best thing about these nifty machines is you can be 3,000 miles away on a job interview and not have to worry about losing valuable messages. No matter where you are, make it a habit to retrieve your messages twice a day.

A fast word about personal messages: Avoid cutesy, staged and especially dumb messages. Don't play 10 seconds of Beethoven's "Ninth Symphony" or the Coasters' "Get a Job." Or any silly diatribe that begins, "We're not home right now, but your message is important to us," etc. Give callers credit. If they don't hear a human voice, they'll conclude you're not home as soon as the machine answers.

For the time being, the answering machine is a business, not a social, tool. In as few words as possible, get your message across. "You've reached John Halderman. Kindly leave your name, telephone number and time you called at the beep. I'll be back to you soon."

Day Organizer.   An inexpensive all-in-one day planner, appointment book and calendar is as important as your wallet when in the field.

Job Search Log.   Like your day organizer, the job search log helps you run a systematic job search. When you're running to interviews, gathering and sending out information and spending hours on the phone, it's easy to get sloppy and jot notes on slips of paper. Hours later, you've forgotten about them. A hastily written note to call an important contact is lost forever. Enough faux pas like that and you're bound to miss out on jobs. Like morning coffee, log entrees ought to be a daily ritual. The log also permits you to evaluate your search as you go along. The job search log can be set up on a pad, better yet in a computer, if you have one.

There are many ways to set up your log. Whatever method you use, keep it simple. Consider the format below as a guide:

Correspondence Sent (Date)	Company	Contact	Follow-Up	Status
1.				
2.				
3.				
4.				
5.				
6.				

Bulletin Board and Calendar.   I'm a big advocate of bulletin boards. You're asking for trouble by letting important documents pile up on your desk. I like seeing reminders about upcoming appointments in bold letters in front of my nose. For double protection, note appointments on both a bulletin board and in an appointment book. Even if you forget to pop in your contacts, you can't miss them.

Typewriter/Computer.   Ideally, you ought to have both. That doesn't mean a top-of-the-line IBM personal computer (PC) or Macintosh. An inexpensive clone or a second-hand PC is just fine. A PC increases efficiency and saves time. Letters and notes can be stored, updated and instantly retrieved. Rather than constantly rewriting cover letters, simply add or subtract names and alter information to fit the prospective job. Decent software also permits mass mailings. An inexpensive portable typewriter is recommended to quickly dash off notes or address envelopes. Or rather than own both a PC and typewriter, check out some of the memory typewriters on the market. The combination typewriter/computers are inexpensive and easy to use.

Office Supplies.   Pencils, paper, eraser, paper clips, stationery, stamps, stapler, file folders—sounds so basic, you wonder why I mention them. That's precisely why. They're so basic, they're the most commonly overlooked items when stocking home offices. Try to run an office without them. Imagine the frustration of not having a lowly stapler or paper clip when mailing information?

A Day in the Life of a Job Hunter—Make Time Count

Rather than plan your day in the early morning, it's more efficient doing it the night before. Many of us overworked mortals need an hour or two to rev up to full throttle. By planning each day the night before, you start each day with a sense of mission.

There are hundreds of ways to carve a day. Test the following order and see how it works:

8 a.m. to 9:30 a.m.   The earlier you start, the more you accomplish. Check classified ads in local papers to see if anything appeals to you. Follow them religiously to get a sense of when new listings appear and older ones are filled. If an ad has been running for a few straight weeks, assume something is awry. A company or agency is likely shopping the market to see what the applicant pool looks like or the company doesn't have the foggiest idea what kind of applicant it wants. More on this in Myth 3: "The Best Jobs Are Always in the 'Hidden' Job Market." Also check general business pages to see what's happening in the world and in your industry particularly. You never know when you're going to pick up a potential job lead.

Question everything you read. A company in the throes of expanding or relocating, for example, ought to be pursued posthaste. The former may need full-timers, the latter, part-time or temporary help. Go with your gut, even though you're playing a long shot. No matter how far out or remote the lead, play it! You'll kick yourself if you don't.

Schedule employment agency interviews and return the prior day's calls.

9:30 a.m. to 10:30 a.m. Send out correspondence and note it in your job search log. Again, fanatical bookkeeping is the only antidote against sloppiness. Know where your correspondence is so you know when to follow up. Allow 8 to 10 business days before chasing answers. Doing it sooner is bad form.

10:30 am. to 12 p.m. Ideal time for scheduling appointments and going on interviews. Within the hallowed halls of Corporate America, coffee and pastry have been digested and the pace is picking up.

12 p.m. to 1:30 p.m. Don't waste time trying to schedule appointments during lunch hour. Even if employers or human resource workers are not eating out, chances are they don't want to see people. Many busy executives deem it an ideal time to get things done. This is an excellent time to call your machine for messages and possibly kill a few hours doing research in the library or catching up on reading.

1:30 p.m. to 3:00 p.m. This is also a good time to see people. Some experienced job seekers swear this time is better than mornings for scheduling appointments. With less than half a day left, they contend human resource folks are in a better mood and are less likely to put job prospects through the wringer. In fact, Monday morning is touted as the worst time to schedule interviews. Many corporate types have not come off their weekends. They're still thinking about their golf or tennis scores and are having trouble changing gears. Face it, not everyone loves their job. Be careful, they're not beyond displacing some hostility on you. Could you think of a safer target?

3:30 p.m. to 5:00 p.m. By now, you're wrapping up field business and heading home to finish the day. But your work's not over; there's plenty to do. First return calls, then get out correspondence before the last mail pickup.

Secrets of Reaching Busy People

The more important the person and the bigger the job commanded, the harder she or he is to reach. The reasons are obvious. Believe it or not, most are actually busy; the rest can't be bothered with piddling calls from unimportant people like you. You may be a budding Bill Gates, Lee Iacocca or John Sculley, but you're the only one who knows that.

Rest assured, if they do intend to return your calls, you'll be way down on the list—maybe even last. Strategy is called for, since there are good and bad times to call people. Executive search professionals, better known as headhunters, are polished practitioners when it comes to nailing people by phone. They say the worst times to reach busy executives are Monday morning between 9 a.m. and 10:30 a.m. and Friday afternoons between 4 p.m. and 5 p.m. On Monday mornings, they're planning their week ahead, and late Friday afternoon, they're winding down and can't be bothered. The rest of the time, you're taking your chances. Tuesday through Thursday are the best days to reach people. Even then, you'll have to run an annoying gauntlet of intermediaries before you reach the right person.

Don't Alienate Assistants—Swallow Your Pride and Be Nice

The last—and toughest—of the lot is the executive's personal secretary or assistant. Brace yourself. This person may have all the charm of the Terminator and Frankenstein combined. Some secretaries and assistants have elevated rude to an art form. Part of their job is screening calls from annoying job seekers like you. What's more, they don't have to be nice to you. If their boss is giving them a hard time, watch out! You're a factory-approved scapegoat, and there is nothing they'd enjoy more than guillotining you over the phone. Snubbing you amounts to unbridled fun.

Swallow your pride and be nice *no matter what*. If you get snippy, you've destroyed part of your meal ticket. Befriend them and you'll have a built-in ally, a friend in high places. They'll intercede on your behalf, put your application at the top of the list, interrupt meetings and do their best to get you an audience with their boss. But whether they're charming or have the personality of a serial killer, you must display the patience of Job and the tact and diplomacy of a ranking diplomat.

Make Calls during Off-Hours

If you're real clever you can bypass these guardians of the gate. A suggested tactic is calling during nonbusiness hours. What rulebook says you must call between 9 and 5? No busy fast-track executive works 9 to 5. It's more like 8 a.m., sometimes 7:30 a.m., until 6:30 or 7 p.m. Call at 7:45 a.m. or at 5:45 p.m., and you may hit pay dirt and be surprised when the boss answers the phone.

This is the moment of truth, a time to deftly explain who you are and why you called. An absolute no-no is badmouthing this person's secretary who wouldn't put your calls through. Remember, the executive hired that assistant and is fanatically loyal. Don't say you've been trying to reach this person for the past week and you're foiled every time you try. Instead, apologize for either calling so late (or early) and get to the point. "Mr. Raskolnikov, I apologize for calling so late. I am applying for the job of systems analyst, and I have all the qualifications you are looking for. I would appreciate it if I could see you so I can tell you about myself and how I can be valuable to your company."

Push all the right buttons in a few sentences. Summing up: Quickly explain the reason for the call. Offer a skill or service rather than ask for a job. Don't come on like you are looking for a handout or, God forbid, are desperate. Ask for a 15-minute interview. You're more likely to be seen if you promise not to take up too much time. Once you're in the door, be brilliant and cross your fingers.

Five Phone Rapport Commandments

Until an employer claps eyes on you, your voice is your spokesperson. It reflects who you are, revealing age, attitude, personality characteristics, whether you're introverted, extroverted, troubled, etc. If you're the least bit intuitive, you can learn a lot about a person from a brief telephone conversation. Your voice is your spokesperson. It must sell, convince and sound professional all at the same time. It is a credential in and of itself.

Remember these five phone rapport commandments:

1. *Be yourself.* Don't try to sound like a radio or TV announcer. You'll come off sounding pompous and pretentious, making less than a favorable impression.

2. *Plan conversations before making calls.* Start by assuming the person you're speaking to is extremely busy. Don't waste time searching

for words. Know who you are speaking to, the information you want to impart (or get) and the best way to get your point across. Until you're a skilled phone practitioner, jot down what you plan to say in some kind of logical order before you make calls. Nothing is more embarrassing than jumbling your thoughts or forgetting to make important points.

3. *Pronounce names correctly.* If you're not sure how to pronounce a name, find out before you embarrass yourself. All it takes is an additional call to a company operator to find out how names should be pronounced.

4. *Form a mental impression of the person you're speaking to.* You'll have a better idea how to proceed. It isn't always possible, but it's a game well worth playing. Many voices fall into a nondescript category, while others transmit definite vibrations. You can almost picture what the other person looks like (even though the image you build around a person's voice may be the furthest thing from reality).

5. *Adjust your voice to the same speed and volume as the person you're speaking to.* It makes communication easier. If the voice sounds rushed and anxious to get on to other things, move quickly before the person loses patience and abruptly closes the conversation. Conversely, if the person is a turtle-like talker, speak more slowly than you normally do so he or she feels comfortable with your voice. Strive for harmony and a fleeting, yet positive connection. Remember, you're laying the foundation for an important relationship.

There Are Only Twenty-Four Hours in a Day

Give yourself about a week to build a job-hunting momentum. You'll be surprised how motivated you are. You'll be a self-propelling machine. That initial anxiety of not knowing how to organize your day will disappear forever. Once you realize there is an awful lot to do and you're spending 9 to 10 hours doing it, you'll throw yourself into your job search routines with a vengeance. You won't be like a tired locomotive trying to get up a head of steam before chugging down the tracks. You'll be an SST Concorde taking off.

Myth 2: Mapping Out and Following a Predetermined Career Track Leads to the Emerald City.

Reality: *Rigid career tracks lead to confusion and bad choices. Job-hopping is the way of the future.*

Chapter Snapshot

- ☐ Where the Heck Is My Career Path?
- ☐ Careers Reflect Our Personalities
- ☐ I'll Take Next Year's Model
- ☐ Get on Board Now!
- ☐ Pouncing on Opportunities
- ☐ Survival Thinking and the Quest for Meaningful Work
- ☐ Work as the Foundation of Our Lives
- ☐ Building a Career—You Are the Architect of Your Own Life
- ☐ Jobs and Blind Dates Have a Lot in Common
- ☐ What Do You Want, a Job or a Career?
- ☐ Figuring Out Tomorrow
- ☐ Career Tracks, Then and Now—Off-the-Shelf Stability versus Self-Crafted Career
- ☐ The '90s Promise a New Work Ethic
- ☐ The Sprinter Philosophy
- ☐ Relish the Journey as Much as the Destination—Plotting Your Career Map
- ☐ Indulge Your Fantasies—Create a Fantasy Job
- ☐ Focus on the Reality Thread

❋ ❋ ❋ ❋ ❋ ❋ ❋ ❋

Wouldn't it be nice if everything fell neatly into place like a grade-B TV sitcom? You found the job you wanted and latched onto a benevolent boss who recognized you for the genius you are and put you on an aggressive career track leading to your dream job.

If the above happened a decade ago, it would have been too good to be true. Today, it ranks with striking oil in your backyard. Benevolent bosses will always be around, but the notion of getting on one career track and staying there for an entire career is like searching for old dinosaur bones.

When Corporate America offered secure jobs—and meant it—career tracks had real meaning. The career track served as a carefully planned direct route up the corporate ladder avoiding dead-end jobs.

In theory, career tracks make sense if you know precisely what job you ultimately want and if the job market is stable. But how many of us have such precise career goals? What's more, the job market will be in a state of flux for as far as we dare project.

By the late '70s, career advisors made decent livings plotting career tracks for clients. Aggressive young professionals wanted the fastest route to the top, and career consultants happily designed it for them. In the early '80s, career books quantified the job market, highlighting career tracks. In *Career Stages, Surmounting the Crises of Working Life* (Seaview/Putnam), Auren Uris and John J. Tarrant went a step further by carving a lifetime into career stages. It starts with late teens— Getting Ready; Stage II—The Learning Decade (20–30); Stage III—The Power Decade (30–40); Stage IV—The Win/Lose Decade (40–50); Stage V—Consummation Decade (50–60); and Stage VI—The Wrap-Up Years. What could be simpler? If you hadn't accomplished all you think you should have in the appointed time slots and you're the least bit insecure, you questioned your abilities and self-worth. Open the window, *please!*

Where the Heck Is My Career Path?

Even in the best of times, the concept behind the career track needs to be overhauled. Whether we change jobs or careers, most of us will alter our career courses several times throughout our lives. Typically, changes are unplanned.

The best we can strive for is finding something we love doing early on so we can devote the rest of our lives to excelling at it. In this job market that's no small feat.

In the early '90s, financial services firms (banks, brokerage and investment banking houses) hired people only to fire them a couple of months later. Many of these stunned employees spent close to six months looking for work. Until corporations are fully consolidated and slimmed down to fighting weight, expect more of the same.

As I said earlier, you'll have many jobs throughout your lifetime. And maybe a couple of career changes as well. Job and career changing is no longer a sign of instability but a reflection of the times, not to mention a natural inclination to dabble and learn. More important, it's the healthy evolution for a human being.

Careers Reflect Our Personalities

We define ourselves by what we do for a living. Our careers reflect innate abilities, goals, creativity, attitudes toward others and a host of other mysterious variables. "You are what you eat" may be the silliest summation of a human being, but "You are what you do for a living" is a true barometer of what we're all about. It casts an illuminating ray of sunlight on our personalities. In that skewed path to fulfillment, it's human destiny to taste many jobs and experiment with new careers before we settle on something that gives us true pleasure.

I'll Take Next Year's Model

We're living in a period of accelerated change, making frequent job changes almost a necessity. Many of today's staples—cars, planes, computers, fax machines—are already becoming obsolete.

The computer has transformed our lives. Who could have imagined that the power of a gigantic mainframe computer could be condensed into a lightweight portable computer? In the early '80s, the desktop PC was considered a milestone in compressed efficiency. By the early '90s, notebook and pen-based computers weighing between 5 and 7 pounds debuted, replacing 12- and 14-pound laptop computers.

We're only years away from Microsoft founder Bill Gates' vision of a PC in every home. It won't be long before the PC with all its bells and whistles will be as indispensable as a wallet or pocketbook. Computer visionaries say we ain't seen nothing yet.

Get on Board Now!

The pace is speeding up. The rapid-fire evolution of the computer is a metaphor for change. Technology is changing our world and creating

new opportunities in its wake. Just as rapidly as new careers are created, others are rendered out of date. If you hope to be successful, you
must keep pace. If you don't, you'll be as obsolete as laptop computers will be in another decade. We must change with our machines.
Better still, we must adjust to change before it happens. Call it the
twenty-first-century survivor's mindset.

Stay alert. Past and future are practically licking at each other's
heels. Corporate America may be consolidating, but it's not slowing
down. When the restructuring of U.S. business is completed, we'll be
shifting into fast-forward as entrepreneurs aggressively compete for
international markets.

Pouncing on Opportunities

The billion-dollar question: Is it possible to forge a long-term career
track when we don't know what the world will be like next year?
Answer: No. The majority of successful careers are loosely planned
and involve erratic movements toward changing goals. Job transitions
happen more by accident than by design. We pounce on opportunities
as they arise.

Countless success stories can be cited as examples. William Sonoma,
founder of William Sonoma Corporation, a national housewares retail
empire, never saw beyond a few small retail outlets in the San
Francisco Bay Area. Wendy's founder R. David Thomas never
dreamed he'd head one of the largest fast-food franchises in the
world. And Richard and Henry Bloch, cofounders of H & R Block, the
largest tax preparation service in the world, never intended to build a
billion-dollar company whose shares are traded on the New York
Stock Exchange. These entrepreneurs merely took advantage of
opportunities as they presented themselves. Their success owes as
much to luck and timing as it does to astute business planning.

Maverick billionaire entrepreneur H. Ross Perot, founder of
Electronic Data Systems (EDS) and heavyweight 1992 presidential
contender, once said it is the individual's ability to deal with the
unexpected that characterizes the difference between success and failure. Perot believes accidents create opportunity. His career is living
testament to that fact. A former IBM salesman, Perot launched EDS
with $1,000 borrowed from his wife's savings. Initially, EDS bought
unused computer time from owners of large units and sold it to companies that could not afford expensive equipment. Twenty-two years
later, in 1984, Perot sold EDS to General Motors for $2.5 billion.

Looking back upon your own life, how often have things worked out precisely as planned? If you're lucky, maybe it's 25 percent. For me, it's about 10 percent—and I'm overestimating. When I was 18, I thought I knew what I wanted from life. A hopeless romantic, my immediate plan was to join the Navy and see the world, George Orwell style, followed by college and then a career as a journalist. I wanted to be the music critic for *The New York Times*. With free aisle seats to major concerts in New York City, I deemed it the ideal job to have. My folks had other ideas. My father wanted me to be a doctor; my mother felt law made sense, since I hated the sight of blood and failed most of my science courses. My teachers stamped me a hopeless misfit and suggested I find a cheap shrink and then take the first job offered. My favorite uncle insisted I follow my instincts. No wonder I was confused.

Miraculously, I managed to conquer a college degree after rocketing through a series of jobs that included hauling printing ink, packing snowsuits, frying burgers and home fries in an all-night diner, waiting tables in a sleazy restaurant, pumping gas in a gas station and delivering newspapers at 6 a.m. After college, I worked as an investigator for New York City's Welfare Department followed by a short stint as a placement manager in an employment agency before landing my first reporting job for $95 a week. How's that for a career track? If you detect a common theme in that tangled mass of jobs, call me immediately—I'm all ears.

There are no rules or formulas for jumping on opportunities. More important than a plan, you need an open mind allowing you to follow the wind.

Survival Thinking and the Quest for Meaningful Work

Remember the landmark 1967 film *The Graduate*, where the young college graduate played by Dustin Hoffman was given prophetic career advice by a friend of the family. "Plastics, get into plastics," said the friend, as if he were delivering the Sermon on the Mount.

Relatives and friends enjoy giving career advice. It's ritual. Big families, in particular, are top heavy with pundits who take pride in passing on the wisdom of the ages. My family had a half dozen of them. Synthesize the long-winded messages and you get something like this: Find something that pays well and stick with it. If you're lucky, you'll get some satisfaction as well. (More on this topic in Myth 5: "Super-Growth Fields Offer the Best Opportunities.")

Most of the advice is rooted in first-generation thinking. My relatives who emigrated from Eastern Europe weren't thinking about finding work that was personally fulfilling or altruistic. They wanted jobs that brought in enough money to feed and clothe their families and themselves. There were no alternatives. Later on, they hoped to amass enough money to start their own businesses. They were driven by money and security, potent forces that oddly enough often led to actually loving what they were doing.

Similarly, families who lost jobs and fortunes during the Depression thought along the same lines. A job was a survival ticket to a better life.

The idea of aligning work and pleasure is fairly recent. As life became more comfortable during the '40s and '50s for the United States' melting pot population, values about career and work changed. Bigger, more ethereal issues began to play a part in people's career choices. We started thinking about values, goals, achieving satisfaction, peace of mind. By the early '70s, career heavies conjured complex theories about the meaning of work. Work was tied to metaphysical, psychoanalytic and spiritual issues. It was aligned with goal-setting, the foundation for forging career tracks. Work was no longer something you did to keep body and soul together. It was a vehicle leading to satisfaction, accomplishment and fulfillment. Rather than "working to live," the trademarked advice of our grandfathers' generation, we ought to "live to work." Along that winding road to fulfillment, the concept of career tracks took root.

Work as the Foundation of Our Lives

As we approach the twenty-first century in our apocryphal quest for happiness, we only think we have our priorities straight and understand the value of work. We know it is the fulcrum upon which our world revolves, the steel underpinning of our lives. Yet the question remains: How do we achieve our goals? Knowing where we want to be and designing the vehicle to get there are different parts of the life equation. Knowing you're a potentially talented programmer, lawyer, accountant, securities analyst, teacher, writer or architect is only the first step. The hard part is planning your route and getting there.

Dreamers can be riveting conversationalists when they're sitting in crowded bars nursing beers, solving life's problems surrounded by a captive audience. Give them enough time and encouragement and they'll convince themselves they can achieve anything. Worlds are conquered and wars are won after dark. But daylight and sobriety severs dreams with laser beam reality.

Dreams are wonderful if we can make them happen. The would-be and could-be dreamers live in a conditional world, whereas the doers and achievers connect present and future. They understand the difference between "I could be" and "I will be." They envision the finish line. They can practically taste success. They know what it takes to get something done and are prepared to cope with drudgery. A career is seldom one or two jobs but a string of related ones. Building a career doesn't happen overnight.

Building a Career—You Are the Architect of Your Own Life

Successful people share common traits. They set out on life's journey primed for a variety of jobs. At the end of their journey, however, they envision a career that turns them on. Rather than forging rigid career tracks, they search for jobs that enrich and expand their horizons, that take them a little further on the mystical journey through life.

That quest reminds me of a wrinkled old bluesman wailing timeless lyrics in a tiny, smoke-filled Memphis bar in the mid-1970s: "I know what I want outta life," he screamed in a hoarse voice. "It's just a question of findin' the road to it." The message is never stop searching for fulfillment.

Ideally, there ought to be a comfortable marriage between career and personal fulfillment. Think of each job as another brick in a custom-made home you're building for yourself. See yourself as the architect of your own life. When all the bricks are in place, your house is completed. You've arrived. The 8 to 10 jobs you've logged over a lifetime amount to a fulfilling career.

But it's going to take a while before your metaphorical home is built. All the bricks aren't going to fit. Some will be chipped or broken, others won't be sturdy enough. Count on boring jobs and maybe a couple of dead-end ones as well. They call it job-hopping, but it's actually dues-paying or kicking around the career waterfront.

Jobs and Blind Dates Have a Lot in Common

Be realistic. Every job isn't going to be a winner. A new job is like a blind date. There is no predicting how it will work out beforehand. You'll quit some jobs and be fired from others. The only way to appreciate a great job is to leave a couple of duds in its wake.

I Quit!   There are real virtues in quitting a job you don't like. Every time you start a new job, you're given a new opportunity. Hopefully, you're in a better job than the one you left.

Quitting takes guts, especially if you're leaving for good reasons. You've given the job plenty of time and worked hard, but it's just not for you. Rather than lie to yourself by saying everything will eventually work out, you find another job and quit. A bad move is quitting before you have a new job to replace it. It's common sense, but you'd be shocked by how many people throw reason to the wind and just walk out. It's fine if you can find a new job immediately; it's a disaster if you don't see another paycheck for months.

You're Fired!   Being fired—an inescapable fact of life in this market—forces you to look at yourself. If you're honest, you'll figure out what went wrong. Was it because of you, them or circumstances beyond your control? It's not always an easy question, but one that must be answered honestly if you hope to build a satisfying and successful career. No matter how smart you are, it's hard to step back and admit you screwed up.

There Is No Master Plan.   Whether you quit or are fired, don't get bent out of shape when it happens. Things seldom work out according to a master plan. Like a prize fighter prepared to take any punch thrown at him, be ready for the unexpected when building your career.

The idea is to latch onto jobs that get your juices going, that give you a reason to get up in the morning. Accomplish that feat and you're on your way.

What Do You Want, a Job or a Career?

Know the difference between a job and a career. A job is a paycheck; a career is a future. A job, according to *Webster's New Collegiate Dictionary*, is "an undertaking, a role or function." That's a pretty icy definition. A career, however, is something bigger. Webster defines it this way: "A passage, a field for pursuit of consecutive progressive achievement, a profession for which one trains and which is undertaken as a permanent calling." That's only a little better, but it's also a cold and dispassionate definition.

A career has just as much or more impact on our lives as our family or lifestyle. Picking the right career is as important as finding a compatible mate.

Figuring Out Tomorrow

Short- versus Long-Term Thinking

There are two ways to approach career planning. You can take a long-term view and lay out a succession of hypothetical jobs leading to a jackpot, the career of your dreams. Or you can adopt a short-term attack plan that starts with a goal followed by the first two jobs leading to it. I recommend the latter strategy. The first is a traditional approach, assuming constant variables and little change; the second is realistic, flexible and geared for the moment.

This is a short-term market calling for short-term, 6- to 18-month thinking. It is ideal for leapfrogging obstacles. We have no choice but to keep pace with industry. As it changes and contracts, we must be chameleonlike and change with it. Yes, it's nerve-wracking and frustrating, but like your mother used to say before she shoved the castor oil down your throat, "You'll be better off for it." Actually stronger—and flexible. We're moving so fast, it's often hard putting everything in perspective. It's information overload or too much information too soon. (More on that in Myth 6: "The More Information You Can Get Your Hands On, the Greater Likelihood You Have for Success.")

Apply the brakes and you find a volatile market offering incredible opportunities never dreamed of by career counselors pushing career tracks. It's making job-hoppers out of all of us.

Design Your Own Experience Belt

Job-hopping may be frustrating and stressful, but it's also a staircase to opportunity. Each job is another notch on the experience belt. You're shopping the market, learning about jobs and people. It sure beats sitting back in a comfortable job contemplating whether you'll ever get to take next year's vacation. Even if you're able to chalk up a decade or more with a company, count on the organization reshaping itself several times, forcing you to rethink your career options. Organizations reflect the people running them. They change as they grow. Small, entrepreneurial companies often become towering bureaucracies. But, don't assume you'll change with the organization. The question is who outgrows whom? If the marriage isn't working out, it's time to push on down that long lonesome highway. It may not be worth the time and effort trying to make it work.

Career Tracks, Then and Now—Off-the-Shelf Stability versus Self-Crafted Career

Career track used to mean stability, security and quick success. If you were hell-bent on conquering wealth and power, you'd lace up your running shoes and hop on a fast career track. If you bolted ahead of everyone else, you were envied. Reaching the top in your thirties meant you were a superstar. Achieving it in your twenties meant sure fame—maybe a record or film deal as well.

Lee Iacocca was a favorite idol of fast trackers. He inched up the Ford hierarchy with clear goals in mind, even the salary he envisioned for himself. The consummate team player, he achieved every one of his goals—along with becoming a media personality.

There are countless success stories of young multimillionaires who worked themselves into coronaries trying to be imitation Iacoccas. Now they're in analysis trying to figure out whether they're happy.

Future corporate heroes will be taking different paths. Their models will be entrepreneurs like Steve Jobs and Michael Dell, men who became industry leaders by breaking rules and doing things their own way. Jobs did it with Apple Computer; Dell with Dell Computer Corporation. Both men became millionaires in their twenties. If they had followed traditional career tracks, they would have been canned. Neither man was destined to be an organizational clone. What's more, they had no stomach for organizational life. Their success points up the importance of finding your own career path.

When Dell was a teenager, he envisioned himself leading his own business and owning an entire floor of an office building, complete with flagpole in front. Dell's vision came true. But he doesn't own just one floor of an office building, he owns the whole building—corporate headquarters for Dell in Austin, Texas. The self-motivated over-achiever started his company when he was a freshman at the University of Texas at Austin.

Jobs was just as driven. Prior to launching Apple, he discovered he was cut from a different mold when he did a short stint at videogame maker Atari. Jobs didn't fit into the corporate culture. He was going at a mile a minute and everyone else was bringing up the rear. But he also had a knack for turning people off. The engineers found him arrogant and brash. They recognized his talent, but they didn't want to work with him. Eventually, an agreement was made for Jobs to come to work at night.

The '90s Promise a New Work Ethic

What path will future business leaders take? Some will follow traditional career tracks; most will create their own. Whether part of a large organization or start-up, new paths will be forged as new products and services are created. The remainder of the '90s promises a new work ethic in which career transcends power and wealth and is bound to personal satisfaction, responsible products or services and altruism.

The '60s pointed the way to change. Radicals of the day screamed for socially and environmentally conscious companies and ethical business standards. Back then, these standards were just lofty ideals of overzealous students. It took 20 years to discover they were not only attainable, but essential for our economic and moral salvation.

Fierce international competition will force businesses to focus on quality and innovation. From an environmental vantage point, they'll channel more money and time into turning out safe and healthy products that improve rather than deplete the environment. Where the young professionals of the '80s were concerned with acquiring the toys of success, the '90s professionals are quieter, philosophical, less flamboyant. Having experienced a recession and watched the job market shrivel, they're leery of overspending and concerned about socking away for tomorrow. They realize job security is a myth. A corporate squall could erupt tomorrow, even today. They're frightened and cynical for good reason. They're wary of the present and intent on preparing for the future.

Make intelligent choices based not solely upon money, but upon gratification and satisfaction. These are the bedrocks of a fulfilling career.

The Sprinter Philosophy

Compare your quest for a satisfying career to a race. See yourself as a sprinter rather than a long-distance runner. Each job experience is clearing another hurdle. Put them all together and you have a career.

Be realistic. Don't expect an easy or predictable race. Along the way, you'll encounter obstacles, hills, valleys or ravines that you'll either hurdle or avoid through detours. There will be delays, wasted time, unforeseen accidents, and mistakes along that exciting path to fulfillment. You may be blown off course by political or economic events beyond your control. Or mysterious moods or altered values will steer you in unexpected directions.

You'll be moving through a series of cycles. The idea is to gain ground and progress. Whether your moves are voluntary or forced, count on lots of jobs. Unlike our relatives, you're not going to feel like abandoned sheep every time you're put out to pasture. You'll be prepared. Constantly dealing with the unexpected makes jungle fighters out of all of us.

Relish the Journey as Much as the Destination—Plotting Your Career Map

Instead of creating tracks for yourself, plot your career as you would a trip on a map. Just as you search for alternative routes to a destination, think about alternative paths to a career goal. If you find yourself in a dead-end job, find the path leading to a better one. Just as there are hundreds of auto routes from New York to San Francisco, there are untold ways to reach your career destination. There is no prescribed path leading to job fulfillment. The right path is the one that works for you.

Start with that attitude, and you'll enjoy the journey. Not all successful journalists graduated from prestigious journalism schools, and many of the world's brilliant computer minds hold neither masters nor doctorate degrees in computer science. And dozens of familiar entrepreneurs never completed high school.

Take their cue. Have an open mind and be ready to change directions. You never know when opportunity will force you onto a side road. It doesn't matter whether the alternate course is faster or slower as long as it gets you where you want to be. It's hard to accept, but speed ought not to be the issue. Reflection, learning, and satisfaction are ultimately more important.

Indulge Your Fantasies—Create a Fantasy Job

Along that long dusty road to the right job in the right career, sketch a picture of your fantasy job. Nothing so far-out that it's unobtainable, but one that's real and achievable. It's an illuminating exercise. I recommend it to all job seekers, experienced and inexperienced.

All things are possible in this best of all possible worlds, even fantasies. We all have them. Some of us wallow in rich ones, others keep them in check, afraid to unleash hidden desires for money, power, romance and adventure.

Indulge yourself. You have nothing to lose, everything to gain. Unleash your imagination and create a fantasy job. It's the dream job you've always wanted, one that makes you get up at 6 in the morning because you can't wait to get started.

Focus on the Reality Thread

The hard part is plugging the fantasy job into the real world to see if it can be turned into reality. You say you want to head General Motors or become a famous trial lawyer or surgeon? Terrific. But what are the chances of you're actually doing it? Possible? Remote? Impossible?

The game is separating the impossible fantasies from those with a strong reality thread. Most of us don't realize that many fantasies can actually be realized. The hard part is making them happen. You'd be surprised what serious thinking and hard work can accomplish. There are countless success stories of people of all ages who are actually working at their fantasy jobs. A social worker turned his investing hobby into a career and became a stockbroker. A 25-year veteran teacher landed a job with a national jewelry company. A high-priced corporate attorney became a stand-up comic. An accountant opened a gourmet restaurant. The best is a nun who became an FBI agent.

The fantasy was the romantic part; making it happen required old-fashioned hard work. Career changing is a painful process. Yet successful career changers say it's worth all the sweat and aggravation.

Think about it. Look at your skills, talents, education and motivation level and evaluate if it's possible. Take this quickie self-test to see if your fantasy can be turned into a career:

1. Do I have the necessary skills?
2. If training is required, how long will it take and what will it cost?
3. Is there a demand for my skills?
4. What is the competition like?
5. What can I earn?
6. How far can I go?

What do the results tell you? Is it worth it? If you have to go back to college for three years to get another degree, are you willing to do it? And can you afford to? Or if the competition is great in your fantasy field, are you up for the fight? These are big questions with no simple answers. Somewhere between practical thinking and sensible risk taking lies the answer.

Now let's move on and find out where the jobs are. They are out there. Some can be found in obvious places; others require sophisticated detective work.

Myth 3: The Best Jobs Are Always in the "Hidden" Job Market.

Reality: *The hidden job market is not the only game in town. What about classified ads, employment agencies and temporary service firms?*

Chapter Snapshot

- □ The Shotgun Tactic
- □ Playing the Markets
- □ The Back Door Advantage
- □ The Visible (Open) Market
- □ New Strategies for an Old Market
- □ The Temp Route—Hooking Up with the Right Firm Can Pay Off
- □ Working with Employment Agencies and Executive Recruitment Firms
- □ Separating the Wheat from the Chaff

✽✽✽✽✽✽✽✽

Just as the Bible holds timeless messages, the mysterious hidden job market is touted as the place to find the ultimate fantasy job. It's the smart job searcher's first line of attack. So goes conventional wisdom.

Millions of words have been expended on the hidden job market. Tom Jackson and Davidyne Mayleas wrote a book about it, *The Hidden Job Market, a System to Beat the System.* But what is it exactly? The term has been bandied about since the '70s, yet most job searchers don't have a clue as to what it really means or where to find it.

The late great career guru John Crystal, whose theories about life and work inspired Richard Bolles to write the perennial *What Color Is Your Parachute*, alluded to the hidden job market when he told me, "There is no such thing as a centralized job market."

The easiest way to get your hands around the job market is by carving it into two broad categories: the hidden or unpublished market and the open one. The hidden market holds most of the jobs, in contrast to the published market where employment agencies, temporary service firms and many companies advertise the remaining openings. Conversely, the open market is accessible; the hidden one is not.

Jackson and Mayleas say 90 percent of the available jobs can be found in the hidden job market, and Ronald L. Krannich in *Re-Careering in Turbulent Times* contends that 75 percent or more of all job opportunities are found there. These authors, along with other experts, advise job hunters to put most of their energies into exploring the hidden market and marginal effort into the published area.

The Shotgun Tactic

Focusing to such a degree on the hidden job market is a mistake in any market—especially in today.'s. Everyone agrees the hidden job market is mighty powerful, yet so is the traditional, but downplayed, published one. A realistic breakdown is 60 percent of the jobs are in the hidden market, the remaining 40 percent lie in published sources. Yet these are only guesses and are to be taken with a grain of salt.

The more important reality is that there are jobs in both markets. The trick is finding them. In a stable market offering plenty of jobs, you're better off concentrating on the hidden market, especially for high-demand jobs that seldom reach the want ads. But in a tough market, a shotgun approach exploring both markets is recommended.

I'll show you how to tap both markets with equal zeal. You can't afford not to. Before we begin with the secretive hidden market, a little about how the markets work.

Playing the Markets

The published market is accessible. Buy a daily paper, open the help-wanted section and there they are—hundreds of jobs. Find the ones that appeal to you and go after them.

But you also pay a price for accessibility. The odds of securing interviews are much lower because you're competing with hundreds of applicants whose credentials are as good as or better than yours. It's a numbers game. You stand a chance with knockout credentials that dazzle placement managers and human resource people. But even if you're a jewel of an applicant, it could be weeks, even months, before anyone calls you for an interview—if you're called at all.

Tapping the hidden market, however, takes digging, ingenuity and street smarts. These jobs never reach the want ads, making the odds more attractive. They surface many ways: Someone is fired, retires or dies; a new department or division is formed; a start-up company hires a staff; an out-of-town or foreign company relocates to your city creating new jobs. But like the published market, things don't happen immediately. Connecting with it requires patience. And when you unearth a job, it might be months before you are interviewed for it, especially if it's a soft rather than a hard opening.

A hard opening is an immediately available job, contrasted to a soft opening, which is an evolving undefined position. A new department is created, for example, yet it's unclear what job functions will be needed. Soft openings are common after mergers and reorganizations. Following a reorganization, departments are often eliminated and divisions trimmed. Two or three jobs are often consolidated into one function. What seems like a simple process often takes months before the powers in a mazelike organization sign off on it. New job titles have to be approved, and the corporate organizational chart has to be reworked and approved before it's etched in stone—two monumental tasks right there. That's enough to keep bureaucrats working double-time.

The Back Door Advantage

The tricky part is finding the back door leading to the hidden job market. The following are the most popular sources.

Publications.   There are truckloads of reading materials ranging from local and national newspapers to trade, consumer and special interest magazines and newsletters to alumni and government publications. *Bacon's Publicity Checker, Directory of Magazines and Newsletters* (published by Bacon's Information Inc., 332 S. Michigan Ave., Chicago, IL 60404), for example, offers a comprehensive listing of magazines and newsletters in the United States and Canada. If you're interested in the management side of health care, for instance, publications like *Health Care Management Review* and *Health Care Strategic Management* will give you an inside track. Virtually every industry has at least a handful of publications covering it. Even the livestock industry boasts a slew of trade magazines, including *Holstein World, Hoof Beats* and *Illinois Beef.* And the U.S. Department of Labor's Bureau of Labor Statistics publishes the yearly *Occupational Outlook Handbook,* the *Occupational Outlook Quarterly,* plus other publications covering the national and regional job market.

Organizations.   If you've never been a joiner, this is a good time to start. There are alumni, fraternal and professional organizations you ought to consider joining. All of them can be a source of job leads.

Heading the list are trade and professional organizations. Every industry has a number of trade and professional organizations or associations. The engineering and scientific/medical professions, for example, have dozens of organizations offering information and services. Every engineering speciality has its own membership group. Industrial engineers have the American Institute of Industrial Engineers; electrical engineers, the Institute of Electrical and Electronics Engineers; fire protection engineers, the Society of Fire Protection Engineers and so on. Computer professionals have the American Federation of Information Processing Societies. In the medical field, biomedical technicians can contact the Association for the Advancement of Medical Instrumentation; cytotechnologists, the American Society of Cytology; diagnostic medical sonographers, the Society of Diagnostic Medical Sonographers, etc. Nuclear energy workers can contact the Atomic Industrial Forum. Communications workers also have plenty of information outlets. The broadcast industry has the National Association of Broadcasters and the exploding cable industry has the National Cable Television Association.

Two good sources listing trade and professional organizations are the U.S. Department of Labor's Bureau of Labor Statistics, *Occupational Outlook Handbook* and the *Encyclopedia of Associations* (Gale Research).

Depending upon the school, many alumni organizations offer job-hunting tips and career information. A few schools offer mentor relationships with graduates well-situated in solid companies. It pays to get political and know what's happening. Even if you can't attend every meeting, speak to people who do.

Knowing People in the Right Places, or Networking.   This is the most popular tactic, which will be covered in detail in Myth 4: "Aggressive Networking Is the Key to a Successful Job Search."

People Are the Best Conduit

All the above avenues should be tapped, yet people are ultimately the best conduit to the amorphous back door. Find it and you've discovered the inside track. Months in advance, you'll hear about pending openings in the discussion phase. A random call to a trade organization president may alert you to openings in a well-funded start-up company; lunch with a colleague may tip you off to a corporate reorganization in progress. When completed, six new jobs will surface. Your sources know the players and are willing to pry doors open to get you a first crack at interviews. This beats dealing with human resource departments, often the last to know about corporate shake-ups. Employment agencies may be contacted when the hiring wheels are already in motion. More on building such priceless connections next chapter.

Not All Employers Expect to Fill Jobs *Yesterday*

Many firms are wary of putting jobs on the open market. Trusting neither classified ads nor employment agencies, they prefer to hire people through their own methods. Victor Lindquist, director of Northwestern University's placement center in Evanston, Illinois, and author of the widely respected annual *Lindquist-Endicott Report*, says not all companies are frantically rushing to fill job slots.

A corporate recruiter at a *Fortune* 100 firm told me to beware of the high-speed "New York mentality." Unlike New Yorkers, people in other parts of the country are not rocketing through the day at 150 miles per hour, he says. In contrast, many midwestern and southern employers, for example, are taking a wait-and-see attitude toward hiring. They reason that by spreading the word, the right people will eventually surface. Once a job opening reaches the grapevine, it's only a matter of time.

Easy and Painless

It's easy to see why employers prefer the hidden market over conventional methods. It is controllable and cheap. Executives can bypass the headaches and paperwork of dealing with human resource departments, who in turn negotiate with employment agencies. At the same time, applicants skirt the tiresome multistep process of passing from employment agency to company human resource departments to the person actually doing the hiring.

All it takes is a few telephone calls to fire up the hidden job market machinery. A friend or a recommendation of a friend has instant credibility. There is a built-in willingness to accept these applicants before they even show their faces. In more instances than employers will admit to, interviews are more a formality than a critical pass-or-fail test.

Even without an inside track, employers respect applicants who have the ingenuity and cunning to uncover jobs on their own, especially from leads from unconventional sources such as a nondescript announcement in a trade publication or newsletter. Employers deem these applicants potential problem solvers, ready and willing to do more than their jobs. Even potential leaders.

The High-Demand Hidden Market

Traditionally, most glamor jobs in the broadcasting, cable, film, performing arts, journalism, public relations and advertising industries were filled through the hidden market. Now practically all jobs in high-demand fields, executive to entry level, are found through hidden market sources. Even plum blue-collar jobs are quietly filled behind closed doors. Try and get a job running a forklift on the docks or hauling cement on a construction crew without connections. Check out the New York, Boston or Chicago docks, and you'll find an unwritten code that says jobs are seldom, if ever, given to outsiders. Sons, daughters, cousins and people owed favors are given these secure jobs with high starting salaries and excellent medical benefits.

Money Isn't the Issue

For entry to mid-level positions, salary is seldom an issue for many hidden market jobs. Among high-potential careers, particularly, job searchers deem any job a career stepping stone, even nonpaying internships. The idea is to break in. After that, it's survival of the fittest. The smartest, most talented and most driven stand the best chance of lasting.

Although most of the jobs are filled through inside sources, a significant number find their way to the published market. It pays to stay alert and tap into it.

The Visible (Open) Market

Meet the Players—Companies, Employment Agencies, Temporary Services, Executive Search and Career-Counseling Firms

Classifieds (or job or want ads) are run in daily newspapers, consumer and special-interest trade magazines and newsletters by companies, employment agencies, and temporary, executive recruiting, and career counseling firms. Company advertisers need little explanation, yet many applicants are not quite sure of the differences separating the remaining players. The most frequent mistake is calling employment agencies "headhunters," which offends both groups.

You'll soon see they not only function differently but cater to separate categories of job applicants.

Companies. Most companies use classified advertising to a certain extent. To control the hiring process, many run their own job ads. Sources at the *Personnel Journal,* the trade magazine for human resource professionals, say 95 percent of its human resource director readers use newspapers to fill positions. The companies range from tiny firms to *Fortune* 500 conglomerates, privately held to publicly owned, not-for-profit to profit making.

Employment Agencies. Employment agencies earn money by getting applicants jobs. They're paid by the company doing the hiring. Agency interviewers are called "placement managers." By the early '80s, disgruntled applicants tagged many such managers "flesh peddlers," because of their penchant for aggressively hustling bodies into job slots with little concern about whether it was an appropriate fit. Since then, agencies have made a concerted effort to topple that image. With tougher employer demands and fewer job orders, they're working harder selling applicants.

Temporary Service Firms. Temp firms have come a long way since they opened for business following World War II. Up until the mid-1970s, the bulk of their revenues came from supplying low-level clerical workers, secretaries, stenographers, bookkeepers and back office workers to companies with cyclical needs. The firms suffered a poor image. "Temp" work was considered a second-rate, low-paying resource for job hunters unable to capture full-time jobs.

Not any longer. By the early '80s, the temp industry captured respectability among clients and job hunters. Now it represents a valued labor source for companies large and small. The National Association of Temporary Services (NATS) in Alexandria, Virginia, reports that revenues for its 7,700 members are derived from supplying four categories of workers: 63 percent office/clerical; 15 percent industrial/manufacturing (blue collar); 10 percent licensed caregivers at institutions and home settings; and 12 percent technical/professional (managerial, accounting, sales and marketing).

According to the U.S. Bureau of Labor Statistics, well over 1 million temporary jobs exist in the United States, compared to 184,391 in 1970. Approximately 1 percent of the nonagricultural work force, or one in every 109 jobs, is employed by temp firms, compared to 1990 when one out of 384 nonagricultural jobs was a temp position.

As established as they are, most people think temp firms are employment agencies supplying temporary help. Temporary firm owners bristle when their organizations are called agencies.

Unlike employment agencies collecting fees (a percentage of an applicant's first-year salary) from client companies for pairing them with acceptable applicants, the temp company *is* the employer. Temp firms furnish their own employees (or temporaries) to handle customers' temporary staffing needs. Although the employees work somewhere else, they're paid by the temp firm. Temp service firms' profits come from marking up your hourly wage. Depending upon supply-and-demand conditions and worker skill level, markups range from 20 to 35 percent. A computer programmer, for example, earns significantly more than a secretary with word processing skills.

Beyond a competitive hourly wage, many temp firms offer their veteran workers a variety of perks unheard of 15 years ago. Many of the large, established firms provide health insurance at discounted corporate rates, vacation pay, referral bonuses, even profit sharing.

Executive Search Firms.   Often called "retainer firms," search firms work exclusively with companies rather than applicants. Their client is the company searching for an applicant rather than the job applicant.

Search firms specialize in finding executives at the supervisory, middle-management and senior-management levels. Salaries range from as low as $45,000 and climb to $400,000 and more for chief executive officer slots.

Search firms research, identify and recruit the best person in a given field and match that person to a management-level job. They're paid a retainer, which is about 33 percent of the executive's first-year salary, whether or not they actually find the right person. They're popularly known as "headhunters," because of the aggressive networking methods employed to track down applicants.

Career-Counseling Firms.   These include career managers, career management consultants, career guidance professionals, career guidance executives, recruitment advisers, recruitment consultants. Ethical career-counseling firms do nothing but counsel applicants on job-hunting techniques. *They will not find you a job.*

Many less-than-reputable firms lead clients to believe they can find them jobs. Thinking they'll get jobs, unsuspecting clients have been bilked for exorbitant fees. During the '80s, the Better Business Bureau (BBB) and attorneys general offices received thousands of complaints about fraudulent counseling firms. After lengthy investigations, the BBB uncovered high-pressure sales tactics, ridiculously priced aptitude tests, letter writing services and promises of employment that were never met. The problem is career-counseling firms, like employment agencies and temp service firms, are virtually unregulated.

Not all career-counseling firms are taking advantage of naive, often desperate, job searchers. Plenty of reliable firms legitimately help applicants get their job-hunting acts together by identifying aptitudes and teaching job-hunting techniques. From the onset, they make it clear you're paying for professional career assistance, nothing more.

New Strategies for an Old Market

In the mid-1970s and early-1980s, there were plenty of jobs to be had, and the suppliers—employment agencies, temporary service companies and executive recruitment firms—were cleaning up. Bodies were practically placed as soon as jobs surfaced. High-grade charming applicants with super grades and work experience secured jobs immediately.

Not any longer. In this buyer's market everyone but specialized temporary service companies is singing the blues. Almost all sectors of the placement community are hurting. Applicants are plentiful, and full-time jobs are not. And that's the way it's going to be through 1995 and beyond.

The National Association of Personnel Consultants (NAPC) in Alexandria, Virginia, the public relations arm of some 2,000 U.S. employment agencies, reports that business is off significantly. Yet its members are responsible for a conservative 10 to 12 percent of the national hirings, according to recent NAPC surveys.

With fewer jobs to fill, employment agency placement managers have time to kill, which can be turned to your advantage. Just a short while ago, placement managers at busy agencies barely spent 15 minutes with a client. Before résumés were shuttled to employers, managers perfunctorily interviewed applicants to see if they were breathing, presentable and reasonably articulate before being stamped acceptable.

The fast-moving conveyor belt of applicants from employment agencies to employers has ground to a crawl. Because agencies are hurting, applicants have an opportunity to work closely with placement managers exploring job opportunities. The relationship can work to both parties' advantage. It could even evolve into a career-long association.

The Temp Route—Hooking Up with the Right Firm Can Pay Off

Until a full-time job materializes either through an employment agency, company-placed classified ad or a hidden job market source, consider temporary work. You may be surprised by walking away with more than just a few weeks' pay.

Most experienced temporary workers are registered with a few different temp companies. Employment agencies expect loyalty from applicants, whereas temp companies encourage employees to work with more than one temp company because it makes them more marketable and competitive.

Working for a temp company in the best of times makes sense. In a down economy, it's an opportunity to sample many companies without being branded a job-hopper. There is a growing army of highly skilled workers, computer technicians, programmers and health care workers to name three, who move around the country working temporary assignments. Knowing their skills are always in demand, they relish the adventure and excitement of perpetual job changing. Where else could they experience new surroundings, people and corporate cultures and not be branded unstable recluses? The paycheck culture isn't everyone's cup of tea.

More and more companies are using temps as an auditioning process for full-time jobs. In the space of a few months, these companies can test six candidates and make a full-time job offer to the best of the lot. It's certainly cheaper and more efficient than hiring people based on credentials alone and then firing them when they don't work out six months later.

There are countless success stories of temp workers asked to stay on full-time. It sounds like a fairy tale, yet it happens all the time.

Temping is a ready-made networking platform. Where else can you get an opportunity to earn a salary and shop the job market at the same time? Do a first-rate job and you'll work continuously, shuttling from company to company as needs arise. Within 18 months, one temp employee I spoke to worked for Mobil Oil Corp., Grace & Co., BMG Music, McKinsey & Company and Bank Leumi before a hospital offered her a permanent job as a human resources interviewer.

Lastly, more and more temp companies are offering computer training to their regulars. Everyone benefits. When applicants master the latest software and computer systems, temp companies market the skills to conquer new accounts, all the while charging premium rates. As new or updated software is released, temp companies will either upgrade your skills or cross-train you so you're knowledgeable in many software packages. You can't lose. As you learn more, your hourly pay scale jumps.

A recently commissioned NATS survey of 2,508 temporary employees revealed the following: 70 percent of the participants saw temping as a way to improve job skills, and 54 percent said they were asked to continue on a full-time basis for the company they were assigned to.

Downside of Temping

Although temping has improved and employers expect to make greater use of temps as corporations continue to reshape themselves, there are caveats.

Beware of overzealous salespeople. Many temp firms operate like real estate agencies. Overzealous salespeople hungry to build a qualified stable of workers may promise more than they can deliver. They'll guarantee nonstop work, when realistically all that's available is two to three days a week. If you register with many temp firms, you'll avoid this.

Be prepared for monotonous work firms can't unload on full-time workers. Many companies use temps to handle expanded workloads and crunch deadlines.

Then there are companies who hire temps to do dirty, boring jobs they wouldn't ask full-timers to do because it's distasteful. A move is in the works, cartons have to be packed and unloaded or new filing and bookkeeping systems have to be set up. Worse yet, you may be sequestered to a dusty storeroom or basement and asked to work several days by yourself.

Ask Questions and Get It in Writing

Most temp firms are legitimate, but there are plenty of fly-by-night, fast-buck operations that are not. Be on your guard. Ask questions and get your working arrangement in writing. Find out what your hourly pay is, when you're going to be paid (like most companies, expect to be paid either weekly or biweekly) and approximately how long the assignment is. Since you're an employee of the temp firm, you ought to receive a W-2 form, not a 1099 form for independent contractors or consultants. The W-2 entitles you to worker's compensation and unemployment insurance, a 1099 does not. If the temp firm says you'll receive a 1099 and be paid when the client company pays its bill, head for the door. This is not a bona fide temp service company. Its collection problems are not your concern. What's more, it's violating the Federal Wage and Hour Law.

Working with Employment Agencies and Executive Recruitment Firms

Be practical. Unless you have a high-priced, marketable skill or impressive executive credentials, don't spend too much time pursuing executive recruitment firms. Instead, invest most of your time cultivating relationships with employment agencies. There are shortcuts for working with both. First, employment agencies.

Finding the Right Agency

Rather than waste time contacting every employment agency in your city, find one that specializes in your field. Start by checking the want ads daily to find out which agencies best serve you and then consider purchasing *The National Directory of Personnel Consultants*, published by the National Association of Personnel Consultants (3133 Mount Vernon Ave., Alexandria, VA 22305). Published yearly, it lists 1,500 to 2,000 agencies, specializing in 100 categories. You'll save time by taking advantage of its geographic and specialty listings.

Once you've located agencies that can help you, consider the following tips:

1. *Visit the agency.* Let instinct and gut feeling guide you. I'm not suggesting avoiding dingy offices in low-rent districts. But it could be a warning. It's safe to assume that a company operating out of a nicely furnished office in a prosperous location does a brisk business, has a good rapport with clients and thus has a steady flow of jobs coming in.

2. *Size up the placement manager.* A 10-minute conversation should give you a good idea whether you can work with this person. If the vibrations are negative, proceed cautiously. To be on the safe side, give the agency a couple of weeks to prove itself before investing time elsewhere.

Most important, make that first meeting count by plying the manager with questions. How good is this person's contacts? Get a reading on the manager's success rate.

3. *Understand the agreement.* Read the agency agreement carefully so you know exactly how the agency earns its fee. Most agencies are paid

a placement or contingency fee by the company when their applicants are hired. The majority of agencies advertise "Fee Paid" jobs, which means the company pays the agency anywhere from 10 to 35 percent of the applicant's first-year salary. But there are other fee arrangements as well:

- *Applicant-paid fees.* The employee assumes full responsibility for the fee. NAPC estimates some 10 percent of the agencies run applicant-paid fees. Thanks to the recession, that figure jumped a couple of points by 1990. What with companies struggling to stay afloat, many reason they don't have to pay a worker's agency fee. After all, the person may not work out.
- *Partially paid fees.* Prior to job acceptance, employer and employee reach an agreement to each assume a portion of the fee.
- *Fee reimbursed.* Employee pays fee, but employer agrees to reimburse it after a certain period. Employer is playing it safe by finding out whether the new person works out before coughing up the agency's fee.
- *Partial fee reimbursed.* Employer agrees to reimburse a portion of the fee after a stipulated period of employment.
- *Fee advanced.* Employer pays the fee initially and deducts the amount over a period from employee's paycheck.

Understand the fee arrangement before signing the employment contract. Read the fine print carefully, and don't be squeamish about asking questions. Just because a contract is printed doesn't mean it can't be amended. If a statement seems ambiguous or unreasonable, ask if it can be changed to your liking.

4. *Maintain contact.* Don't expect placement managers to give you a weekly progress report. They're tracking many clients, so it's virtually impossible for them to provide you with follow-up calls. Don't make a pest of yourself by calling every day. However, a weekly follow-up call is recommended. Naturally, agencies waste no time contacting you when employers are interested, but they may not consider you for every new job that comes in. Stay in touch.

Don't Expect Much from Headhunters

Jim Kennedy, editor and publisher of *Executive Recruiter News* and the *Directory of Executive Recruiters,* says job applicants expect too much of search firms. If you happen to match some or all of the specifications of an assignment they're trying to fill, you've hit paydirt. If not, don't give up. Instead, correspond with as many search firms as you think might help you. The larger-retainer search firms keep files on as many as 400,000 potential candidates in dozens of industries.

Kennedy's *Directory of Executive Recruiters* (Templeton Road, Fitzwilliam, NH 03447), updated yearly, lists recruiters alphabetically by industry, job function and geography.

Here are some pointers for working with search firms:

1. *Don't visit or call.* Unlike employment agencies, do not try to schedule an appointment, or worse yet, pop in unannounced. You're wasting time and it's inappropriate. Chances are you'll alienate the very person you want to befriend. Similarly, do not call unless you're returning their call. It's as simple as this: If they don't call you, they *ain't* interested.

2. *Be visible.* The best way to be discovered by a recruiter is to stand out. Successful headhunters have a knack for gathering information and being omnipresent. If you're hot, a shining star, a superstar in your field, they'll find you.

3. *Keep in touch.* Many search firms clean their files every few months. Don't assume you're permanently on file. As long as you're building a career, employed or unemployed, it pays to keep them apprised of your qualifications by writing to them about your accomplishments. You never know when they may get a call for your particular talents. It's a gamble worth taking.

4. *Don't expect acknowledgment of your correspondence.* Don't take it personally. They neither have the time nor staff to respond to every letter they receive.

Separating the Wheat from the Chaff

Combing the Classifieds—Who Said All Ads Are for Real?

Finally, some fast tips on interpreting want ads. There are three kinds of ads: real, phony and blind. Within a couple of weeks, you'll be spotting the differences. The trick to understanding them is to study them seven days a week. Like brushing your teeth and morning coffee, make it a daily ritual.

The heaviest ad day is Sunday, followed by Wednesday and Friday.

But it pays to scan them daily. You never know. Some perverse employer may run an ad on a Monday just to see how smart you are.

Unfortunately, not all ads are legitimate. Don't fault the newspapers' running them. They have no way of knowing which ads are legitimate and which ones are phony. Companies call in ads and pay for them. Publications only follow up if there are complaints. And then it's after the fact. You've already wasted time trying to make contact.

Some unscrupulous employers have no jobs to offer yet run enticing ads to see what the applicant pool looks like. What better way to upgrade your staff than to pick the cream of the crop from a vast unemployment talent pool? It's common practice in highly competitive industries. But don't expect anyone to admit doing it.

Initially, it's virtually impossible to separate bogus ads from real ones. Only time will tell. If the same ad appears for four or five straight weeks, write it off. Either the company doesn't know what it wants or it's a fake.

Finally, if an ad doesn't read right, chances are it's phony. A good ad is specific. For example:

SALES ASSOCIATE

National software company needs motivated self-starter with three to five years' sales experience to work on commission-plus basis. Generous end-of-year bonus if quota met. Salary negotiable.

Taking Your Chances with Blind Ads

Blind ads, however, pose other problems. Rather than a company or employment agency, you're responding to a post office box number. First, you don't know who you're responding to. The worst scenario: It could be *your* employer who ran the ad. Needless to say, this could turn into an embarrassing horror story. And second, you don't know whether it's a hard or soft opening or if the company is just fishing for talent.

Like the ad's name, you're in the dark and out of control. All you can do is take your chances and keep your fingers crossed. Although blind ads seem devious and underhanded, many reputable companies and executive search firms use them for good reason. For efficiency's sake, many understaffed, small companies prefer to conduct job searches in secrecy. By listing the company name and address in an ad, a company is forced to field hundreds of calls and answer an equal number of letters and résumés. In a normal market, an enticing ad can draw hundreds of applicants; in a tight market like ours, the number rises into the thousands. No wonder companies opt for anonymity. It's not to foil job searchers; it's just a practical tactic for finding the right person by limiting paper and phone work.

Even big companies with large human resource departments occasionally use blind ads to save time and paperwork. Blind ads have always been a favorite for executive search firms. The majority of search firms are small, three- to ten-person operations, which conduct their searches in total secrecy.

Want Ad Checklist

Here are some pointers that will help you get the most mileage from want ads:

1. *Don't limit yourself to one publication.* Naively, job seekers rely solely on want ads published in daily newspapers. Large industries are tracked by a few trade magazines and newsletters, many of which run want ads. Contact your industry's trade association to get a list of publications serving your industry.

2. *How exclusive and timely is the information?* Magazines work with at least a two-month lead time. By the time you read the ad, the job could be filled. Newspapers offer the freshest information. Ads are placed as late as 48 hours prior to publication.

3. *Don't assume employers are advertising in one publication.* They could be pursuing several as well as working with employment agencies to see what the market looks like.

Myth 4: Aggressive Networking Is the Key to a Successful Job Search.

Reality: *Networking is the recommended career tactic for the '90s. But not all networking efforts reap the same results. On one hand, aggressive, blind networking is self-defeating, inconsistent and politically incorrect. Creative and productive networking, on the other hand, is subtle, understated and strategic.*

Chapter Snapshot

- ☐ What the Heck Does the Word Mean?
- ☐ Networking as a Social Tool in Childhood
- ☐ The Networking Formula
- ☐ Formal Networking and the Pitfalls of the Blitzkrieg Approach
- ☐ Where Are the Power Brokers?
- ☐ Informal Networking's Tactical Strategies—You Never Know Who the Person You're Talking to Knows
- ☐ Traits and Attitudes of the World's Great Networkers
- ☐ Aggressive Tactics Don't Work!
- ☐ Networking Global Style
- ☐ Finding the King-Makers
- ☐ Milking the Information Interview
- ☐ Four Networking Commandments

❋ ❋ ❋ ❋ ❋ ❋ ❋ ❋

At this split second, there are hundreds of thousands of people networking, the well-publicized technique of using friends, business acquaintances and referrals to uncover job leads.

"Networking" has developed into a popular aphorism for success. If you're not a whirling dervish networker, you're doomed to mediocrity. You'll land a respectable job and earn a conservative living, but you won't go to the head of the class. Only killer, aggressive networkers will. So goes the well-entrenched myth.

The truth is, networking is important. It always was and always will be. It's critical in this tight job market where the supply of workers far exceeds demand, especially for choice jobs from entry level to senior management. But for many, networking has become more like a sport than a carefully nurtured career strategy. True networking reaping hefty long-term dividends is neither obvious nor aggressive. It's persistent, studied, cautious and political.

What the Heck Does the Word Mean?

I'd love to tell you about famous networkers from the past, but unfortunately, no one chronicled them. Suffice it to say, the concept of networking dates back to the beginning of civilization. It began when people realized they needed each other not just to mate but to survive.

Although no one knows for sure when the word *networking* was first used, most career experts trace its origins to the mid-1970s when women formed groups, or networks, to help each other secure job leads and career guidance. A solid network was made up of a tight chain of contacts threading itself through virtually every crevice of an industry, top to bottom. Once career and business writers endorsed networking, it wasn't long before it became widely touted as a crucial career-building technique.

Networking as a Social Tool in Childhood

Networking is usually associated with career building, yet the process of forming networks actually starts when we're children. Unknowingly, we develop a variety of networks throughout our lives. As children, the core "network" is our families. Growing up, our parents thrust us into the world and initiate our early networks that begin with play groups, followed by school classes and participation in clubs (chess, acting, collecting) and athletic teams.

By then we've picked up the ball. It's on to college where we gravitate toward networks that appeal to us—academic, athletic and social. Before even tasting our first jobs, most of us have already participated in more than a dozen informal and formal networks.

The Networking Formula

The process of making connections can be reduced to a simple formula. It begins with a need or goal, followed by the identification of others who share the same need. The result is contact and relationships. Or,

$$\text{Need (goal)} + \text{identification of others} = \text{contact}$$

For some people, networking is practically instinctive; others have to work at it. There are networkers and there are *networkers*. The former achieve erratic results, the latter have an uncanny knack for being in the right place at the right time. It's no accident either. If a layoff or bankruptcy is two months away, they're the first to know about it. While their colleagues are scurrying around in a panic wondering what to do next, the real networkers are quietly making calls and preparing to jump ship before it sinks. You can bet your entire bank account they'll be employed before anyone else. And they'll rocket through their careers with their network taking care of them.

In fact, this network is their lifeline to the world. It keeps them wired, plugged in, connected. But if you ask them how they network, they'll be at a loss for words. They're not being secretive; it's that most successful people go about networking intuitively and informally. They understand group dynamics and respect the differences between people. They have an uncanny knack for being everywhere and for finding information in the most unlikely places.

They shrewdly go about the contact-building process with adroit sophistication. At parties, business or informal gatherings, they always manage to be where the action is. Life is an adventure for these masterful communicators. After all, you never know where you'll unearth juicy tidbits of information or gossip—boardrooms, bars, poolhalls, street corners, even bathrooms of posh hotels and restaurants. Hang out long enough and the information will come to you.

The great networkers are meticulous information gatherers, unobtrusive schmoozers, professional minglers, born-again snoops. They could easily earn their livings as detectives or even journalists—perish the thought. If nothing else, give them honorary doctorates in social chemistry.

Watch them and learn. It's an apprenticeship yielding career-long dividends. Like learning a craft, a textbook takes you only so far. To bolt down that track ahead of the pack, you have to learn by doing. Observe networking virtuosi in action so you can imitate them. For these seasoned practitioners, networking is a combination philosophy, technique and art form all rolled into one.

Formal Networking and the Pitfalls of the Blitzkrieg Approach

This is a true networking saga: Over 200 advertising types crowded into a brightly lit, poorly ventilated Manhattan hotel conference room to network. It was the quarterly get-together of a local advertising association. Account executives, copywriters, production and finance professionals gathered to talk shop and trade information, hopefully leading to jobs.

It was a circus of well-pruned, neatly coifed professionals, sipping wine, scrambling about the room searching for prey—anyone who will listen to them for 15 seconds or more. Seasoned networkers worked the room like stand-up comics hungry for a break. A wired, stick-thin 34-year-old copywriter managed to paper the room with his business cards in less than 45 minutes. An incredible feat when you consider he had to slither around 150 sweating human beings.

Events like the above take place all over the United States. They're organized by professional career societies, business groups like the Chamber of Commerce, nonprofit organizations, churches and synagogues, college placement offices and alumni organizations. When you get beyond the tumult, cheap wine, stale crackers and moldy cheese, about the best anyone can hope to get out of these events is some short-term companionship.

Where Are the Power Brokers?

Most organized networking events are more successful as social events, opportunities to talk shop in a neutral setting, rather than meaningful career-building sessions. Put 100 copywriters, lawyers, computer programmers, engineers, doctors or safecrackers in the same room and ask them to network and it doesn't take a statistician to project the results. It's an exercise in futility, since they're all there for the same reasons. If by some stroke of luck, there are a couple of prime contacts in the bunch, only a few blessed attendees will walk away knowing something helpful. The very power brokers they want to meet—senior management, corporate recruiters, headhunters and trade association heads—are not there. So why bother?

Relying solely on formal, prearranged networking channels yields half-hearted results. The depressing result of an exhausting night of networking is often nothing more than a bad case of laryngitis.

Think twice before investing time in networking parties. Your chances of scoring a brilliant contact are a lot better sitting in a saloon all evening nursing a few beers. Don't take my word. Attend some networking parties as an observer rather than participant. Suddenly, the events take on new meaning.

Informal Networking's Tactical Strategies—You Never Know Who the Person You're Talking to Knows

Informal networking is harder and more time-consuming but ultimately more successful and gratifying than formal networking. Like searching for the back door to the hidden job market, informal networking forces you to be creative.

Rather than an organization making the rules, the informal approach relies on your own self-styled system of finding and developing leads. It embraces the thousands of casual calls to friends and colleagues, the countless hours playing golf, tennis or racquetball or nights spent in smoke-filled bars talking shop with cronies and potential leads. It's the unofficial "nonpaid" time invested in building your network. Many seasoned employed networkers say it amounts to more than 25 percent of their time.

For fast-trackers, it's practically a 365-day, 16-hour-a-day obsession. It sounds compulsive, but if you love what you're doing, why not? The difference between amateur and pro networkers is that amateurs think they're wasting time talking to people who can't do anything for them; the pros insist every contact is helpful, directly or peripherally. You just never know who you're talking to, or who the person you're talking to *knows*. Major players and decision makers, the folks you want to meet and impress, are not going to have spotlights on them. In fact, they may not be all that impressive-looking. They may be dressed like everyone else and meld right into the crowd. Some even work at keeping a low profile, preferring to be inconspicuous. Subtle networking teaches you to stay on your toes at all times. Be ready for the expected, look great and be armed with prepackaged brilliance, charm and wit.

Traits and Attitudes of the World's Great Networkers

Superstar networkers can be found in all fields, occupying all rungs of the organization ladder from CEO down to mailroom clerk. Some are leading the pack, others are strategically positioned at the bottom and middle. But they all share common traits. Uppermost, they know how to make things happen.

But whether they're running or starting companies, managing a division or ambling up the career ladder, the great networkers of the world have an intricate web of contacts working for them which they can call any time. They're so well positioned, information either starts with them or reaches them and then filters out to everyone else. They're at the heart of the grapevine.

The world's great networkers share these traits:

1. *Healthy attitude toward people.* Simply, great networkers like people, which immediately sets the tone of their relationships. Many of us have a nasty habit of quickly sizing up people and being off base in the process.

We've been taught first impressions count. More often than not, they're dead wrong. How many times have you met people who, on first meeting, seem hostile, belligerent or mean-spirited? But get to know them and you're shocked when you discover they're actually nice, even special. What you thought was aloofness or hostility was actually shyness. Great networkers start with a good attitude and an open mind.

2. *Don't give up.* Take bad days as a given. Everyone has them; you're not alone. The only way to cope with them is don't let yourself be swallowed up by them. Depression is like quicksand, it can smother you if you let it. The only antidote is stay busy and productive.

3. *Willingness to share information.* The backbone of good networking is reciprocity. Jump at the opportunity to help someone out. That doesn't mean sharing exclusive information with anyone. But if you trust someone, share freely. Like my mom used to tell me when I was a neurotic teenager, "Whatever you do for someone else comes back to you twofold." Or as the New Testament (Matthew, 7:12) says, "Do unto others as you would have them do unto you." Sooner or later, you'll be paid back. And ofttimes, it happens unexpectedly. People don't forget; more amazing, most enjoy helping others. Putting payback aside, it's a nice feeling.

Aggressive Tactics Don't Work!

We've been brought up thinking aggressiveness pays off. If you want to be successful, you must be aggressive. Just think of all the books written on how to liberate your aggressive side. How else do you conquer big accounts and seduce wavering clients? Be like the late John Wayne in the 1949 classic, "Sands of Iwo Jima." Take one hill after another until the enemy is vanquished. Don't stop until you get what you want.

We relish using war and sports analogies to describe business tactics. We "strategize" and "capture" accounts with the feverish intensity of military logicians plotting invasions. Or we "go the distance" and "run with the ball" when hot on a new account trail. When we screw up, we are guilty of "Monday morning quarterbacking." Sports jargon is so basic to our vocabulary, we hardly think about how silly it sounds to someone from another country who doesn't have the foggiest idea what we're talking about.

But when it comes to the noble art of networking, blind aggressiveness repels rather than attracts people. It's harsh, abrasive, lacking tact and diplomacy. In the worst situations, it alienates the very people we want to connect with rather than sows seeds for friendship. The war and sports analogies don't work.

True networking is not like conquering an account or hitting a homerun playing baseball. Productive networking is about building ironclad, self-sustaining long-term relationships. As one high-level corporate executive put it, "I don't believe in fast friends. If I'm hiring someone for a big job, I want someone I can trust."

Aggressive networkers are motivated by immediate gratification. They share information begrudgingly or as a bargaining tool, not for the sake of sharing. Obsessed with overtaking the competition, they don't know the meaning of the word reciprocity. They don't realize they're playing a losing game.

Good networking is a slow and persistent building process. As a rule, world-class networkers are understated, subtle and fair-minded.

Networking Global Style

Networking is not simply identifying leads and contacts and pouncing. You could get away with that kind of frontier tactic a century ago, but it's not the way business is conducted in the '90s. The world has changed and so have business styles. With the official launching of the

European Community on December 31, 1992, and the privatization of Eastern Europe and many Latin American countries, U.S. business-people are wheeling and dealing in an international arena for the first time. There is no universal business ethic, but rather a potpourri of cultures and styles. Welcome to the global economy.

Americans can no longer assume everyone conducts business the way they do. They must respect and understand Japanese, British, French, German, Italian and Russian customs and cultural styles; so if Americans do network, they can do it on an international plane. Europeans still consider Americans culturally backward. American businesspeople are fast learning that Europeans do business different-ly. Deals are seldom consummated instantly.

Even networking styles differ from country to country. Americans have no lock-and-key on the contact-building art. The British, for one, have been at it for centuries. Unlike American businesspeople, who create their own rules as they go along, the British are ruled by tradi-tion and protocol. Business, for example, is relegated strictly to the office, whereas lunch, dinner and weekends are strictly for socializing. They're offended by Americans who are always "doing business." They don't understand why it's a constant obsession. Americans, however, don't think twice about melding business and social activi-ties. A business opportunity is a business opportunity, regardless of time, place or event.

Not so in Japan. In Japan, the business day never ends. In America, the whistle blows at 5 p.m. In Japan, the business day is just shifting into second and third gear. True networking takes place after hours. The movers and shakers spend their evenings with business cronies at a local bar. This is when they let their hair down and get to know each other, mixing business and pleasure. It's networking Japanese-style. A saying among Japanese businessmen is, "You get through to a man's soul at night." It's not uncommon to stay out until the wee hours of the morning and then crawl into work the next morning at 9 a.m. Not an easy feat. But while the rest of the world sleeps, relationships are cemented and deals consummated.

Whether you're dealing with American or foreign businesspeople, keep in mind that networking is a sophisticated process requiring time, effort and an understanding and respect for the people you hope to connect with. That's the secret for building career-long associations.

Ineffectual networkers never quite master the game. They either network when it occurs to them or more frequently, when they've lost their jobs. Whether they're too aggressive or downright lazy, their connections are flimsy and temporary rather than concrete solid.

Finding the King-Makers

In your quest to build a solid network, you're going to be meeting all kinds of people. In *Throw Away Your Résumé and Get That Job!* (Prentice-Hall), Warren J. Rosaluk estimates that we all have access to 40,000 people who may be in a position to steer us toward a job. He contends that everyone is acquainted with 200 people, who in turn are acquainted with another 200 people. Simple multiplication tells you talking to 200 people gives you a potential network of about 40,000 contacts. It would a veritable utopia if you had this tiny army of people funnelling you information. Incredible fantasy. Realistically, the majority of those people can't help you, nor do they care to.

According to a survey of Goodrich & Sherwood Company, a human resources management consulting firm, serious networking reduces your job search. If you see 2 people a week, you may expect the search to last up to a year; if you meet 10 people a week, your search will usually be cut about six months. But if you see 20 people a week, you're likely to conquer a new job in 90 days or less.

Within any network of friends, family, colleagues and casual contacts, you'll encounter four types of contacts. According to Northwestern University's Victor Lindquist, they are:

1. Those who are insulated and can't be bothered.

2. People who mean well and will help you when it occurs to them.

3. Sincerely interested contacts who will do whatever they can for you.

4. King-makers who attract information and are politically well positioned.

The king-makers are the most valuable, as well as the most impressive contacts. Every organization has them. They are strategically positioned at the apex of the information loop with gossip and news flowing to them from all directions. They're so well connected, they know about events months before they happen.

Although king-makers relish their power, they seldom abuse it. They are master communicators who instill trust because they have no ulterior motives or axes to grind. Holding the confidences of the world, they are the ultimate power brokers. Hypnotize them and you'll be amazed at the wealth of information, dirt to classified, that pours out from their vaultlike brains. These networkers are the only ones who can separate fact from fiction. No wonder they're CEOs' chief confidants or, in government, high-ranking advisers. When crisis strikes, they're the first ones called.

They exist in every company, field and specialty. Get to know them. Not only can they be a valuable information source, they'll show you how to tap into the information chain.

Milking the Information Interview

Another excellent strategy for extending your networking chain is the information interview, which is nothing more than an informal conversation with an employer to find out about an industry, company and, of course, job prospects. College placement advisors tout it as an excellent technique for getting a bird's eye view of an industry. But it's also an excellent networking tool.

Don't assume that because employers are not hiring, they can't be a valuable information source. Rather than call, write a brief letter to either the employer or a high-ranking associate politely requesting 15 minutes of their time. You'll be pleasantly surprised by the results. After all, you're not asking for a job, just information and advice which carries no price tag or obligation. For good public relations alone, it makes sense for them to respond.

Once in the door, take advantage of the opportunity. Not only will you learn about the company and its hiring policies, but you'll hear about other companies that might be hiring now or in the future.

Don't waste time. Prepare yourself beforehand by learning about the company and, if possible, the person you're seeing. Busy people are giving you precious time, so get to the point. And don't leave without politely asking if there is anyone else this person can suggest you speak to.

Even if you don't uncover a job lead, you'll add another link to your networking chain.

The information interview is also excellent preparation for job interviews. You'll get a different perspective of the interview situation. Rather than the employer controlling the interview, you're piloting the ship.

Be brilliant and you may be pleasantly surprised. Imagine the employer spinning around in his upholstered chair and saying: "You know, I like the way you handle yourself. You ask insightful questions. You're a thinker. I could use a person like you. Have you ever considered working for Cellophane Surfboards?" Don't bank on it, but as comedian Judy Tenuta says, "It could happen."

In the course of your job search, try and schedule as many and as wide a variety of information interviews as you can.

Four Networking Commandments

Finally, some priceless advice for profitable networking:

1. *Network daily and set goals.* The cardinal rule of networking is never lose touch with people. Rather than wait until you're in trouble, always keep the networking wheels in motion. Let too much time pass (six months to a year), and you've lost a potentially valuable contact.

Set flexible networking goals. Try to make 5 to 10 networking calls a day, either to make new contacts or to keep existing ones warm. If you make 10 calls a day, that's 50 calls a week or 200 calls a month. By the law of averages, you're bound to add at least a dozen valuable links to your networking chain.

2. *Everyone is reachable.* Busy people are hard to pin down, but it doesn't mean they can't be approached. Don't waste your time or theirs calling during conventional business hours. Busy people are either in meetings, on the phone or out of the office. We touched on this topic in Myth 1, in the section "Secrets of Reaching Busy People."

Picking up where that section left off, successful networkers rate early evening, between 6 p.m. to 7 p.m., as the prime time for reaching busy people. The secretaries and drones have gone home and the workaholics are hunched over their desks intent on impressing their bosses. This is the best time to connect with unreachable bosses and senior executives. In peace and quiet, they're either getting important work done or doing some networking of their own. It's the perfect time to find out what your colleagues and friends are up to.

Summing up, start with a healthy attitude toward people in power. Don't put them on pedestals because they have big jobs. Everyone is reachable, if you know how and when. The tough part is breaking through the fortresslike structures which insulate and protect them.

Every organization has gatekeepers. Your job is to find, connect with and impress them. They have the power to open the creaking doors to the inner circle, selectively doling out keys to the executive washrooms. Alienate them and your career is on permanent hold; befriend them and there is no telling how far you'll go.

3. *Information is everywhere.* Whether ambling down the street or in hotel lobbies, airports, bus stations, bars or at parties or family gatherings—you never know who you're going to meet. Talk to someone for a few hours and you'll be surprised what you'll learn. Even vacations are incredible networking opportunities.

4. *Keep a networking diary (or log).* Keeping a journal or diary can be a real drag. It takes discipline, yet it's worth the effort. If you're con-

scientious about building a network, you're going to be speaking to hundreds of people. The only way you're going to keep track of them and separate the hot from the lukewarm leads is by noting contacts every time they're made. Don't wait days or weeks before jotting down your impressions. Do it while your insights are fresh.

List names, addresses, phone numbers, observations and proposed strategies. Keep entries brief and to the point. A few sample entries might look like this: .

Week Ending September 18, 1993

Sept. 14—Information interview with Clide McFatter at Stevens International. Nice guy. Picked up dirt on Stevens. No jobs, cutting back. Told me to call old friend Fanny McPherson, information specialist at Twiggy Time. She's well connected and will candidly tell me what the possibilities are at her firm.

Sept. 16—After-work drink with Ben Bozo Smith at alumni association who promises to hook me up with buddy at Bartol Bromlett International. Will call on Sept. 18 to find out if he laid groundwork by contacting his friends.

Sept. 18—Called Bozo Smith who gave me green light on calling friend Teddy Tritchett at Bartol. Call Tritchett at 8 a.m. on Sept. 23. Expecting my call. Again, Bozo Smith said Tritchett is a shooting star. An important cog.

Fruitful networking takes work. But it can also be exciting meeting new people all the time. Once you get into it, you'll be pleasantly surprised when you discover networking is not the necessary evil you thought it was. It's actually fun. Done right, it can yield big rewards. Done wrong, it can sink you.

Myth 5: Super-Growth Fields Offer the Best Opportunities.

Reality: *Using history as our guide, high-growth fields are not the only game in town.*

Chapter Snapshot

- □ Question Conventional Thinking
- □ Don't Believe Everything You Read—Trends Are Short-Lived
- □ Create Your Own Opportunity—Don't Be Afraid to Take Chances!
- □ Position Yourself for the Future
- □ Six Skills Employers Most Want
- □ Following an Old-Fashioned Career Route—Check Out Apprenticeship Programs
- □ Hot and Cold Careers
- □ Hot Careers for the '90s—Information Technology to Travel Management

* * * * * * * * *

Squash a half century of career advice into one sentence, and it would sound something like this: "Get into a high-growth field offering plenty of opportunity." Between early adolescence and late teens, most of us can rake up memories of well-meaning advisors pointing us toward such hot fields. Right behind mother-in-law jokes, comedians are still getting rich recounting stale shticks of coercive parents pushing kids into medicine, law or accounting because they're safe, profitable and respectable professions.

Parents will always be telling their children what to do with their lives. It's genetic. They can't help themselves. I even gently warned my actor son that the odds of making it on screen or stage are staggering. I insisted it was tougher than journalism. What impact did my fatherly warning have? He went right on shoveling scrambled eggs and toast into his mouth at conveyor-belt speed. He wasn't worried.

Thankfully, few of us heed warnings about uncertain careers. Pursuing a career is like falling in love. There are no rules, formulas or pat solutions guiding us to smart decisions. Like picking a mate, it is often just as much an emotional as it is a rational decision. You never quite know how things will work out. You cross your fingers and hope for the best. The very unpredictability of your decisions makes life exciting, challenging and fun. Choosing a career amounts to one of life's most exciting adventures.

Don't expect all your decisions to bear fruit. They may be right for the moment, but wrong for the long term. No matter what the futurists say, no one knows what lies ahead. Mistakes are part of the equation. You'll take some wrong turns and detours, but if you're honest with yourself and in touch with your needs, you'll find the road leading to career fulfillment. If you stay attuned to yourself and the marketplace, you'll realize opportunity lurks everywhere. Just because everyone is following one path, don't assume it's the right one. It might be the very path to avoid.

Let's take a look at the entire career waterfront, covering high- to low-growth fields, as well as unconventional career paths.

Question Conventional Thinking

If you have two equally appealing jobs to choose from—one in a trendy high-growth industry, the other in a slow-growth or evolving industry—which one do you choose? The former offers immediate opportunity, the latter has enormous potential. One is secure, the other risky. I'd take my chances with the job in the slow-growth industry. A good part of job hunting is about following your instincts and making informed judgments based upon accurate information. That's about as scientific as playing the commodity market. If you don't listen to that inner voice, and the field takes off, you'll beat yourself up later.

Naysayers laughed at stereophonic sounds, color television, personal computers, compact discs and every major innovation that has come down the pike. Take cable television. Fifteen years ago, it was hardly a poor stepchild to the well-entrenched broadcasting industry. Cable was experimental and untried. Yet cable visionaries touted it as television's future.

Cable innovators are enjoying the last laugh. No longer in its infancy, we're fast approaching the day when cable will be a staple in all homes. Ironically, compared to broadcast TV, cable TV is underplayed. Yet it's an ascending industry. In *Future Shock,* Alvin Toffler predicted that we would become a world of niches as the mass audience breaks down into segments and subgroups. One innovative cable company announced that it won't be long before subscribers have 500 channels to choose from.

Can you think of a better medium for a melting pot society? Question conventional paths. A better one just might be right under your nose.

Don't Believe Everything You Read— Trends Are Short-Lived

Like fashion and music trends, there are also hiring trends. Within a decade, growth fields can become no-growth fields. A paring of government budgets, for example, may put a hold on defense and aerospace projects. Companies heavily dependent upon government contracts react by temporarily freezing hiring. When the news spreads to engineering campuses, students panic and switch out of aeronautical and mechanical engineering into electrical and chemical engineering. A monumental error.

Companies may retrench, but they *never* stop hiring. The very companies that delayed hiring spin on their heels and soon find they need engineers to meet new needs. And what was an oversupply of engineers turns into a shortage. It happens all the time.

Similarly, prolonged recessions often trigger real estate slumps, pushing residential and commercial properties down as much as 50 percent. Since most people stop buying or selling property, the related construction, electrical, plumbing and home furnishings industries suffer as well. Meanwhile, smart real estate agents and developers, along with contractors and architects find other income avenues. By working harder and longer, they're tapping survival skills they never knew they had. When they ride out the storm, they'll be in better shape than they were before. Hard times fine-tune coping mechanisms.

Look at financial services, an industry that has endured a roller coaster history. Expanding in the '60s, consolidating in the '70s, tumbling and then shrinking following the 1987 stock market crash, it slowly turned around and picked up by mid-1991.

There are lessons to be learned from all of this.

Create Your Own Opportunity—Don't Be Afraid to Take Chances!

Rather than trying to fit into a job because it offers immediate opportunity, find one that excites you and create your own opportunity. Even in tough markets, there are jobs to be had. The challenging part is finding them. In some industries they're plentiful; in others they're not.

The odds of breaking into cutthroat jobs in journalism, film, TV, radio, advertising and fashion, for example, will always be staggering. Once you break in, the chances of succeeding are equally forbidding. Does that mean you shouldn't try? That's like a fighter throwing in the towel before the first bell clangs.

Compare it to a marathon race. If all the runners are perfect human specimens—lean, muscular running machines—do you pack up your running shoes and go home? If you've trained for the event, quitting is cowardice. The same goes for breaking into a tough career. If you think you have the talent, drive and creativity to make it, not trying is a mortal sin. You'll be another wannabe who crawls through life blaming everyone but yourself. Like Marlon Brando's legendary line in *On the Waterfront,* the 1954 film classic, "I coulda been a contenda." There are thousands of "contendas" out there, and they're all singing the same tired dirge. Watch out or you could be wailing the same lament if you're not careful. "I could have been a great copywriter if I had taken that low-paying copy job offered to me." Or, "I should have listened to my gut instinct and taken that gofer job with a small Indiana radio station. I could have produced better programs than they're airing now. Those guys have no talent." Hollow excuses. Like they say, criticizing is easy, but doing takes guts and initiative.

Whether it's a high-demand field hiring only a few or a low-demand, shrinking field, hard-working job searchers willing to hustle can go far. Barring agriculture, which has been declining since the turn of the century, many low-growth industries offer mouth-watering opportunities. The U.S. Department of Labor reports manufacturing jobs will decline by more than 600,000 jobs through the year 2005, yet the industry will still account for almost 14 percent of total U.S. employment. It's a dismal outlook for bank tellers, service station attendants and butchers, yet they're still finding jobs. A decade from now, however, they may all be replaced by computers.

While technology eliminates jobs, it also triggers countertrends spawning niche industries. The crafts and health food industries are good examples. Back in the "drop out" '60s when thousands of disgruntled young college students snubbed materialism and headed for the hills "to do their thing," selling crafts and organic foods were favorite livelihoods for the disenfranchised. It was the counterculturally correct thing to do. Today, many of those former hippies have turned their rebellion into successful businesses. Many are multimillionaires. Necessity and maturity turns idealists into pragmatists.

Back in the '60s, rebellion propelled many career seekers. Today, it is a healthy combination of survival and personal conviction. Old-fashioned job hunting as well as the notion of staying in one job for most of your career have been debunked. The doors have opened; you can follow any course that makes sense.

Position Yourself for the Future

The key to a bright career is knowledge, information and training. "Technology is changing so fast, we are forced to train and retrain to stay alive," said the president of an Indianapolis printing company. He went on to say education and training are crucial to the survival of U.S. business.

To keep up, U.S. industry is investing more in training. Yet, the average American worker lacks the necessary skills to take him or her into the next century. According to the American Society of Training and Development (ASTD) in Alexandria, Virginia, by the mid-1980s, the United States was spending some $30 billion on formal training programs and $180 billion on informal, on-the-job training. The U.S. Department of Labor's Bureau of Labor Statistics estimates that 1.5 percent of payroll is funnelled into training programs. And that's hardly adequate. We ought to be spending 2 percent in the near term and 4 percent over the long term, say ASTD economists.

Solution? Don't wait for someone to spoon-feed you career skills. Do as much as you can on your own. Don't make the same mistakes as prior generations and assume benevolent bureaucrats will take you under their wings and be career guides and mentors. It won't happen, and if it did, you would suffer the consequences by abdicating control of your career.

The Hudson Institute, a not-for-profit research organization and think tank in Indianapolis, confirms the growing complexity of most jobs. Its report, *Workforce 2000*, says that by the year 2000 "below-average" skills will be good enough for only 27 percent of jobs created after 1985, compared with 40 percent of the jobs existing in the mid-1980s. About 41 percent of the new jobs will require average or better skill levels, up from 24 percent.

Get ready for the future so you'll have the skills to capture jobs that are on the drawing board right now. Stay on top of the technologies that affect you. Don't wait for change; learn about it as it's happening.

Get used to the idea that updating your skills *must* be a career-long obsession. You must change with technology. Getting comfortable in a job is the first step toward stagnation. *Knowledge is your best defense against change.*

Six Skills Employers Most Want

You have incredible success fantasies that perhaps include cars, homes, vacations, expensive clothes. And you've got the right attitude too. You're ambitious, committed, motivated, driven and a plugger. In short, you've got what it takes. So what! They don't count for much if you don't have the skills employers deem essential for success.

Employers used to say, "Give me people who can read, write and do simple math and I'll train them for the jobs I have available." Not any more. As work became more complicated, they discovered they needed workers who could conceptualize, organize and verbalize thoughts, work in teams, and integrate new technology and sophisticated production processes. Easier said than done. To master all of the above, you need these six skills:

1. *Three Rs.* Incredible as it seems, the most common reason for rejecting potential job candidates is inadequate reading, writing or math skills. Unfortunately, educational standards throughout the United States aren't uniform.

A Department of Labor study found that 60 percent of Americans between the ages of 21 and 25 lack the basic reading and writing skills needed in the modern workplace. Equally shocking, placement managers and human resource professionals routinely receive poorly written résumés and cover letters full of spelling and grammatical errors, many of them from college grads.

Companies aren't looking for scholars, but they do expect job applicants to write simple, error-free sentences. Don't be upset if you're weak in these basic academic skills. You're not alone. It doesn't mean you have to go back to school either. Recognizing the problem is the tough part. The rest is easy.

The solution lies in a basic grammar handbook, a variation of the text your junior high school teachers should have made you memorize cover to cover. Read it carefully and do the exercises. Practice writing every chance you get. Write letters, compose fictitious memos, let your imagination run away with itself. And Read! Read! Read! You don't have to reread the classics. *The Wall Street Journal, Barrons, Newsweek* or *Time,* for example, are fine. The best way to learn to read is start with what you enjoy and then, every once in a while, push your limits.

Rather than reading for comprehension, read for style, sentence structure and spelling. Try it: The exercise will prove invaluable in your job search. Reading will make letter-writing easier and help you score well on skill tests, which many employers inflict on hopeful candidates. When you land a job, you'll be able to dash off pithy memos and reports. If you can't produce crisp memos, what good are you? We'll get into letter-writing skills in great detail in Myth 8: "You Don't Stand a Chance without a Knockout Résumé."

2. *Communication Skills.* Reading and writing are core communication skills, yet we spend most of our time listening and speaking. According to the ASTD, most people spend 8.4 percent of communication time writing, 13.3 percent reading, 23 percent speaking and 55 percent listening.

Only idiosyncratic geniuses can get away with mumbling monosyllabic phrases and speaking in non sequiturs. The rest of us must make sense. When we're not talking, we're listening, another vital skill everyone must master.

Any successful salesperson can tell you how important speaking and listening skills are. These salespeople are gifted communicators who have elevated communication to an art form. You'd never doubt their willingness to stake their lives on their products. That's real talent. More on the importance of selling ability in Myth 7: "The Candidate with the Highest Qualifications Always Gets the Job."

3. *Adaptability (Problem Solving and Creativity).* Companies can no longer amble along offering a single product or service. They must either improve current products or offer new and better ones. The pressure to stay competitive and grasp for market dominance has put a premium on problem solving and creativity.

Not only is getting a job tougher than it ever was; holding onto it is even harder. In the '50s, an old family friend who held a secure job with a large publishing company unloaded his secret of permanent employment. You don't have to kill yourself to make a decent living, he confided. Getting a good job was the hardest part. But once your foot is in door, you can coast for the next 30 or 40 years and walk away with a fat pension and plenty in the bank.

"Get on the good side of your boss and stay there," he advised. "Remember his birthday, keep your mouth shut and don't badmouth anyone. Nobody likes a troublemaker. If you have a problem, solve it quietly." He wasn't kidding. It worked for him. He left the company after logging 40 years.

Today, that kind of advice seems as dated as the Model T Ford and black-and-white television. The days of free corporate rides are over. Try and hide in a corner and your days are numbered. As you read this page, corporate America is dumping organizational sponges like my old family friend. Profits are more important than loyalty.

Employers have not gotten meaner, only smarter and more practical. Time is money, as they say. Put yourself in an employer's shoes and you'll see the job-searching process in a realistic light.

Employers can't afford to hire drones. They need people who understand their mission and who help them achieve it. If you can't fatten the bottom line, you're useless. More on this in Myth 10: "Employers Are Autocratic Powerlords Who Know Exactly What They're Looking For: Ergo, They Hold All the Negotiating Cards." But if you make money for an employer, you've written your own insurance policy. Once employers latch onto creative, hard-working problem solvers, they'll do everything they can to hold on to them.

4. *Personal Management (Self-Esteem, Motivation, Career Development)*. Productivity is directly correlated to self-esteem. Studies reveal that workers with good self-images take pride in their work. They set and meet goals and work hard to better themselves. That's no small feat in a business environment as uncertain as the weather. Jarring disturbances—mergers, acquisitions, consolidations, layoffs—erode self-esteem, creating stress. Workers feel powerless and out of control because they can't move toward their goals. Their career destiny is up in the air. That's enough to keep anyone up nights.

Despite all this chaos, rather than keep your fingers crossed and hope for the best, you're expected to come to work wearing an emotional flack jacket, ready for the unexpected. Even well-established grapevines don't always know when and where the axe will fall.

Despite turbulence, employers need people who keep their cool and who have a strong sense of self-worth and value: the fuel propelling them to reach their potential. The ideal workers, according to motivation experts, are self-directed, high-functioning and autonomous. Rather than just putting in time to collect their paychecks, they feel good work carries intrinsic value.

Everyone reaps rewards from that kind of attitude. The employer turns out better products and services; the worker builds a career.

5. *Organizational Skills (Leadership)*. Organizations are a complicated labyrinth of explicit and implicit power structures. In the explicit

structure, leadership is bestowed by title and authority; in the implicit structure, it is subtly woven and cultivated by the respect of peers. In *America and the New Economy*, economist Anthony Patrick Carnevale (also executive director of the ASTD's Institute for Workplace Learning) says knowing how to function within an organizational maze has never been more important. He says workers need strong organizational skills to participate in the tight networks that have replaced rigid hierarchies.

Those workers who master the organization game will go the furthest. They're functioning at the razor's edge, armed with a network that has them wired to news on all fronts. Organizations actually offer training in "organizational effectiveness," the corporate term for making friends and influencing people to help companies reach their goals and further your career at the same time.

Gifted practitioners at organizational politics become leaders with the power to either help manage organizations or start their own. Leaders have priceless assets employers need. They are power brokers with the persuasive energy to be either allies or traitors. They can rally workers for a common good and simple-mindedly boost productivity. Or they can be negative forces, subtly undermining and weakening the organization like a malignant cancer.

Employers need and rely on leaders. And they're willing to pay premium dollar to keep them.

6. *Interpersonal Skills* (*Negotiation, Teamwork*). The ASTD reports that interpersonal and negotiation skills are the foundation for successful teamwork. A better term for interpersonal skills is "people skills." Rather than hiring people with skills to get the job done, they're buying people who can motivate others. They can mesh their talents with others to achieve greater results. That's teamwork. No wonder management heavies have been making a big deal about teaching teamwork skills in order to build self-directed groups. Do it right and you have motivated workers, better products and, naturally, bigger profits.

Although management aggressively combs organizations to find and train teamwork builders, they usually surface by themselves. Every organization has them. When I was growing up in Brooklyn, I used to call them "street corner shrinks." You had a problem, they solved it. If there was a mission, they helped get it done. They worked better in groups than they did alone. If someone had to be coaxed or persuaded, they found the best people for the task. When two guys were about to bludgeon each other to death over a point in a stickball game, they jumped in to strike a harmonious chord. If there was a controversy over an important task, they had a knack for separating people from problems. When they got older and took their people-building skills to the assembly line, they put their egos aside to work for the greater good, the team's goals. When these charismatic souls were christened organizational assets, they were called "team play-ers."

Combine the above skills with technical know-how and you have a model twenty-first-century worker, whom employers call "gold-collar workers." The have everything going for them, technical smarts as well as finely honed communication skills. The most difficult to recruit, they'll never want for a job.

Following an Old-Fashioned Career Route—Check Out Apprenticeship Programs

In search of high-potential workers, many employers are taking a fresh look at an antiquated model—the apprenticeship. This crazy job market has proven a college education is not the surefire ticket to a career everyone thought it was. Another career route is an apprentice-ship, an option enjoying a renaissance. Traditionally popular with job seekers with high school vocational school diplomas, the U.S. Bureau of Labor Statistics reports an increase in the number of apprentices with a college education. Unable to find suitable jobs in their own fields, an increasing number of college graduates are turning to the skilled trades for work. In fact, this trend has put high school gradu-ates at somewhat of a disadvantage when competing for apprentice-ship openings. Often, college graduates are more sought after by pro-gram sponsors because they show greater management potential.

An apprenticeship is a relationship between an employer and an employee during which the worker, or apprentice, learns a trade. The apprenticeship covers all aspects of the trade and includes on-the-job training and related instruction. Apprenticeships last one to six years, most running about four years. During this time, apprentices work under experienced workers known as journeyworkers—the status attained after successfully completing the apprenticeship. Typically, the apprentice's pay starts out at about half that of an experienced worker and increases steadily throughout the apprenticeship.

Apprentices who successfully complete registered programs receive certificates of completion from the U.S. Department of Labor or a fed-erally approved state apprenticeship agency. For the past 55 years, the apprenticeship system has relied on federal and state funds, with business and labor designing specific programs. Registered programs offer apprenticeships in over 830 occupations. About 100,000 new apprentices are registered each year. Many are in the following occupations:

1. Electrician
2. Carpenter
3. Plumber
4. Sheet metal worker
5. Machinist
6. Roofer
7. Firefighter
8. Bricklayer
9. Cook/Chef
10. Correction officer
11. Automobile mechanic
12. Diesel mechanic
13. Welder
14. Cement mason
15. Toolmaker

Currently 27 states, the District of Columbia, Puerto Rico and the Virgin Islands have apprenticeship agencies. To apply, visit or write a local job service office (listed in the state government section of the telephone directory under such names as Employment Security Commission or Employment Service); a local office of the Labor Department's Bureau of Apprenticeship and Training (listed under U.S. Government in many large cities); a state apprenticeship agency; or a joint apprenticeship, union or employer engaged in the craft you want to enter. For information, write the Bureau of Apprenticeship and Training, Employment and Training Administration, U.S. Department of Labor, 200 Constitution Ave. NW, Washington, D.C. 20210, or one of the department's 10 regional offices in Boston, New York, Philadelphia, Atlanta, Chicago, Dallas, Kansas City (MO), Denver, San Francisco or Seattle.

Now let's turn corners and look at some hot and cold careers plus some projected to show superior growth.

Hot and Cold Careers

Capsulized Job Prospects for 12 Occupational Groups

Let's wind down and give a down-and-dirty peek at the job market through 2005, according to the U.S. Department of Labor's Bureau of Labor Statistics (BLS). First, a guide to BLS terms:

- *Grow much faster than average.* Increase 35 percent or more (projected employee increase between 1990 and 2005).

- *Grow faster than average.* Increase 25 to 34 percent.

- *Average growth.* Increase 14 to 24 percent.

- *Grow more slowly than average.* Increase 5 to 13 percent.

- *Show little change.* Increase or decrease 4 percent or less.

- *Decline.* Decrease 5 percent or more.

Executive, Administrative and Managerial. The growth of complex organizations plus the continuing expansion of the economy will contribute to *faster-than-average growth* for this group. Because they're employed in every industry, employment prospects will vary. Managers and administrators employed in the service industries will experience faster-than-average growth, especially business, engineering and management services. Yet, those working in government will face average to slower-than-average growth. Many businesses will reduce administrative costs and employ fewer managerial workers.

Professional Specialty. This large group includes engineers, architects and surveyors; computer, mathematical and operations research occupations; life, physical and social scientists; lawyers and judges; social, recreational and religious workers; teachers, librarians and counselors; health diagnosing, assessment and treating occupations; and communications, visual arts and performing arts occupations.

The group as a whole will grow *faster than average*. However, growth rates for individual occupations vary. Physical therapists, human service workers, operations research analysts and computer systems analysts will grow much faster than average while physicists, astronomers, librarians, musicians and mining, nuclear and petroleum engineers should grow more slowly than average. Most new jobs will be in education and health services.

Technicians (and Support Occupations). This category includes health technologists and technicians, engineering and science technicians, computer programmers, tool programmers, aircraft pilots, air traffic controllers, paralegals, broadcast technicians and library technicians.

Overall employment will grow *faster than any* other major occupational group. One of the *fastest-growing* occupations is paralegals. And increased demand for medical services has boosted demand for radiologic technologists, medical record technicians, surgical technologists and electroencephalographic technologists. Jobs for health technologists and technicians will account for about half of all the jobs in this group. Employment of computer programmers will grow rapidly as more organizations use computers and take advantage of new software.

Employment of broadcast technicians will record little change, but employment of air traffic controllers and library technicians will grow more slowly than average.

Marketing and Sales Occupations. With an increased demand for financial, travel and other services, employment will experience *average growth.* A large number of part-time and full-time positions will be available for cashiers and retail sales workers because of the size of these occupations and high turnover as well as employment growth. Higher-paying sales occupations (securities and financial sales workers, for example) are more competitive than retail sales jobs.

Administrative Support Occupations (Including Clerical). These workers prepare and record memos, letters and reports; collect accounts; gather and distribute information; operate office machines; and handle other administrative tasks. Even though this group employs the most workers, employment growth will be *slower than average.* As a proportion of total employment, these occupations will decline by 2005.

Increased automation will limit growth in many clerical occupations such as typists, word processors and data entry keyers; bookkeeping, accounting, and auditing clerks; and telephone operators.

Teacher aides and hotel desk clerks will grow faster than average, and receptionists and information clerks will experience much faster-than-average growth.

Service Occupations. Demand for protective services; food and beverage preparation; health services; and personal and cleaning services workers will grow *faster than average.* Reasons? A growing population and economy, combined with higher personal incomes and more leisure time. This group is expected to add the largest number of jobs of any occupational group by 2005.

Because of the size, high turnover and fast growth of many food service occupations—chefs, cooks and other kitchen workers—full- and part-time jobs will be plentiful.

In the health service sector, medical assistants—one of the fastest growing occupations—and nursing and psychiatric aides will grow much faster than average.

Agriculture, Forestry, Fishing and Related Occupations. Although demand for food, fiber and wood is expected to increase as the world's population grows, the use of more productive farming and forestry methods and the consolidation of small farms are expected to result in *little or no employment change* in most of these fields.

Mechanics, Installers and Repairers. Workers in this group adjust, maintain and repair automobiles, industrial equipment, computers and other types of machinery. Projections vary by occupations, but overall *average growth* is forecasted because of the continued importance of mechanical and electronic equipment throughout the economy.

Computer and office machine repairers will be one of the fastest-growing occupations in this group. However, communications equipment mechanics and telephone installers and repairers will decline because of labor-saving advances.

Construction Trades (and Extractive Occupations). Practically all the new jobs will be in construction. *Average employment growth* is expected because of an upturn in the residential and commercial real estate markets, along with programs to modernize plants and repair infrastructures (highways, bridges, dams). But continued stagnation of oil and gas industries and sluggish demand for coal, metal and other minerals will mean meager employment prospects for extractive workers.

Production Occupations. This includes workers who set up, adjust, operate and tend machinery and use handtools and handheld power tools to make goods and assemble products. *Little change or a slight decline* in employment is expected due to increased imports, overseas production and automation.

Some growth is expected for plastics machine operators because plastics are increasingly being substituted for metal.

Transportation and Material-Moving Occupations. Workers operate equipment moving people and materials. Although overall employment will *grow about as fast as average,* again prospects vary by occupation. Faster-than-average growth is expected for bus drivers, and average growth is projected for truck drivers. But slower-than-average growth is forecasted for material-moving equipment operators because of the increased use of automated material-handling systems. And water and railroad transportation industries will experience an employment decline as technological advances increase productivity.

Handlers, Equipment Cleaners, Helpers and Laborers. Thanks to automation, employment will increase *more slowly than average.* High turnover and cyclical economic swings will affect employment prospects, especially for construction laborers.

Fastest-Growing Occupations

Here's where the action is, according to BLS statistics. Below is a list of the 30 fastest-growing occupations through the year 2005 by percentage ranking. (Note: The percentage figure reflects the projected difference between the number employed between 1990 and 2005.)

1. Home health aides—92 percent
2. Paralegals—85 percent
3. Systems analysts and computer scientists—79 percent
4. Personal and home care aides—77 percent
5. Physical therapists—76 percent
6. Medical assistants—74 percent
7. Operations research analysts—73 percent
8. Human service workers—71 percent
9. Radiologic technologists and technicians—70 percent
10. Medical secretaries—68 percent
11. Physical and corrective therapy assistants and aides—64 percent
12. Psychologists—64 percent
13. Travel agents—62 percent
14. Correction officers—61 percent
15. Data processing equipment repairers—60 percent

16. Flight attendants—59 percent
17. Computer programmers—56 percent
18. Occupational therapists—55 percent
19. Surgical technologists—55 percent
20. Medical records technicians—54 percent
21. Management analysts—52 percent
22. Respiratory therapists—52 percent
23. Childcare workers—49 percent
24. Marketing, advertising and public relations managers—47 percent
25. Legal secretaries—47 percent
26. Receptionists and information clerks—47 percent
27. Registered nurses (RNs)—44 percent
28. Nursing aides, orderlies and attendants—43 percent
29. Licensed practical nurses (LPNs)—42 percent
30. Cooks, restaurant workers—42 percent

Finally, a list of the 20 fastest-growing occupations requiring a college degree through 2005:

1. Systems analysts and computer scientists—79 percent
2. Physical therapists—76 percent
3. Operations research analysts—73 percent
4. Medical scientists—66 percent
5. Psychologists—64 percent
6. Computer programmers—56 percent
7. Occupational therapists—55 percent
8. Management analysts—52 percent
9. Marketing, advertising and public relations managers—47 percent
10. Podiatrists—46 percent
11. Teachers (preschool and kindergarten)—41 percent
12. Teachers (special education)—40 percent
13. Securities and financial services sales representatives—40 percent
14. Recreational therapists—39 percent
15. Lawyers—35 percent

16. Accountants and auditors—34 percent

17. Aircraft pilots and flight engineers—34 percent

18. Social workers—34 percent

19. Engineering, mathematics and natural science managers—34 percent

20. Teachers (secondary school)—34 percent

Hot Careers for the '90s—Information Technology to Travel Management

The Rochester Institute of Technology in Rochester, New York, touts a number of hot fields for the '90s. A few of them are:

1. *Information Technology.* Despite our Information Age, people are still uptight about using computers. Enter information technologists (ITs). ITs apply knowledge of computer functions to everyday use, rather than focusing on theory or programming. Wherever there is a need for information processing, an information technologist will work to help people understand how the computer can be used as a tool to make their jobs easier.

2. *Microelectronic Engineering.* The need for these high-demand engineers is expected to double over the next 15 years. They're involved with the design and manufacturing of semiconductors—the key ingredient for all types of electronic devices, from computers, space shuttles and VCRs to high-definition television.

3. *Packaging Science.* Preserving the environment is more than a hot issue; it's high priority. Proper disposal, sorting and recycling of packaging, as well as source reduction of materials, is critical to contributing to a healthy environment.

4. *Telecommunications.* Opportunities exist for both the technical and management-bound professional. Approximately 30 percent of our work force is involved with telecommunications technologies beyond telephones, such as data transmission and computer networks. Examples: banking, facsimile reproduction, reservation systems and nationwide inventory management.

5. *Food Marketing and Distribution Professionals.* There is a growing need for professionals who understand issues such as reduction of labor costs, longer product shelf-life, waste reduction and complex distribution channels. Who hires them? Food service distributors,

manufacturers, food exporters, government agencies, growers/shippers and commodity market analysts.

6. *Electronic Still Photographers.* The future of electronic still photography is very bright. This young technology is based on digital and electronic memory. Electronic cameras record images magnetically, and the recorded image is then brought to life on a computer screen. By combining electronic and film cameras with personal computers, electronic still photography's benefits range from cost efficiency to time savings.

7. *Biomedical Photography.* Biomedical photographers are needed to photograph everything from landmark surgery in an operating room to cell growth to a rainbow of colors in a butterfly wing. They're needed in hospitals and research and nonprofit organizations.

8. *Travel Management.* With the cost of business travel expected to jump dramatically, corporations need travel managers to coordinate meetings and conventions and find the best hotel and conference center rates. This job requires organized and meticulous people who can work under intense pressure and tight deadlines.

Finally, visit your library and skim the latest four-volume *Corporate Technology Directory* (published by CorpTech, Woburn, Mass.) listing data on 35,000 technology manufacturers throughout the United States. The annual directory offers a glimpse at companies you may want to contact. A typical listing includes address, phone number, company description, sales, product information and key executives. They also publish a monthly newsletter, *Technology Industry Growth Forecaster,* projecting new jobs for the year, growth rates of hot companies, choice locations and private companies to watch.

That's where the jobs are. Now let's find out how to uncover information leading to them.

Myth 6: The More Information You Can Get Your Hands On, the Greater Likelihood You Have for Success.

Reality: *Information overload creates confusion and stress.*

Chapter Snapshot

☐ Remember the Good Old Days?

☐ Declutter Your Life

☐ Organize and Summarize Your Information Sources

☐ Playing Information Hunches

☐ Filing, Tracking and Storing Information

☐ Information Housecleaning

❋ ❋ ❋ ❋ ❋ ❋ ❋ ❋

A favorite college professor once told me to read everything I could get my greedy little hands on. Never stop gathering, reading and questioning. It's part of the learning process. Become an information junkie, he urged. Make it a lifelong habit. It's essential not only for job searching but for keeping abreast of our frenetic world. I believed him.

Fifteen years later, I realized his well-meant advice missed the mark. In theory, it made sense, but practically speaking, it was impossible. He was right about the "never stop questioning" part, wrong about trying to randomly absorb information like a sponge. The human mind has its limitations. Today, with information bombarding us from morning till night, from all points on the globe, all we can hope is to absorb a miniscule percentage of it.

Like excess TV, junk food or caffeine, too much information is not good for you. Overdosing on TV can turn you into a comatose couch potato, overindulging in junk food can make you sick and trying to ram too much information into your overstimulated head creates confusion and stress. Hence, the term *information overload,* another popular buzz-term describing yet another nasty by-product of the Information Age. If we're trying to absorb more information than we can process, it is information overload. Once again, Alvin Toffler was a step ahead of everyone in 1970 when he predicted such effects in *Future Shock.*

Too much information too soon, too fast and in huge quantities causes stress, says Toffler. There are limitations on the amount of information we can receive, process and remember. It will slow you down under any circumstances, especially during job hunting, when you must gather, interpret and quickly act on information. The tough part is confining yourself to information that gets you interviews with companies you want to work for.

Remember the Good Old Days?

Our great-grandfathers never scratched their heads in a bored moment and asked, "Should I read the paper; buy a magazine or book; watch television; go down to the square to watch the divisional bungee jumping championships; listen to the radio; pop a compact disc in the stereo system or boot up the PC to check out the local bulletin boards?" Not an easy decision for sure, especially if all options are appealing.

Information overload didn't exist back then because there wasn't that much information available. Our grandparents were spared myriad choices. Spare time was spent either reading the local newspaper (maybe there were two to choose from), perusing a book or flipping the dial on the radio to choose from a half-dozen weekly serials.

Back then, staying on top of the world was easy. High-speed communication networks, interactive television, teleconferencing, voice-activated computers and facsimile machines were the subjects of sci-fi/fantasy writers. Nobody even dreamt such technologies would one day change the world. Not that they didn't have problems back then, but too much information wasn't one of them.

Declutter Your Life

It doesn't take a degree in quantitative analysis to get a job. The hardest part about job finding is organizing yourself—finding and interpreting information and making good decisions.

Combat information overload by separating the useful from the superficial. Start by putting together a list of information sources that may be useful in your search. A few obvious ones come to mind:

1. Want ads (daily newspapers)
2. College sources
   a. College placement office
   b. Alumni associations
   c. Fraternities/sororities
3. Professional associations
4. Corporate sources (Moody's, Standard & Poor's, Value Line)
5. Trade associations (*Encyclopedia of Associations*)
6. Trade magazines and newsletters
7. Business magazines
8. Employment agencies
9. Executive search firms
10. Job fairs

Don't worry. You'll be narrowing these choices down to a more manageable list.

Organize and Summarize Your Information Sources

Try to pursue all your sources at once and you'll run smack into the information overload wall. Simplify your life by organizing information sources into two groups: timely sources and background sources. Accomplish this simple task and you'll feel better. Already your life is more organized.

Timely Sources

The following is a list of some timely information sources:

1. *Want Ads* (*Daily Newspapers*). The ads ought to be monitored daily, not just on Sundays and Wednesdays, the traditionally popular days for running want ads. You never know, a clever employer might test an ad on a Monday or Thursday just to see who responds.

2. *Employment Agencies.* Constantly keep a lookout for new agencies advertising jobs in your industry.

3. *Trade Associations.* Invest a couple of hours in your local library combing the *Encyclopedia of Associations* (Gale Research), noting trade associations that directly and indirectly represent your industry. You ought to be on all their mailing lists. It doesn't hurt to befriend trade organization insiders. As we said in Myth 4: "Aggressive Networking

Is the Key to a Successful Job Search," all it takes is one friendly tip to open doors.

4. *Trade Magazines and Newsletters.* Trade associations can tell you which magazines and newsletters track your industry. Another overlooked source, a favorite of public relations professionals, is the *Gerbie Press All-in-One Directory*. It lists daily and weekly newspapers, general and consumer magazines, business papers, trade press, news syndicates and radio and TV stations. Each listing provides essential information including address, audience and circulation. A publication's circulation is meaningful for public relations folks hungry to get their clients press exposure. But it's also important for job seekers looking for inside information. High circulation indicates broader coverage and, often, more news.

Better still are industry newsletters for tips and exclusive information. On the quality scale, newsletters range from exceptional to weak. Don't put much stock in the way a newsletter looks. There is no correlation between gloss and quality. Some of the ugliest ones, which are hardly more than photocopied sheets of paper stapled together, are considered must reading. The purpose of a newsletter is to present hard, exclusive information in a no-nonsense format so busy executives can quickly scan it. A busy exec deems exclusive information priceless. That's why some industry newsletters, carrying yearly subscription rates of up to $500, are considered mandatory reading for insiders. A newsletter's circulation is also a telling indicator of the quality of editorial coverage and following. If a newsletter is read by over 100,000 high-ranking industry executives, I'd get my hands on it.

Find out which newsletters carry the most clout. A well-stocked trade association library carries all the publications catering to its industry.

5. *Executive Search Firms.* Once again, unless headhunters just happen to be searching for your particular skills, don't expect them to acknowledge you. Nevertheless, it doesn't hurt to periodically correspond with headhunters specializing in your field. You never know. If they think they can use you, they'll find you.

6. *Business Magazines.* It's impossible to read all of them, but make it a habit to skim major ones that cover the nation, such as *Forbes, Fortune, Business Week, Nation's Business, INC., Entrepreneur.* Most of the national business magazines are excellent for staying on top of either career, industry, economic or financial trends.

Background Sources

The following are background information sources:

1. *College Sources.* No matter how relieved you are to be rid of college, don't cut yourself off from college connections. They can be valuable not only for short-term job leads but throughout your career.

- *College Placement Office.* University placement offices are hotbeds of information. Many placement directors are plugged into career opportunities throughout the United States. It pays to keep in touch.
- *Alumni Associations.* Many alumni associations boast far-flung networks. A fairly recent trend is hooking up recent grads with older, established alumni. They can be bottomless wells of advice and support.
- *Fraternities/Sororities.* They are not everybody's cup of tea, yet many colleges boast a handful of them. At many rural schools, they are social lifelines responsible for building lifelong friendships. Just as you would gladly pass along career tips or advice to other fraternity/sorority members, don't be squeamish about asking them for leads.

2. *Professional Associations.* Where fraternities and sororities amount to a hit-or-miss proposition for career advice, professional associations ought to be pursued aggressively. They can offer networking possibilities as well as job leads. Each connection represents a potential information avenue.

3. *Corporate Sources.* There are at least a half dozen sources that are excellent for background information on corporations and business trends. For quick snapshot information on companies, books by Moody's, Standard & Poor's and Value Line are excellent. Investment banking firms and brokerage houses depend upon them. In minutes, they'll tell you what the company does, how big it is plus its earnings and track record. All libraries stock these reference books.

4. *Job Fairs.* Staged by schools and organizations, job fairs can be valuable for quickly gathering information on many companies. Typically, a cross-section of companies participate, ranging from giant *Fortune* 500 companies to startups. Job fairs provide opportunities to ask company representatives questions and come away knowing something about the company and its industry. Companies use these events as recruiting tools.

But don't get your hopes up. You'll be one of hundreds, even thousands, who will attend. A well-publicized job fair staged in a large hotel or stadium looks more like a cattle call than a career opportunity. Don't make the mistake of thinking that attending companies are looking for people. Often, they're just scouring the market to see what the applicant pool looks like, or they deem the event a good public relations tactic. Go with the purpose of learning about companies. If anything else comes of it, you've lucked out.

Overlooked Information Jewels

You're not through. There are information sources most job seekers miss. The following are four favorites of hidden job market watchers.

People (Information Interviews).   The information interview was discussed in Myth 4: "Aggressive Networking Is the Key to a Successful Job Search," as a marvelous networking tool. As we said earlier, the information interview serves a dual purpose: It's both a networking and information gathering tool, particularly effective in a tough job market. When jobs are scarce, employers are more likely to give you 30 minutes of their time if there are no strings attached. They're also flattered because you're asking them for advice. Missing is standard interview protocol with accompanying angst and formality. Instead, it's a relaxed conversation between job seeker and employer.

It's also an opportunity to ask candid questions you couldn't ask during an actual job interview. After all, you're not about to ask a prospective employer career tactic and political questions. For example: What sectors of the industry offer the best career potential, and what strategies get you the furthest quickest? Which is the best route to the executive suite or up the sales/marketing or technical ladder?

In sum, milk the information interview for all it's worth. It's an opportunity to fill in the spaces by absorbing a lot of inside information quickly. If you are fortunate, some of it may be exclusive.

U.S. Government.   Few people realize our government is an enormous publishing house, producing numbing quantities of information on a smorgasbord of topics. Combine all the material published by every government agency and you have a neighborhood full of material. The best part: Most of it is *free*. Unfortunately, only journalists, academics and researchers take advantage of it.

There is no point mentioning the reams of material published by the 13 federal government departments. But many of the publications of the Commerce Department and Department of Labor are excellent background sources. The Commerce Department publishes reports on the state of U.S. industry, including five-year projections. Its yearly *U.S. Industrial Outlook* is a weighty tome covering business forecasts for over 350 industries. Each section is a 3- to 10-page sketch of the industry, its current and future prospects and its place in the world industrial market. For information, write: U.S. Department of Commerce, Office of Business Analysis, 14th and Constitution Ave. N.W., Room 4885, Washington, D.C. 20230. And the Department of Labor's Bureau of Labor Statistics publishes monthly labor reports for the nation as well as regional job markets.

For information on specific careers (job descriptions, qualifications, salaries, outlook and where to get information), skim the BLS's recent edition of the *Occupational Outlook Handbook*. Most libraries have at least one copy. BLS also publishes the *Occupational Outlook Quarterly*, covering industry forecasts and job market projections until 2005. If your library doesn't have it, consider subscribing to it. Write the Superintendent of Documents, U.S. Government Printing Office, Washington, D.C. 20402, or the U.S. Department of Labor, Bureau of Labor Statistics, Publications Sales Office, P.O. Box 2145, Chicago, IL 60690.

The BLS has eight regional offices throughout the United States. Call the one nearest you to be put on its mailing list or periodically stop by to peruse publications covering your state's job market. Note the BLS office nearest you from the following list:

Boston: 1 Congress St. (10th Floor), Boston, MA 02114.

New York: 201 Farrier St. (Room 808), New York, NY 10014.

Philadelphia: P.O. Box 13309, Philadelphia, PA 19101.

Atlanta: 1371 Peachtree St., N.E., Atlanta, GA 30367.

Chicago: Federal Office Building (9th Floor), 130 South Dearborn St., Chicago, IL 60604.

Dallas: Federal Building, 525 Griffin St. (Room 221), Dallas, TX 75202.

Kansas City: 911 Walnut St., Kansas City, MO 64106.

San Francisco: 71 Stevenson St., P.O. Box 193766, San Francisco, CA 94119.

On-Line Computer Services.   A decade ago, only hard-core hackers plugged into on-line databases. (A database is an organized collection of related information.) Today, computers are easy to use. All it takes is a few hours and you're up and running. If you stick with it, within a few days you can plug into vast computer databases via modem and discover a mind-boggling world of endless information. The modem, a small device connected to the guts of your computer and your telephone, transforms digital computer signals to analog tone signals used on phone lines and then back again into signals understood by the computer.

Once you get used to a modem, the world is literally your oyster. You can just as easily communicate with another computer on the other side of the globe as you can with one next door.

Don't panic if you have neither computer nor modem. Although a computer is practically a necessity, most PC owners don't have modems. If you're on a tight budget, you can do without a modem. Granted, they're valuable, but they can also be expensive. Many large public and research libraries have computers which can hook you up with on-line databases. Speak to the library's information specialist to see what's available.

If you have a modem or are considering purchasing one (you can buy an inexpensive unit through one of the dozens of mail-order computer companies), carefully research databases before subscribing to any. You'll be amazed how much is out there. Databases are a multimillion-dollar industry; each year dozens spring up. Consider the following:

Free On-Line Job Information. Before you explore commercial databases check out the free ones. For the past 20 years, most states have been providing job banks to job seekers through the 2,000-plus state employment services scattered through the 50 states. Despite massive government cutbacks, most people don't realize all states are federally funded to operate a labor exchange or employment service. It's free to both employers and job applicants. Most employment services offer a smorgasbord of jobs ranging from menial to professional. Now most states are offering easy-to-use on-line job listings. Applicants sit in front of a terminal and, by touching selected keys, move through a series of occupational categories and hone in on jobs they're qualified for.

In Manhattan, New York, the N.Y. State Employment Service provides colorful, easy-to-use software that lets users search for information and print out job listings by touching buttons on the screen itself. These computers can be linked to the Labor Department's main computer system or be used as stand-alone units that can be set up anywhere they can be plugged in. The system contains information on jobs and employment, civil service examinations, education and training, labor market information, labor market and community directories, a list of job-related services and a catalog of Labor Department publications and videos.

Check your telephone book to find the nearest state employment service. Stop in, you may be surprised.

The U.S. Bureau of Labor Statistics makes many of its press releases available on-line through a commercial contractor. The data are free. Users can access all or part of the releases, paying only for computer time used. For information, contact: The Bureau of Labor Statistics Electronic News Release Service, 441 G St., Room 2822, Washington, D.C. 20212.

Research Databases.   Most libraries have a number of excellent database sources, such as:

The Gale Directory of Databases (Gale Research). The two-volume directory covers about 5,800 databases, embracing business, technology, law, humanities, social sciences and medicine.

Database Directory (Knowledge Industry Publications, Inc.). Offers helpful information on databases, such as price, source, origins and which company to contact for specific databases.

Be careful when selecting an on-line database vendor. Do some homework beforehand. The guiding word is *exclusivity.* You're paying for information. Just because it's on-line, don't assume it's hard to come by. An association, government agency or trade association may provide the same information free.

Costs vary among vendors. Many on-line computer services charge over $50 an hour to search a database. Multiply that times four or five hours a couple of times a week and you're looking at towering monthly on-line charges. Find out what you are paying for. Is there a startup fee or subscription fee? Are rates the same throughout the day? Is there an evening discount? How easy is it to use the database? If you have to be a programmer to use it, look elsewhere. Finally, how often is the information updated?

Use an on-line service when (1) the information is exclusive or hasn't been published, and (2) speed is a critical factor—you've got a surprise interview tomorrow and you need up-to-the-minute information immediately so you can turn in a stunning performance.

The following are a few career databases worth looking into:

America Online, Inc. (8619 Westwood Center Drive, Vienna, VA 22182, 800-827-6364) offers a number of databases for job seekers and entrepreneurs. Its Career Center database, updated weekly, boasts 4,000 jobs throughout the United States on its network that can be accessed 24 hours a day. Jim Gonyea, its creator, touts it as the first electronic career guidance and employment center in the

United States. Its Occupational Profiles database profiles 700 occupations, with information about specific companies, working conditions, training, job outlook and salary range.

CompuServe Information Service (P.O. Box 20212, Columbus, OH 43220, 800-848-8199). Members can take advantage of what they call a "headhunting service." Your qualifications go on-line and are available to hundreds of *Fortune* 500 and emerging companies. If a company likes your background, you're called in for an interview. According to CompuServe, more than 100 new companies log on each week. It's a fast and inexpensive way for companies to find bodies without dealing with intermediaries (employment agencies and human resource departments). Jobs include business, technical, engineering and health care positions.

Career Placement Registry (CPR) (302 Swann Ave., Alexandria, VA 22301, 800-368-3093). CPR is an on-line database containing résumés (or qualifications) of experienced personnel and recent college graduates who are actively seeking employment. More than 8,000 employers—practically all the *Forbes* 500 companies—have access to the database. The database can be searched by skill levels, experience, geographical preferences for employment, etc.

Peterson's Guides (P.O. Box 2123, 202 Carnegie Center, Princeton, NJ 08543, 800-338-3282). Peterson's offers Connexion, an on-line service similar to the above. Applicants are made available to over 200 companies and headhunters across the United States.

Information Kinetics (640 North La Salle St., Suite 560, Chicago, IL 60610, 800-828-0422). This company offers KiNexus, an on-line service which the company touts as the largest candidate database in the United States with over 125,000 candidates. Although it boasts a variety of jobs in all fields, this database is a particularly good job source for recent college grads. Some 1,600 colleges plus alumni organizations are plugged into its database. If you register through a college career office, the service is free. If not, there is a modest charge. Approximately 300 to 500 small to mid-size companies use the service regularly. Applicants fill out a detailed qualifications questionnaire, which is made available to corporate subscribers.

Reference Texts. Check your library or local bookstore for timely job reference books. Timely is the operative word. Once you find a helpful text, check the copyright date (usually in small type in the first 5 pages of the text) to see when it was published. If it's more than four years old, assume much of the information is dated.

Two recommended reference texts are *The American Almanac of Jobs and Salaries* (Avon Books, 1984) by John W. Wright and Edward J. Dwyer and *Find It Fast: How to Uncover Expert Information on Any Subject* (HarperCollins, 1990) by Robert I. Berkman. The *American Almanac* gives short descriptions of hundreds of occupations, including comprehensive job descriptions and requirements, salaries, benefits and career prospects for each field. *Find It Fast's* author is an information junky who's mastered the art of information gathering. He helps readers think like journalists to uncover information sources most people never consider.

Last, but by no means least, try *Bacon's Publicity Checker.* Published once a year, this is practically a bible for public relations professionals. This source can connect you with a wealth of information about your field. It offers editorial profiles and advertising and editorial contacts, plus lists of trade shows and conventions with dates, locations and contact information. Most libraries carry it. To find out where to get a reference copy, write to *Bacon's Publicity Checker,* 332 S. Michigan Ave., Chicago, IL 60604, or call 800-621-0561.

Playing Information Hunches

Since childhood many of us were blindly taught to follow rules and do what we're told. We often thought someone smarter than us built and paved the road we're on. All we have to do is follow it and never veer off onto the shoulder.

That's dangerous thinking leading to mediocrity, disillusionment and boredom. The great leaders of our time never completely bought that viewpoint. Somehow they found the guts to find their own paths and do their own things. Whether it was out of curiosity, cynicism or rebellion, they had an irresistible urge to play a hunch even though they had no idea where it would lead. Something beckoned to them, drew them like a magnet—even if it was only a promise of new information or leads. Sometimes the journey led to incredible discoveries, but most of the time it led nowhere, a dead end, a blind alley. Yet even a trip down a blind alley or to a deserted cul-de-sac can be fascinating. You never know what you'll discover along the way. If nothing else, the journey may inspire new ideas. That one special discovery, insight or precious idea, no matter how infrequently experienced, makes every excursion worth the effort. That one overwhelming gust of radiant creativity changes lives forever. Whatever the outcome, great leaders are ready to take the gamble.

I urge you to do the same when running down information leads. Don't be afraid to play hunches. Nothing is lost by trying, only by not trying. The achievers among us are the risk takers and gamblers. They have the guts and initiative to strike off on their own and follow their instincts. When an idea strikes, they act on it. If we're lucky, brilliant ideas or spontaneous flashes of insight strike a couple of times during a lifetime.

Information is a job searcher's ammunition. Whether it be a hunch, lead, tip or even a dream, act on it. Don't put it off. If you don't act on it immediately, it'll be forgotten and lost. If a great idea strikes in the middle of the night, drag yourself out of bed and write it down so you remember it. If you don't, all you'll have the next day is a fleeting memory of the event.

Let's wind down with some tips on storing, filing and tracking information.

Filing, Tracking and Storing Information

The best tool for housing information is a personal computer. It's efficient and you avoid the hassle and clutter of keeping paper files. There are plenty of choices to consider.

As new models are introduced each year, the price drops dramatically. Rather than buy at a retail computer store, consider buying through a large discount chain or through a mail-order house. You'll save hundreds of dollars. With technology changing monthly, don't buy the newest model. You don't need it. Last year's, or even five-year-old models are more than adequate. Unless you're a professional hacker, it doesn't matter.

And don't buy a popular brand like IBM or Apple. Buy a recommended clone from a small company. It will do the same job and cost half the price. Check out the computer magazines, especially *Computer Shopper*, for great buys.

As for creating files, most decent software has its own filing system. All you have to do is follow instructions.

If you're planning on sticking with typewriter and paper, create logical filing systems so documents and correspondence can be easily retrieved. Don't get fancy. Rather than file by industry or category, do it alphabetically by company. It is the fastest and easiest way to find things. And don't let information pile up on your desk. Get into the habit of filing every day.

Information Housecleaning

Finally, the surest way to avoid information clutter and overload is to constantly houseclean. Like filing, make it a daily task. In fact, the two tasks can be done together. As you decide what to save and file, don't hesitate to discard. It adds up to efficient harmony.

The discarding process becomes so automatic, you'll get to a point where you don't even think about it. You'll just do it. Fight the tendency to save things you don't need. If something serves no immediate or long-term purpose, get rid of it. As for my professor's advice to read everything you can get your hands on—fight that urge. It's not humanly possible.

Myth 7: *The Candidate with the Highest Qualifications Always Gets the Job.*

Reality: *Sales and marketing skills are just as important as qualifications.*

Chapter Snapshot

- [ ] Coming to Terms with a Cruel World—So What If You're Phi Beta Kappa?
- [ ] Honing Marketing and Sales Skills
- [ ] Marketing Yourself '90s-Style
- [ ] Selling, Then and Now
- [ ] Selling and Marketing Skills Are Vital for Success
- [ ] Selling 101 and Other Basics
- [ ] Building a Selling Style

✻ ✻ ✻ ✻ ✻ ✻ ✻ ✻

We've all been brought up thinking supertalented, head-of-the-class brainiacs with high IQs capture big jobs. We are weaned on that kind of thinking. Most of us believe it. But it's only true in your fantasies.

Academics, in particular, ram that thinking down our throats. Sitting comfortably in safe, tenured environments, surrounded by ivy and tradition, insulated from the world they're supposed to know about, they teach students how to live in an idealized world. Sadly, few tell students great qualifications account for only a fraction of the success equation.

The scalding truth is all honor students don't wind up heading *Fortune* 500 companies. And all brilliant computer hackers don't head departments at international software companies.

Glowing qualifications get you in the door. But it takes sales and marketing skills to capture the job.

Coming to Terms with a Cruel World—So What If You're Phi Beta Kappa?

Success is doled out to those who play the game well. Playing well is knowing how to market and sell yourself into a job.

"What the heck does marketing and selling yourself mean?" you scream. "I didn't go to business school. I have a degree in electrical engineering, computer science, English literature, philosophy, history, mathematics or psychology. I am not a salesperson nor do I have any intention of being one!"

With that kind of attitude you are not going far. Maybe a business degree would be helpful to let you see the connection between selling a product or service and selling yourself to an employer. But even business students don't always make that connection. Maybe it's too obvious. But the cold reality is qualified applicants who master selling basics snatch jobs quickly.

Nobody is going to hand you a job based solely on your qualifications. So what if you're Phi Beta Kappa, summa cum laude, and a straight-A student who's a member of every prestigious academic organization. Big deal. Prove to me you're right for the job. Sell me and you're hired. There lie the nuts and bolts of getting a job. Credentials and qualifications are calling cards. The next, and most important, step is convincing a potential employer you're the right person for the job. The only way to do that is by marketing and selling yourself.

Honing Marketing and Sales Skills

Selling is convincing someone to buy a product or service. "You gotta try this regenerating womsicle. It's guaranteed to change your life. As soon as it's finished, it regenerates itself and starts over. It's indestructible—and cheap! Try it. If you don't like it, we guarantee a full refund."

Selling yourself into a job is explaining and touting yourself so employers rapidly come to the conclusion: "I need this person. That's all there is to it."

Right alongside selling is its blood relative—marketing—the process of getting product (or service) to buyer. As we said in the introduction, "you are the product." You can be likened to a human automobile, lawnmower, washing machine or microwave oven. Merely performing well is not going to get you bought. But wrap and package yourself appropriately, and then find the right vehicle (people, publication or organization) leading to the job you want, and you're marketing yourself.

Combine qualifications with a creative selling and marketing campaign and you're on your way. All eight cylinders are firing, and you're going to get a job faster than you realize.

Let's start with marketing ourselves and move on to the crucial selling process.

Marketing Yourself '90s-Style

Think of yourself as a multiuse product that can be bent and molded 100 different ways. You're a human Gumby, the infamous green rubber toy that bends in all directions.

Just as the corporate marketer looks for better and more creative ways to get product to buyers, you must think the same way. Here are four timeless marketing commandments to guide your career:

1. *Identify buyers.* Stay tuned. Since the market is always changing, be quick on your feet, and know where the action is at all times. Stay on top of hiring trends. In this hectic market, they change practically every year. Know who's hiring, who's firing and what you're worth. (More on this in Myth 11: "In a Competitive Market, Job Seekers Have Little Negotiating Power. They Should Take the First Salary Offered and Be Happy They Got It.")

2. *Don't try to be all things to all employers.* Position yourself accordingly so you can target yourself to an employer's needs. Successful corporate marketers drive home the importance of strategically positioning product. Push the wrong product to the wrong market and you strike out. Xerox and RCA lost billions when they tried to jump into the computer market. What do you think would happen if Burger King tried selling sushi to its loyal customers? It would lose its shirt.

Apply that principle to yourself: Concentrate on marketing and promoting your skills to employers who need them. Otherwise, you're wasting precious time.

3. *Get there first.* The first product to market stands the best chance of capturing it. If it's exceptional to boot, there is an excellent chance of long-lasting success. Everyone knows Charles Lindbergh was the first pilot to fly across the Atlantic Ocean. But only trivia freaks know that Bert Hinkler did it second. Similarly, IBM was first in computers, Coca-Cola in soft drinks and Hertz in rental cars. Now there are hundreds of successful imitations. But as irrational as it is, we associate

"first" with "best." Marketing gurus Al Ries and Jack Trout, authors of marketing classics *Positioning, Marketing Warfare, Bottom-Up Marketing* and *Horse Sense* (all published by McGraw-Hill), insist that people never forget firsts. Take the hint and adopt a similar strategy when marketing yourself. As soon as you uncover a job lead, pounce on it.

4. *Be the best.* Oreo Cookies, Kentucky Fried Chicken and Haagen-Dazs ice cream have been around a long time because they're excellent. Even though health food addicts insist they're not good for you, millions of loyal consumers think otherwise. Hence, the companies are still around and very profitable. The message is obvious: There is no such thing as perfection. Nevertheless, try your best.

Now let's do some creative selling.

Selling, Then and Now

Your Dad's a What?—Two Hundred Years of Bad Press

A decade ago, few experts were clear about the role selling played in getting jobs. Some even insisted there was no connection, primarily because of the poor image salespeople have suffered with since the Industrial Revolution. Despite our supersonic lifestyles, we still cling to unpleasant stereotypes surrounding salespeople. They are the pushers and shovers of the world—drummers, hucksters, con men, scam/flimflam artists, tin men, snake charmers, fast-talkers, hustlers, grifters, you name it. Glib conversationalists and smoothies, they coax you into spending your hard-earned money on things you don't need or want. They lie, deceive and dupe you into buying. Once again, revisit *Tin Men,* Barry Levinson's timeless 1987 classic film about a bunch of aluminum-siding salesmen in Baltimore, in 1963, prior to a nationwide crackdown by the Federal Home Improvement Commission. Levinson's characters were lovable rogues who carried around a suitcase full of scams seducing unsuspecting homeowners into buying aluminum siding they didn't need at inflated prices. For these rogue salesmen, there was no better game than hustling a sale.

Levinson artfully drove home all the vulgar stereotypes surrounding salespeople for the past two centuries. Tin men had a knack for spotting and suckering unsuspecting "marks," elevating unscrupulous selling to a craft. As they saw it, they weren't doing anything wrong. They were merely convincing folks they ought to buy. And having a heck of a good time in the bargain.

Speak to hundreds of salespeople or people who have known or dealt with them, and you'll unearth colorful stories of characters and places. A deft salesperson is a lay psychologist of the first order. It's a wonder Sigmund Freud didn't study salespeople. But even though they've achieved respectability as legitimate professionals, many of us still harbor old perceptions of carnival-style drummers who'll bilk us out of our hard-earned money if we're not careful. We still wonder whether these articulate verbal acrobats displaying wares are actually for real.

New View of Sales

Only recently have management consultants, industrial psychologists and marketing mavens stressed the importance of selling. What took them so long? An obvious question, with not so obvious answers. Yes, salespeople are crucial. They're the ones who knock on doors, spend as much as 50 percent of their time on the road selling products and services and bring in the dollars that pay salaries, not to mention fuel the corporate machines that buy raw materials to produce more goods. No product flies without aggressive, dedicated salespeople willing to do cartwheels to put the product in buyers' hands. Salespeople are as important as the very product they sell. They're like the wheels on an automobile. Remove them and the engine roars, but the car goes nowhere.

Helping the cause of the salesperson's image was a host of best-selling books by superstar salespeople like Zig Ziglar, *See You at the Top* (Pelican, 1984); Frank Bettger, *How I Raised Myself from Failure to Success in Selling* (Prentice-Hall, 1983); Elmer Wheeler, *Sizzlemanship* (Prentice-Hall, 1983); Harvey Mackay, *Swim with the Sharks Without Being Eaten Alive* (Ivy Books, 1991); and Joe Girard and Stanley Brown, *How to Sell Anything to Anybody* (Warner Books, 1986), plus a half-dozen trendy theories on sales techniques. A truckload of self-help books touting the importance of connecting, making contact, bonding and communicating didn't hurt either.

Flip through history books and you'll learn that people such as Andrew Carnegie, Henry Ford and Joe Kennedy, Sr. were talented supersalespeople who changed the course of history. Some were robber barons who did their fair share of dirty deals, but history long ago cleared them of wrongdoing. Above everything else, we remember they were gifted businesspeople who made things happen.

Channeling people and materials, they single-handedly built industrial empires. No small feat in any age. The nucleus of their talent and success was intuitive sales skills.

It took a recession, intense competition, shrinking markets and demanding consumers for employers to figure out what kind of people they need to survive. Sure, they need the brain power of scientists, mathematicians and computer scientists who could change the world, but they also need people who could knock on doors and sell their creations. And if employers could find one gifted person who could do both, they hit the proverbial jackpot. They didn't have to go any further. They stumbled on utopia in one paycheck.

Everyone Is Selling Something

We've come around to the viewpoint that selling ability is a vital component for success in all careers—mad scientist to professional athlete. It's not only real estate brokers, insurance agents and auto salespeople or big ticket business-to-business salespeople peddling machinery and raw materials. Actually, we're all selling something. It really doesn't matter whether we're selling toothpaste or ourselves, it's the same process. The reality is we must sell to earn. The better we sell, the more we earn and the better our lifestyles. (More on selling ability in Myth 14: "Success Is Guaranteed to Those Willing to Work Hard and Put in Long Hours.")

Selling and Marketing Skills Are Vital for Success

It's easy to see why salespeople are an organization's coveted jewels. Management consultants aren't wrong when they preach that one of the surest routes to the executive suite is via sales. Star salespeople are heroes, proven assets responsible for building organizations from the ground up. They're rewarded with big salaries, commissions and mouth-watering perks. Can an organization afford to lose them? Star salespeople such as Lee Iacocca, Ross Perot, Steven Jobs, Colonel Arland Sanders (founder of Kentucky Fried Chicken), R. David Thomas (Wendy's), to name a few, have ascended to U.S. legend status. Their selling ability created products, markets and thousands of jobs, along with boosting the U.S. gross national product.

Who are they? They are the charmers, convincers, schmoozers, obsessed and driven visionaries who make things happen. They are the single-minded, inspired achievers who found the seminal connection between intelligence, qualifications and selling ability. Not only did they envision the future, they made it happen.

There you have it. To make it in this big, weird, topsy-turvy, funny world, we must sell. It doesn't matter what we do, to succeed we must sell ourselves and we must do it well. If you can't sell, convince and persuade, your options are limited and career potential uncertain. Swallow that reality and start honing your selling skills.

Selling 101 and Other Basics

Hard Sell Went Out with the Edsel

Now that we've driven home how essential selling skills are for success, consider these realities when searching for a job:

1. *Nobody is waiting for you.* You think you're terrific and so does your mom, but you will have to prove yourself to the rest of the world. The problem is there are too many products and not enough buyers. You are the product; a prospective employer is the buyer. Your mission is to make yourself into an excellent product to beat your competition to the good jobs.

Don't underestimate your competition. There is plenty out there. Some of your competitors are as good as or even better than you. But even if you're smarter and more aggressive, assume you're competing with superstars. That's the attitude that keeps you on edge and pushes you to be as good as you can.

2. *Hard sell doesn't fly.* This is especially true in today's market in which there are hundreds of qualified applicants competing for the same jobs. As I said in the introduction, employers want sizzle and steak, a well-wrapped, high-performing package, a chameleonlike worker who does everything well. The days of the one-task worker are gone forever. You might dazzle an employer with fast talk and big promises, but if you can't deliver, employers know there is plenty more product waiting in the wings to take your place. Tin men don't last.

3. *Reaching the right people.* Successful salespeople invest time finding the right buyers. Everyone wants to find a job yesterday. There is no such thing as fast enough. Nevertheless, apply the brakes and proceed methodically. Once again, remember the networking subtleties discussed in Myth 4: "Aggressive Networking Is the Key to a Successful Job Search." Build your network as meticulously as you'd build a house, by precisely laying each brick. More often than not, the

path to the person with the power to hire you is an indirect one. You might have to tap a few contacts before you reach this person. Find an organization's golden king-makers described by Northwestern University's Victor Lindquist in Myth 5. These are the well-positioned contacts who attract information from hundreds of sources. They enjoy amassing information. The unwritten commandment of good networking is reciprocity—sharing information with others, especially king-makers, the seminal connections in any grapevine.

Unless you have a friend or contact working in a corporate human resource department telling you which departments are hiring plus offering insights about politics and personalities, you're not going to uncover inside information from these bureaucratic paper shufflers. Their job is to speedily match bodies with job descriptions. To a human resource worker, you're a letter, résumé, application form, number or alphabetical listing. They don't know you, nor do they care to.

The human resource department is the first step in a traditional screening process—all the more reason to try and sidestep it by getting to the people who will actually hire you. Doing so is not only faster but, ultimately, more effective because it's a chance to get to the right person, eliminating the middle people. Get there first and brilliantly sell yourself. Hopefully, you'll make an indelible impression because you're the first product to market.

Human Chemistry and the Mysterious Connection Bonding Buyers and Sellers

It doesn't matter whether you're selling products, services or yourself, the same selling principles apply. Let's look at a few of them.

Have you ever connected with someone the first time you met? It happens so often, most of us aren't even aware of it. Mysteriously, an almost instantaneous bond is formed, igniting relationships, leading to friendship, intimacy, even marriage.

Successful salespeople forge these connections prior to making a sale. It is a first crucial step in the selling process. Sometimes, it's when the buyer makes eye contact with the salesperson. Other times, it follows a handshake or occurs in the course of conversation.

Recently, it happened to me when purchasing a car. I knew what kind of car I wanted to buy. The big question was finding a dealer who could give me the best price. When I made my choice after visiting five dealers, the deciding factor was not the price, which varied about $200 from dealer to dealer, but the salesperson. Most of the salespeople came on like charging bulls, descending upon me the moment I walked through the door. A couple of them were so persistent, I couldn't wait to leave.

The salesperson I bought the car from had the good sense to back off and give me time to think, ask questions and browse. She didn't present the pending purchase as a life-and-death proposition. Instead, I almost felt like she really didn't care whether she made the sale. Of course, that wasn't the case at all. But she was more concerned with establishing a rapport and building a relationship that may or may not result in a sale. It proved to be a smart tactic that won her a customer. Buying a car is not like buying a pair of shoes where you never see the salesperson again. The relationship often continues, especially if there are problems or if you come back three years later to purchase another car.

Successful stockbrokers, for example, are excellent examples of salespeople who work hard at building long-term connections with clients. Veteran investors often say they're seldom buying the brokerage house, but the broker. Only a tiny portion of the investing population actually investigates broker recommendations on their own. Most investors take their broker's word. Personal recommendations and track record have something to do with it, but the broker's personality is the deciding factor. Every day, investors write checks purely on subjective feelings. And they pray they aren't wrong because fortunes have been won and lost because of these mysterious feelings.

The same kind of chemistry applies every time someone is hired. First an employer checks out your qualifications. Impressive, she or he thinks. Now let's move on to the most important decision. Do I like this person? Are the vibes and chemistry right? Will I connect with him or her?

Like veteran salespeople pitching products or services, once the connection is made and buyer and seller (or employer and applicant) are on the same wavelength, a sale results. This process takes place every time someone is hired. A handshake culminates into a conversation, hopefully cementing a long relationship.

Forging Connections

How do you build these mysterious connections described above? Contrary to what many people think, good chemistry (or positive vibrations) is no accident: It can be created. Here's how.

Be Cool and Let It Happen.   Like my car anecdote, don't make the mistake the other salespeople made by coming on like a jet on a bombing mission. Don't confuse confidence with thoughtless aggression. Be self-assured and in control, yet be cool and laid-back at the same time. Appear too anxious or overzealous and you'll jinx the chemistry. Don't walk into a job interview and start tooting your own horn as soon as you walk through the door.

Let the interviewer make the first move by setting the tone. Is he/she congenial, tense, interrogative, combative, uptight? The first meeting is not unlike the opening round of a boxing match. Seasoned fighters seldom throw the first punch. Instead, they wait for their opponents to make a move and telegraph their fighting style so they can retaliate accordingly. It's just as much a contest of minds as it is of bodies.

Adopt the same strategy when you're marketing yourself to a prospective employer. If your interviewer is flinging questions at you at the speed of light, hurl answers back just as fast. Rise to the occasion or you're out of the race. Or, if it's a rambling conversation in which information is exchanged in teaspoon-full quantities, relax and don't volunteer more than what's necessary. Don't try to outfox your interviewer by being better, faster or smarter. Just be whatever you think this person is looking for. This is all about rapport building, not one-upmanship. You're like an actor auditioning for a role. Play your part well, and you've got the job. Like the salesperson winning the account by creating the perfect harmony between buyer and seller, strive for the identical synchrony between a potential employer and yourself. We'll get into this topic in more detail in Myth 9: "Interviewers Are Sadists in Business Suits."

Get a Reading on the Buyer. Successful salespeople size up the other person's rhythm before they sell. They check out a prospect's body language, trying to get a reading on their personality and temperament. Are they self-conscious, confident, laid-back, hyperactive, cautious? Observing an experienced salesperson at work is worth at least 6 college credits. Prior to aggressively selling, experienced salespeople are like gymnasts stretching their muscles before a workout. Depending on who they're selling to, salespeople will chat about the weather, ball scores, local politics or pollution before getting down to business. By the time the salesperson starts selling, the air is clear, a comfortable rapport exists and you're open to whatever this person has to say.

Adopt the same philosophy when looking for a job. Walk into a company with an open mind. Make no assumptions about the people you'll meet. Like two opponents facing each other on a tennis court, be ready for the unexpected. You may be greeted by an easygoing, effortless exchange or one ignited with tension and rigidity. One day, it will feel like you're walking into a snake pit, the next, a family gathering. As any salesperson can tell you, there is no accounting for human psychology. Some people are constitutionally rude, others are looking for a reason to unleash hostility; most are fair-minded and willing to hear what you have to say. The surprise element keeps you on your toes. The challenge is quickly adapting to the situation by creating good chemistry.

Solving Problems.   Like salespeople, job seekers must be realists. Salespeople don't log thousands of miles each year pitching prospective clients for their health. Like all of us, they're hustling to earn a living. The more they sell, the more they earn. They approach prospective buyers with the sincere intent of offering products that make their buyers' lives easier, more efficient or more profitable, maybe all the above. You ought to be thinking along the same lines every time you meet a potential employer. Don't ever forget you're a walking, talking, thinking, feeling human product. It can't be said enough. No free rides for you. In no uncertain terms, you're presenting yourself as the answer to an employer's dreams. More on the importance of selling yourself into a job in Myth 10: "Employers Are Autocratic Powerlords Who Know Exactly What They're Looking For: Ergo, They Hold All the Negotiating Cards."

Build Confidence and Trust by Being Yourself.   The goal is to build confidence and trust. Once a rapport exists, it's easy. No one will hire anyone they don't think they can trust.

The easiest and safest way to build confidence and trust is by being yourself. Don't try to be a carbon copy of a mentor or idol. You can just pretend so long until your real self screams for freedom. Finally, be sincere, enthusiastic and energetic. That's all an employer needs to draw his or her own conclusions.

Building a Selling Style

Building a selling style takes time. The only way to hone it is through practice, observation and study. Constantly look for opportunities to sell yourself. Your network is a good place to start.

Try to step back and observe yourself when you're selling. Study the interaction and replay the conversations so you can evaluate them. How did you do? Did you talk too much? Were you too aggressive? Did you say the wrong thing? Was your behavior inappropriate?

Finally, the ultimate criterion is how did a prospective employer, the potential buyer, react to you?

Never stop observing and criticizing yourself. It's the only way to improve your selling style. It wouldn't hurt to skim a couple of the better-selling sales books. Most are preachy and simplistic, but they're also crammed with good advice. There is, after all, a reason that they've sold millions of copies.

Myth 8: *You Don't Stand a Chance without a Knockout Résumé.*

Reality: *Résumés are useless.*

Chapter Snapshot

☐ Why Résumés Don't Work—The Standardization of the American Résumé

☐ What the Heck Is a Great Résumé?

☐ Playing the Numbers Game

☐ Shopping List of Résumé Complaints—1 Percent Get a Thorough Read

☐ Sneak Preview of Twenty-First-Century Résumés

☐ Grabbing an Employer's Attention—A Simple Alternative to a Mounting Problem

☐ Why a Letter?

☐ Crafting the Letter

☐ The Winning Structure—A Formula That Can't Miss

☐ Beating the Résumé at Its Own Game

☐ Letters for Career Changers

☐ Letter-Writing Tips

☐ Letter-Writing Dos and Don'ts

✳ ✳ ✳ ✳ ✳ ✳ ✳ ✳

Humorist Gene Perret said it's depressing to think our lives can be reduced to one side of one sheet of paper. That's 250 to 300 words. That's like being asked to sum yourself up in 45 seconds, the average time it takes to read a standard résumé.

It sounds ridiculous but that's the way it's done. One bleak day, some bored drone may clap her eyes on your résumé and classify you as unacceptable. She'll glance at your résumé's objective, scan your qualifications and work history and then toss your résumé in the reject pile. Sorry! You've struck out. Your objective was too long;

you graduated from an obscure grade-C school; your spelling was atrocious and the topper was you worked for tiny, little-known companies.

Too bad! If she gave your résumé an objective reading, she would have discovered your unique skills embedded in the résumé jargon. You were actually a rare pearl in a sea of mediocrity. But a cursory reading branded you unimpressive. Your résumé failed, hence you failed. The hiring process stops dead. Chalk it up to a bad break.

A human resource manager at Bechtel Corporation summed up the résumé-reading process:

> If a company needs people, they're looking for reasons to "read you in." If they don't need people, they'll find reasons to "read you out."

The rest of the time, you're at the whim of résumé readers. If they're in a bad mood, a strange-sounding surname is reason enough to toss your résumé. So what if it's illegal or unethical. No one will ever know.

Our archaic résumé system isn't working. Yet, traditional thinking says you don't stand a chance without a knockout résumé. The problem is no one really knows what this elusive jewel looks like. Confusion rules. The result is millions of qualified applicants don't get a chance at bat because their résumés failed to make an impression.

Why Résumés Don't Work—The Standardization of the American Résumé

A decade ago. résumés worked. The odds of landing interviews were excellent. Today, it's a crapshoot. Thanks to the rampant consolidation of U.S. industry, too many job applicants are chasing too few jobs. Most job searchers never hear from the companies they submit résumés to. More frustrating still, often they have no idea what companies they're applying to because blind ads list only job descriptions and a post office box number.

Résumés used to be personal statements, carrying the preparer's unique stamp. Great care went into their preparation. Before the advent of personal computers with accompanying letter-perfect printers, job searchers actually typed their own résumés, often several times. A common practice was writing them out longhand before typing a first draft. Developing a résumé amounted to a multistep

process before it was right. Some résumés were short, crisp and tightly written, others were rambling, wordy treatises bloated with big
words and exaggerated claims.

Along with a truckload of books about résumé preparation, more
than a dozen résumé software programs are now available, taking the
pain and tedium out of résumé writing. Plug the facts into the right
places and you're halfway there. What used to take job searchers an
entire day—or longer—has been reduced to a couple of hours. Once a
perfect résumé is spit from a computer printer, complete with snazzy
fonts and artsy layouts, it's reproduced and cast off into the ozone.

The modern résumé is a mechanized and depersonalized job summation that looks like it rolled off an assembly line. Like McDonald's
hamburgers, Oreo cookies and Army uniforms, résumés are standard-
ized. Your average résumé has the symmetry of a Hershey Bar and the
depth of whipped cream. Take 200 people applying for the same job
and remove the name, address and phone number from each résumé.
You'll have 200 résumés that could have been written by the same
person. That tells you something.

What the Heck Is a Great Résumé?

Find out by buying a résumé book and learning how to write the perfect résumé! By now, we ought to know what a dynamite résumé
looks like. Like Ponce de Leon's search for the mythical Fountain of
Youth, career experts are still trying to give job searchers the formula
for the elusive perfect résumé. Like the Fountain of Youth, it doesn't
exist. The comical irony is that the 75 odd books on the subject are dis-
pensing the same tired advice. Nothing new has been written about
the résumé in two decades.

All it took was 30 minutes in a well-stocked New York bookstore to
find the following titles:

1. *Résumés for Education Careers*

2. *The Guide to Basic Résumé Writing*

3. *Résumés That Knock 'Em Dead*

4. *Your First Résumé*

5. *Résumé Writing Made Easy*

6. *Does Your Résumé Wear Apron Strings?*

7. *The Damn Good Résumé Guide*

8. *The Résumé Catalog: 200 Damn Good Examples*

9. *Smart Woman's Guide to Résumé & Job Hunting*

10. *Your First Résumé*

11. *Jeff Allen's Best, the Résumé*

12. *The Complete Résumé Book & Job-Getter's Guide*

13. *The Résumé Kit*

14. *How to Write Your First Professional Résumé*

15. *Résumé Writing, a Comprehensive How-to-Do-It Guide*

16. *Résumés for Better Jobs*

17. *Your Résumé: Key to a Better Job*

18. *The No-Pain Résumé*

19. *Résumé Writing Made Easy for High-Tech*

20. *Résumés That Mean Business*

21. *The Complete Résumé Guide*

22. *Encyclopedia of Job-Winning Résumés*

23. *The Executive Résumé Book*

24. *Throw Away Your Résumé*

25. *The Perfect Résumé*

26. *How to Write Better Résumés*

27. *Better Résumés for Sales & Marketing Personnel*

28. *Best Résumés for Scientists & Engineers*

29. *Better Résumés for College Graduates*

30. *Better Résumés for Attorneys & Paralegals*

31. *Better Résumés for Computer Personnel*

32. *Better Résumés for Executives and Professionals*

33. *Résumé Power*

34. *Just Résumés: 200 Powerful & Proven Successful Résumés to Get That Job*

35. *The Guide to Basic Résumé Writing*

36. *Résumés That Get the Job*

37. *The Résumé Writer's Handbook*

38. *Power Résumés*

39. *Résumés for Communication Careers*

40. *Résumés for High-Tech Careers*

41. *Résumés for Sales & Marketing Careers*

42. *Résumés! Résumés! Résumés!*

The local library had a couple of additional titles:

- *How to Write a Winning Résumé*
- *The Smart Woman's Guide to Résumés and Job-Hunting*
- *Designing Creative Résumés*
- *Résumés for Better Jobs*
- *The Résumé Guide for Women of the '90s*
- *Developing a Professional Vita or Résumé*
- *Résumé Handbook*

Get the picture? And you wouldn't be wrong assuming there are at least 25 more résumé books currently in the works. How's that for a chilling thought?

In 1981, when the unemployment rate hovered around 10 percent, my agent asked me to write a résumé book. Now you know. One of the dozens of résumé books out there has my name on it. Those were the good old days when you actually stood a chance with a well-crafted résumé. In 127 pages, I said everything that could possibly be said about the résumé. Trust me, there is nothing very complicated about the chronological, functional and hybrid (combination) résumés.

Yet, publishers keep producing résumé books. Their proliferation only perpetuates the myth that résumés work. Rather than encourage individuality, résumé books stress conformity and the importance of following rules. To say the résumé market is saturated is an understatement indeed. More than obsession or ritual, résumé books are consistent sellers because job searchers still think résumés lead to jobs and that there are new insights into résumé preparation. Until they stop believing it, expect the tired old résumé to be dressed and repackaged over and over again. Why, there is even a Professional Association of Résumé Writers (PARW) in St. Petersburg, Florida, that certifies members after they take a one-hour exam.

Favorite Résumé Buzzwords: *Maximized, Implemented, Utilized, Impacted*

Like a 24-hour assembly line, job applicants keep churning out résumés. Send me a penny every time the words *effected, impacted, implemented, allow, opportunity, challenging, growth-oriented, utilize* and *maximize* appear on résumés, and I'll be able to spend the next two years relaxing in the Scottish Highlands. These words rank among the top-10 most popular résumé buzzwords.

With little encouragement, I could list a dozen more. I dare someone to write a résumé without using the word *implemented* once.

Packaging Bad Taste

Then there are the misguided freethinkers who zap up their résumés by lapsing into bad taste. Under the heading "Personal Philosophy," one job applicant wrote: "I've paid my dues. I won't stop until I go the distance. Like the movers and shakers of this world, I'm ready to kick butt to be successful."

Under a "Personal" heading, another job searcher wrote: "Like James Bond, I love fast cars, adventure and dry martinis." You know what happened to these résumés. Sorry, personal expressions of candid honesty are not appreciated. Robert Half, head of the international recruiting firm Robert Half International and author of several career books, keeps a file of bad résumés which he calls "Resumania." By now, the file is heavy enough to sink an aircraft carrier. In *The Robert Half Way to Get Hired in Today's Job Market* (Bantam Books), an understated Half says most résumés fail.

Job searchers find themselves at an impasse. They're told spiffy résumés get interviews, yet most are not seeing results. They're wasting precious time waiting for the postal delivery person to deliver good news.

Unless you're well connected, get used to the idea you're not going to meet the person with the power to hire you until you summarize yourself on paper beforehand. But the résumé format is not the way to do it. Stay with me and I'll show you a creative alternative.

Playing the Numbers Game

You don't have to be a statistician to figure out the odds of getting your foot in the door when employers comb hundreds, sometimes thousands, of factory-style résumés every week. In companies all over the United States, towering stacks of résumés gather dust before they're read.

If you knew how many résumés companies get each year and how much time is spent reading, make that skimming, them, you'd give serious thought to finding another way to get an employer's attention. Consider these scary numbers:

AT&T and IBM receive over 1 million résumés a year. Johnson & Johnson gets 300,000 résumés over the same period.

During November through April, peak recruiting periods, many large companies receive an average of 1,000 résumés a week.

Other large *Fortune* 500 companies report equally staggering numbers. These are only estimates since many conglomerates' satellite divisions fail to log their résumés. Silicon Valley companies in California's high-tech nerve center also report impressive numbers. Both Apple Computer and Sun Microsystems get close to 3,000 résumés a week. Even mid-size to small companies are inundated with hundreds of résumés a week.

Robert Half says that if 1,000 personnel executives did nothing but evaluate all the résumés circulating, it would take each one of them an average of 71 years, estimating 4 minutes spent per résumé. Half is being generous, since most recruiters think 4 minutes is an eternity. Half also estimates that if all the résumés in circulation were laid out they would circle the circumference of the earth 15 times!

Junk Résumés and the Futility of Mass Mailings

There is so much paper circulating, companies can hardly process all of it. Most of the résumés are "unsolicited," which means job applicants are not responding to advertised jobs. They're mass-mailing résumés to companies, hoping their qualifications match a job opening. For most applicants, it's nothing more than a crapshoot.

You've heard about junk mail and junk phone calls. The latest craze is junk résumés. Desperate job seekers are wasting thousands of dollars mass-mailing résumés around the country hoping for interviews. It amounts to an expensive waste of time. Only the heads of résumé-writing companies are getting rich off this tactic. One executive spent over $8,000 to mass-mail 10,000 résumés to companies across the country. The mailing resulted in 14 interviews and no job offers. Needless to say, the money could have been put to better use.

Jim Challenger, a principal in the Chicago outplacement firm Challenger Gray and Christmas, advises clients to avoid mass-mailing résumés. He estimates a 1 to 2 percent return, making it one of the worst ways to get interviews.

Corporate refugee Robert Hochheiser wrote *Throw Away Your Résumé* after investing several months and mailing out 1,000 résumés during his job hunt. He finally realized he had to find other ways to secure interviews.

Speed-Reading Résumés Is the Newest
Corporate Sport

The situation only gets worse, reports James Link, president of the Professional Development Institute in Horsham, Pennsylvania, an organization certifying career counselors. It amounts to an administrative nightmare with job searchers given short shrift because most résumés are hardly read.

Human resource folks joke about how little time they spend reading résumés. Speed-reading them is practically a sport. A staffing manager at a Connecticut software company spends only 30 seconds reviewing résumés. The head of a Denver bioengineering firm takes half as long. A human resource manager at a Mansfield, Ohio, commercial chemical company confessed she waits until she accumulates a stack of 100 résumés before skimming every tenth résumé, summarily rejecting the other nine. Résumé quality is so bad, she figures 1 out of every 10 deserves a careful read. That makes the odds of getting a fair shake pretty scary.

Résumé Readers Have Been Replaced
by Computers

Michael Silvester, director of sales at Resumix, Inc., in Santa Clara, California, says if a résumé does not grab a reader's attention in 15 seconds, it's trashed. Resumix sells corporations expensive résumé-scanning software that speedily searches for potential applicants. Résumé readers have been replaced by computers, saving companies thousands of hours of reading time as well as the cost of classified advertising. Silvester insists the software yields a 30 to 50 percent improvement in efficiency. Resumix's clients include AT&T, Digital Equipment, Wells Fargo and General Motors, to name a few.

More companies like Resumix will be springing up over the next decade. You can't blame companies for searching for people-weeding techniques that are more efficient than résumés. A property damage restoration firm in Jacksonville, Florida, for example, uses a computer program that matches job applicants' questionnaire responses to a series of success attributes in various positions. The company says it's a real time-saver. Its management figures anything is better than going cross-eyed reading résumés all day.

Need I say more? The facts speak for themselves. *Résumés don't get jobs*. Those four words are more than a catchy book title. They are *cold* truth.

Shopping List of Résumé Complaints—
1 Percent Get a Thorough Read

With a few tons of résumé paper circulating, you'd think we'd have uniform résumé standards. Instead, we have confusion, driving home the point that it's time to bury the résumé for good.

A human resource manager at Motorola reports a 30 percent increase in the number of résumés he receives. Quantity and quality, though, don't go hand in hand. Only 1 percent are given a thorough read, the rest are tossed. The problem? "Most stink," he snaps. The résumé books aren't doing their job, he adds.

The president of a New Jersey textile firm said résumés are "getting cuter and therefore worse." A Wisconsin paint manufacturer said most résumés are "unreadable and sound like they were written by a robot—and a very boring one."

A human resource manager in a nationwide accounting firm complained about exaggerated accomplishments. "If all the applicants did what their résumés claim," he said, "American companies wouldn't be dumping deadweight and consolidating." Other common résumé complaints from seasoned readers: "Too long," "Too short," "Rambling," "Insincere," "Sloppy," "Too Neat," "Confusing," "Silly," on and on.

Most professional résumé readers groaned when the résumé objective was mentioned. That's the line at the top in which you state your reason for seeking employment in the field or at the company you're addressing. Job searchers struggle in vain to find one cohesive sentence that sums up their career aspirations. It's time they realized it can't be done. Yet they keep trying. The result is limp, adjective-dense sentences that say nothing and sound like: "Searching for a meaningful career that allows me to grow professionally and personally and be the best I can possibly be."

Line up 5,000 résumés and you'll get a variation on these objectives: "I'm searching for a high-visibility job that affords me the opportunity to grow with the company." Or, "A challenging position as a salesperson in a multinational company with opportunities to utilize my extensive knowledge of the fashion business." And the cliché words flow like water—*high-visibility, affording, opportunity, utilize, extensive, challenging.*

Even a conservative Robert Half, who devotes a lot of space to résumé preparation in his books, admits most résumé objectives are stiff and best omitted. Half is right, and he opens up a monster can of worms by advising job searchers to drop the objective altogether. Some years ago, he wrote an article for Dow Jones' *National Business Employment Weekly* saying the problem with résumé objectives is that they rule you out for other jobs you might qualify for. A good objective is so targeted that an employer never considers you for anything but the one job you are applying for, according to Half.

So what do you do if you're a Renaissance person capable of doing many things well? How do you come up with a simple, targeted objective? You don't. Instead, you do what smart people have been doing for decades. You have three or four variations of your résumé, each selling different skills. Rather than one all-purpose résumé, each looks like it's custom-designed for a specific job. Each one has a different objective, followed by selected job experiences that sell you best. If you can sell and program computers, or if you've written advertising copy but also developed new clients as an account executive, it pays to have two résumés highlighting each skill.

It can amount to a mountain-size headache keeping track of which version of a résumé was sent where—irrefutable evidence that the résumé is a clumsy and unwieldy tool that ought to be buried for good.

Sneak Preview of Twenty-First-Century Résumés

If you think résumés are bad now, just wait. If the résumé isn't dumped, future résumés will induce strokes. Human resource folks and employment agency placement managers will be jumping from windows en masse.

Résumé objectives will be taken to a new level of banality. As we said earlier, job-hopping, forced or chosen, is the wave of the future. Most job searchers will have worked in so many jobs, they'll be pulling their hair out deciding which ones to include on their résumés. Many career builders will be changing jobs yearly, which means trying to sell yourself with a résumé will amount to a nightmare.

Future résumé writers will have to be not only masterful copywriters, but editors as well. If not, résumés will become unwieldy tomes running 3 and 4 pages or bewildering 1-page shopping lists of jobs.

Grabbing an Employer's Attention—A Simple Alternative to a Mounting Problem

Now that we've debunked the résumé, an institution as established as apple pie and motherhood, we offer a three-step process that increases by more than 50 percent your chances of getting your foot in the door:

1. Research the companies you'd like to work for.

2. Find the person or intermediary (employment agency) who actual-
    ly does the hiring or is a step away from it.

3. Rather than sending a separate résumé with a cover letter, combine
    them into a brilliant, well-crafted letter that sells you.

Ideally, it would be great if you could hook up immediately with
the person doing the hiring, bypassing intermediaries (employment
agencies and human resource departments), but that's unrealistic.
Unfortunately, the published markets are rife with intermediaries
who can't be avoided.

Be prepared to encounter resistance from employment agency
placement managers who still think résumés are the only way to win
interviews. But even skeptical placement managers can be seduced by
great credentials and deft selling abilities.

What do you say when a placement manager doesn't even read
your letter and writes you a note or calls asking for a résumé? "Don't
you know you gotta have a résumé?" he sighs, with a condescending,
"are you some kind of jerky rebel" tone. What he's really saying is:
"Who do you think you are violating a hiring tradition as sacred as
the New and Old Testaments combined?"

Your reply? An emphatic, "A résumé will not sell me as well as a
simple, to-the-point letter. I urge you to read it." Don't even couch
your answer with an "*I don't think* a résumé will sell me as well as a
letter." It shows you're unsure or could be convinced otherwise. Stick
by your guns and be prepared for one of those nerve-bending preg-
nant pauses that makes you want to gnaw your fingernails clear off
your hands before a word is uttered. Keep your cool.

Corporate human resource people, employment agency placement
managers and even executive recruiters will not turn their backs on
blue-chip candidates. The simple truth is that great candidates are
great candidates no matter what their calling cards.

Let's take a close look at each step before crafting the letter.

Research the Companies You'd Like to Work For.   Include a variety of companies, large and small, aggressive and traditional. The longer
the list, the better. Rank the companies in terms of your chances of conquering interviews. The bigger ones with the densest bureaucracies are
always the toughest sales.

Spend time on this vital stage. Rather than just absorbing facts
and figures, evaluate the information and try to get answers to
important questions such as, What is the corporate structure like? Is

there much turnover? How does the company fit into its industry? Is it traditional, aggressive, a trendsetter? Last, and most important, find out what its problems are so you can address those issues in your letter.

Locate the Person Doing the Hiring.   Here's where cunning and street smarts are called for. It's the "Maginot Line" separating Phi Beta Kappa networkers from amateurs. Tap your network, call your trade association, speak to friends and find out what you can about the company. If none of those work, consider a full frontal attack. Muster your courage, take a deep breath and call the company and speak to department secretaries. Remember what we said in Myth 1: "Job Hunting Is a Logical Process." These people are important. Alienate them and you're finished. Friendly and professional are the command words. Whatever you do, don't come on like a Sherman tank!

You'll be surprised what you can learn by a few tactfully delivered questions. If you've got some acting talent, consider a gutsy tactic used by a friend who landed a job at a major broadcasting company. After lining up over two dozen companies, he cold-called departments he wanted to work for by saying, "I'm calling about the opening in your department for a production assistant." After 10 times hearing "There are no openings in our department," he finally hit paydirt with a couple of "You ought to speak to Toby Twaddle or Timmy Tool about that spot. They're interviewing applicants." Or, "You must be talking about the production apprentice job; Todd Twisky is the person to talk to." When his interviewer asked him how he heard about the job slated to be filled internally, he said he just stumbled on it by making several calls. Naturally, he didn't tell the whole story. The interviewer shook his head, laughed and said he admired his tactic. It sure beats the résumé route. The moral of the story: Imagination and creativity pays off.

Once You've Found a Job Opening, Fire Off a Brilliant Letter Selling Yourself into the Job.   The letter is an all-in-one package, eliminating résumé and cover letter.

Why a Letter?

The Personal Touch

Whether it's business or personal, everyone enjoys getting letters. Even badly written letters are fun to read, if for no other reason than to jump all over someone's non sequiturs, poor spelling and fourth-grade grammar.

It's easy to see why direct-mail marketing campaigns are so successful. Most of the direct-mail pieces are long-winded drivel, yet a small percentage are quite good. They ought to be your models. Somehow, they beckon to be read. For a few naive seconds, you actually think it was written just for you. It starts off with a Dear Ms. or Mr. Mark, followed by an enticing lead like: "I bet you never realized you are spending much more on car insurance than you ought to be. If you're a resident of Planet Pluto and you've never had a moving violation since birth, you're entitled to a 250 percent reduction, putting more than $2 billion back in your pocket annually. Mr. or Ms. Mark, no other insurance company is offering this incredible savings. I urge you to take advantage of the limited two-day opportunity."

The above language is a little exaggerated, but you get the idea. A well-crafted letter, even if it's 99 percent hot air, grabs your attention, forcing you to read it.

Of course you're not going to distort facts and make promises you can't keep, but like a well-written direct-mail marketing letter, you're going to try and craft a letter that grabs the reader's attention. Write a great letter and I guarantee readers won't skim it as they do résumés. They'll read every word of it.

The Letter Is a Personal Marketing Tool

Think of the letter as your personal marketing tool. Each letter ought to be tailored to the job you're applying for, while the guts of the letter (your qualifications and accomplishments) remain unchanged. It only sounds more complicated than it is.

Practical Reasons

Additionally, there are two practical reasons why a personal letter is better than a résumé:

1. It makes points faster, bypassing canned objectives. Readers don't have to waste time figuring out what you're qualified for.

2. It's ideal for job-hoppers, career changers and people who haven't worked for long periods. A letter allows you the latitude to focus on what you think is important, rather than every humdrum, meaningless job you've had over the past decade.

If you didn't work for five years because you were raising a child, traveling or in school, you can skirt time gaps and focus on qualifications.

Career changers, particularly, are often crippled by résumés because readers can't reconcile radical changes. "I can't believe this woman. She was a toothpick designer for 25 years; now she's applying for a job as an astronaut!"

A letter, however, creatively uses the experiences of one career as selling points for a new one. "The patience, concentration on detail and problem-solving skills needed in advanced toothpick design will come in handy when piloting malfunctioning ships home to base." You get the idea.

Let's prepare one.

Crafting the Letter

Overcoming Letter-Writing Hang-Ups

Some people get uptight about writing letters. Maybe it's because their folks forced them to write home once a week when they were in summer camp. No letter meant no salamis, no candy bars, no cookies. Letter writing was like homework.

Relax. The letter we're suggesting isn't quite the same thing. First, there is real motivation to write a great letter: a *job*. Second, you don't have to be a great writer. But you do need imagination and creativity. Add time and effort, and you'll craft a great letter. Fundamentally, writing your letter is simple, but it will take practice to perfect the structure and find a comfortable voice.

Striking the Right Tone

Great letters, business and personal, are unpretentious, honest and sincere. They say what they have to say sparing big words, jargon and buzzwords.

Yet, there are clear differences between personal and business letters. Personal letters strike a familiar, congenial or intimate tone. They can take licenses a business letter cannot. Writers can say anything they want without considering style, format or structure. Anything goes. A letter can be one long, mangled run-on sentence or deft prose. It's easy to see why many professional writers use the letter as intimate vehicles for baring their souls.

Not so with business letters. There are rules, regulations and absolute no-nos. It doesn't matter whether the person you are writing to is a low-level manager or the CEO. Respect for the other person's position, power or influence dictates tactful distance and a strict adherence to protocol. Occasionally, you'll be writing to freewheeling, tell-it-like-it-is antiestablishment types who couldn't care less about playing by the book. But you won't know that until you meet them. Pay attention to rank, authority and the hundreds of petty rules and procedures fueling the machine. That's a safe stance to take because you'll come across as a thorough professional. It's better to appear stiff and formal rather than flip or casual. A final consideration; don't assume all businesspeople are the same. Midwest employers, for example, tend to be more formal than Californians or Floridians.

Take no chances and adhere to strict letter-writing form. Rather than indent paragraphs, common in personal letters, use a block format, which will be demonstrated later.

Watch your language, grammar, punctuation and sentence structure. You can get away with sentence fragments in a résumé, but not in a letter. Just one disjointed sentence and your letter will be promptly crunched into a ball and fired into the nearest trash receptacle.

Putting Yourself in the Employer's Shoes

Before you put your first sentence down, put yourself in the employer's shoes. What is he or she looking for? We'll be driving this point home throughout the book, especially here and in Myth 9: "Interviewers Are Sadists in Business Suits" and Myth 10: "Employers Are Autocratic Powerlords Who Know Exactly What They're Looking For: Ergo, They Hold All the Negotiating Cards."

The Winning Structure—A Formula That Can't Miss

Like a catchy print advertisement, the letter must capture attention, make a promise and back that claim. Your attention getter is your opening sentences; your claim is a pitch for the job; and backing the claim is selling your credentials.

Remember what I said in the Introduction. You are the product. The challenge is selling yourself in a letter, a far better platform than a résumé.

Let's look at the letter's components more closely.

Good and Bad Openings

Crafting a letter is like building a house. A house topples without a foundation. The same goes for a letter. The foundation, or support beams, of a letter are its opening sentences.

First, bad openings. A bad opening, like a bad objective, can knock you out of the race. The reader loses interest and you're history.

A good opening can be compared to the lead sentences in a newspaper story. Pick up a daily newspaper and skim the first sentences of a half-dozen front-page stories. They all have one thing in common: They practically beg you to read on. The journalist's goal is to instantly hook you. Like an advertising copywriter's sizzling 5-line ad, you've been seduced in seconds. Your curiosity has been piqued. You're compelled to learn what happens next.

I don't expect you to become instant journalists or copywriters, but you can try to emulate their approaches with compelling, tightly written "grabber" sentences.

What makes a bad opening? The worst thing you can do is make hollow or flip promises. Example: "Dear Ms. Hollyhoodle: I am just the person you are looking for." Or, "I understand you're in the market for a dynamite safe cracker. Your worries are over. I'm the only person for the job." Or, "This job has my name on it and I urge you to see me immediately." All these openers are inane. They make idle claims, accomplishing nothing but incurring the reader's wrath.

Now, a few good openings. Say you heard about a job through contacts or by doing some creative snooping:

Dear Mr. Chiselnut,

For the last five years, I have worked as a research assistant at Consolidated Paints' Des Moines plant. I assisted the line manager and was part of a team that increased output 15 to 20 percent for each of my five years with the company. My experience with automated assembly lines can be very helpful in developing the systems for your new Hackensack, New Jersey, plant. I would like to be considered for the associate plant manager's job, which I learned about through Brad Donaldson, your staffing manager.

If you learned about the job through a want ad, this opening can be used:

My qualifications are identical to those outlined in a recent advertisement in the Mansfield Bugle. For the last three years, I was a senior programmer for Didford Systems, Inc., where I created on-line bookkeeping systems for the company's 12 satellite offices. I am searching for a job that can put my background to good use, plus offer opportunities to take on bigger projects.

The above openings create immediate interest. Neither pompous nor exaggerated, they get right to the point.

In most cases, explain how you learned about the job. However, if you found it through your network, a well-placed king-maker (mentioned in Myth 4: "Aggressive Networking Is the Key to a Successful Job Search") or a low-level contact at the company, don't say so in the letter. The interview is the time to explain how you uncovered the job. It takes too much time to explain it in a letter. Employers are impressed with candidates who have the imagination and drive to chase leads and contacts.

Concentrate on Jobs That Sell You Best

Once you get the opening, the rest ought to follow. The curtain is up, so break into your act by laying out your accomplishments followed by your credentials. Rather than explain your last five jobs, concentrate on recent ones and peripherally mention others. Example:

From 1988 to 1992, I was account supervisor at BCEF Advertising where I:

- Managed five *Fortune* 500 accounts
- Led a staff of three junior copywriters
- Developed strategy and created campaigns for company salespeople
- Spent more than 20 percent of my time traveling to accounts, working closely with senior management

Prior to that, I spent one year at Elcor Advertising as accounts administrator, and from 1984 to 1987 I was a senior accounts executive at Librium Advertising, where I single-handedly built a selling team of salespeople that boosted the firm's revenues 65 percent over the following three years.

Note that each job demonstrates responsibility, accomplishments and growth.

Remember, brevity is important. Concentrate on jobs that sell you best. Do not mention every job you had. Job application forms are the place for lengthy job histories. If employers are interested, they'll ask for details during the interview.

The Home Stretch

Now you're on the home stretch. It's time to wind down with your education and affiliations, if any.

> I have a B.A. from Lempuck University and an M.B.A. from Intercon University. I am a member of the Advertising Society of America.

Time for a brief wrap-up.

> I welcome the opportunity to meet with you and explore your needs and how I can meet them. I will call you on Friday, March 12, to arrange an appointment.
>
> I look forward to meeting you.
>
> Sincerely,
>
> George Blinderbopper

Instead of using conventional closings like "I look forward to hearing from you," "I hope you find my qualifications acceptable," or "I await your reply," which put you at an employer's mercy, try to control the process as much as possible by telling them precisely when you will follow up. That one sentence paints you as assertive and committed to finding a job.

The employer's reaction might be something like: "Hey, this guy is not afraid to say what's on his mind. Let's get him in for an interview."

Obviously, don't forget to call on the appointed day.

Don't get lazy or sloppy in these last paragraphs. They're vital because they open the door to appointments. This is where tactful aggression comes in handy. Lose your momentum inches from the finish line and you forfeit the race. If you wimp out at the end with a weak finish, chances are you'll never hear from them. Remember, these folks are busy. They barely have time to down a cup of coffee in peace.

Rather than requesting to come in and talk about job prospects, ask about exploring their needs and solving their problems. Don't side-step the issue. You want a job. Yet, you're not flip in asking for a paycheck. You're making it clear you want to pitch in, roll up your sleeves and earn your keep. No free rides for you.

Beating the Résumé at Its Own Game

That wasn't so bad. When all parts of the letter fit together, you have a fast, neat, cohesive selling promotional letter. Its advantages over the résumé are obvious: Where a résumé is mechanical and lifeless, the letter bears the job seeker's personal stamp. Where résumés are an unwieldy string of jobs, a letter hones right in on the target, making its point succinctly. Finally, a letter has a beginning and an end. A letter practically forces you to start at the top and end at the bottom. Not so with a résumé. Many veteran résumé readers often start at the middle or end and work their way to the top. If the reader starts at the bottom and gets bored with the applicant's educational credentials, it's on to the next one.

See Figure 8-1 for a complete letter in block format, which means all paragraphs are flush left and not indented. *Important considerations* of the letter are:

- The letter is tight and pointed.

- The letter says what it has to and stops.

- The letter contains no shallow adjectives, self-congratulatory pats on the back or snake-oil-selling tactics.

The advantages of this letter over the résumé speak for themselves. Unless you have a perfect background—three or four jobs that consistently sell you plus glowing academic qualifications—résumés don't work. As I said earlier, the résumé is disastrous for career changers because it confuses readers. "What? This woman wants to be a hanger designer when she spent the last 15 years selling pottery in state fairs." A little far-fetched, but you get the point. Somehow, a cleverly written letter could have gotten around the radical career change by honing in on her qualifications for the career she's pursuing. Similarly, if you've changed jobs practically every year of your career, a résumé will paint you as an unreliable, rootless wanderer.

The beauty of the letter is that it permits the job seeker to focus on *what is important.* Thus, the reader is not distracted by contradictory facts, time lapses and radical changes.

Also note, the writer jumped immediately into her qualifications, enlisting the reader's interest. Rather than saying she was an extraordinary job applicant, she proved it by citing real accomplishments. The reader's response will be something like: "This person has a solid background. She sounds like she can get things done. Let's get her in for an interview."

555 Main Street
Houghtonville, PA 19000
January 4, 19XX

Ms. Elizabeth Carnivour
Bedrock Cereal Company
333 North Street
Philadelphia, PA 19123

Dear Ms. Carnivour:

Attention-Grabbing Opening

Through Jane Hopple, administrative assistant at your Garden City subsidiary, I learned that you're looking for a project engineer at your new Houghtonville plant. I spent the last five years (19XX-19XX) working as a senior project engineer at Howdy Doody Foods, the $125 million international food conglomerate.

Primary Job Experience Stressing Accomplishments

Spending practically 45 percent of my time shuttling between plants in Lancaster, PA, Windsor, VT, and Chicago, IL, I coordinated plant and facilities projects for the cereal, fast foods and snack divisions. I was project leader managing teams of a dozen-plus people and supervising budgets ranging from $500,000 to $5 million. And working closely with vendors, architects, engineers and senior executives, I was solely responsible for completing projects within tight deadlines. Four times, I won the company's "Distinguished Work Award" for completing projects under budget. The challenging and gratifying parts of the work were completing projects to everyone's specifications and being a liaison between management and staff. Typically, I coordinated projects from inception to completion.

Secondary Job Experience Stressing Accomplishments

Prior to that, I was a project coordinator at Piranha USA, the country's largest snack food company, from 19XX to 19XX. I was promoted every year, taking on more responsibility. I joined the company as an assistant engineer and left supervising a staff of four engineers and two technicians. Most of my responsibilities centered around improving productivity for the company's successful line of healthy snack foods. Over a two-year period, I led a fact-finding group which evaluated and found a solution for modernizing and improving productivity on the 40-year-old assembly line. New equipment was purchased and installed, and new techniques for staffing the line were developed, leading to savings of 35 to 40 percent and a 50 percent improvement in productivity. One of the most gratifying parts of the project was that we redesigned the assembly line, increasing each worker's productivity by an average of 25 percent.

(Development) Selling Paragraphs

Figure 8-1. Sample letter in block format.

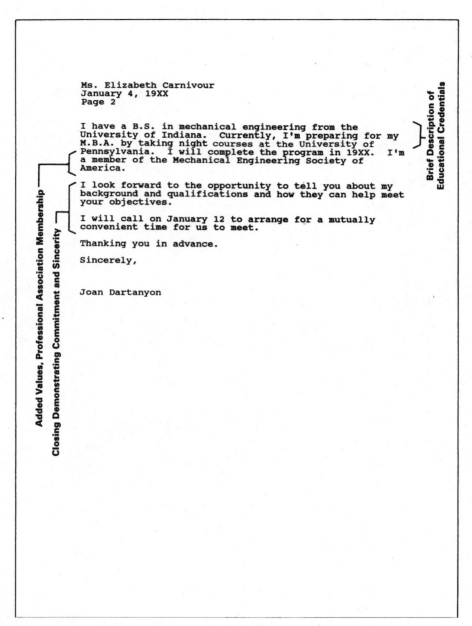

Ms. Elizabeth Carnivour
January 4, 19XX
Page 2

I have a B.S. in mechanical engineering from the
University of Indiana. Currently, I'm preparing for my
M.B.A. by taking night courses at the University of
Pennsylvania. I will complete the program in 19XX. I'm
a member of the Mechanical Engineering Society of
America.

I look forward to the opportunity to tell you about my
background and qualifications and how they can help meet
your objectives.

I will call on January 12 to arrange for a mutually
convenient time for us to meet.

Thanking you in advance.

Sincerely,

Joan Dartanyon

Brief Description of Educational Credentials

Added Values, Professional Association Membership

Closing Demonstrating Commitment and Sincerity

Figure 8-1. (*Continued*) Sample letter in block format.

Letters for Career Changers

As we said above, because of its versatility, the letter is ideal for career changers. If résumés don't work for job changers, how can they possibly work for career changers trying to leverage skills developed in one field to move into another? A letter, however, is a flexible and creative selling platform for actually doing it.

Let's look at two sample letters for career changers: The first letter is from a tool-and-die maker who wants to switch careers and become a computer hardware builder. They're totally different careers, yet the applicant felt the transition was logical and not difficult to make.

Dear Ms. Afguniti:

I'm responding to your ad in *The Daily Worker* (August 10) for a hardware builder. If I'm not being presumptuous and I understand the demands of the position, you're looking for someone with a strong mechanical aptitude who enjoys precise, intricate work and who is self-motivated. I have all those characteristics.

For the past 12 years I've worked as a tool-and-die maker. If you're familiar with the area, tool-and-die makers are highly skilled, creative workers whose products—tools, dies and special guiding and holding devices—are used by other machine workers to mass-produce parts. Toolmakers produce jigs and fixtures (devices that hold metal while it is bored, stamped or drilled). They also make gauges and other measuring devices used in manufacturing precision metal parts. Compared with most other machining operations, tool-and-die makers have a broader knowledge of machining operations, mathematics and blueprint reading. As you can see, the tool-and-die maker and the hardware builder have overlapping skills—knowledge of machining operations and mechanical aptitude, to name just two.

Having worked in an established, traditional trade, I want to get involved in high-technology industries. With my background and inclinations, building computers is my first choice. The demand for tool-and-die makers dwindles each year, yet the demand for hardware builders far exceeds the supply. Aside from being fascinated with computers, I feel I have the mechanical aptitude and creativity to make significant contributions.

Over the past two years, I've taken a number of courses in computer theory, architecture and programming. I have more than enough knowledge to enter your apprenticeship program. Within six months, I feel I could be making a solid contribution to your company.

The above is only a brief sketch of my background. I'd like to get together with you at your convenience to discuss the job opening in more detail. I will call you within the next few days to set up an appointment convenient to both of us.

Sincerely,

Ernest Didley

The second letter is by a social worker who wants to become a stockbroker.

Dear Mr. Ethelbutane:

Lyle Scamster, my broker and friend, told me there were openings for stockbrokers at your office and suggested I apply.

Since graduating college I have followed and studied the stock market intensely, on both a fundamental and technical basis.

It wasn't until a few months ago that I realized I could build a career around my hobby. For the past 14 years I've earned my living as a social worker. Social work and the brokerage business seem miles apart, but in actuality there is a great deal of overlap. For example, the social worker and the stockbroker work closely with people. Success in both fields is contingent upon establishing a workable rapport with people. The skills I developed as a social worker (the ability to reach, understand and empathize with people) will be extremely valuable to me as a stockbroker. You might say that my social work background was an excellent apprenticeship for pursuing a career in the brokerage industry.

My career as a social worker was very satisfying. I learned a great deal about people, particularly how to productively work with them on a one-to-one basis. I got to a point, however, where I could go no further and thirsted to explore new career terrain. Social work no longer excited me. I realized I had the classic attributes of a salesperson. Now I want to use them to good advantage to make myself an excellent broker and to contribute significantly to the profits of your firm.

My fascination with the stock market and my ability to work well with people are the two crucial factors for achieving success in the brokerage industry. I hope you agree.

I would like to come in and discuss the matter with you in greater detail. I will call to arrange a mutually convenient time to meet.

I look forward to meeting you.

Sincerely,

Ed Dillinger

Letter-Writing Tips

Three Commandments of Great Letter Writing

Now that you know what well-constructed letters look like, here are some timeless tips for building them:

1. *Stay focused.* Don't start dashing off a letter until you're clear about how you plan to sell yourself. If you're responding to a want ad or one-line job description from a colleague or friend, think about how you want to position yourself so you impress your reader. Give serious thought to your opening sentences. If they're weak, the letter will get off to a limp start. Like writing a news story or print advertisement, know precisely what you want to say.

2. *Be articulate and find your own voice.* Once you know what you want to communicate, find your own voice and be articulate. Don't try to sound like someone else, a professor or a brilliant scholar, for example. Be yourself. Employers want real people, not clones. Don't use big words, jargon or long-winded phrases. Instead, stick to bite-size words and simple sentences. If your reader has to interpret sentences or read between the lines, you're branded an unclear thinker, and your letter is trashed. Present thoughts in a logical order. A suggested technique is to number the points you want to make. If you have 15 crucial points to get across, build your letter around them.

3. *Rewrite and edit.* Finally, don't ever send a first draft. No matter how anxious you are to get your letter in the mail, exercise discipline and resist the temptation. No letter is perfect after one writing session. Chances are it needs either a rewrite or a heavy edit, whatever it takes to make it as lean and muscular as a gymnast's body.

Sweat a little more and make it perfect. Read every word to make sure it can't be tightened more. You're almost there, but not quite.

The Acid Test

Now that you're convinced you have a Pulitzer Prize–winning letter, take one last step. Put it aside for a couple of hours, or better yet, sleep on it until the following morning. It's a journalistic trick guaranteed to work. When you're working against mind-bending deadlines, it's not always possible to put a story away until the next day. But if you can, the ensuing revision frequently makes a substantial difference in quality.

The mind is a strange thing. Often, the more involved you get in something, the more bogged down you get in trivial details.

Unconsciously, you find yourself getting sidetracked, hovering compulsively over insignificant details. There lies the beauty of allowing breathing time for projects you're immersed in.

Even a couple of hours of distance can make a big difference. I call it gestation, or simmering, time. You are putting it aside so you can come back and look at it with a fresh perspective. You'll be amazed at the changes you'll make. You'll say to yourself: "I can't believe I wrote that." A word here, a word there, an entire sentence moved in another paragraph and you're there. It's perfect. Nothing more can be done.

Neatness Counts

Now for the final draft. As your teachers used to say, neatness counts. Your letter doesn't have to look like it dropped from a laser printer, but it ought to look good.

Once again, I strongly recommend a personal computer. It will make your life easier. Letters can be stored, retrieved, reworked, adapted and edited without having to endure the tedium of endless retyping.

A memory typewriter is a less expensive variable. If you're on a tight budget, invest in a reliable electric typewriter with a pica rather than an elite slug. The pica is larger and easier to read. Stay away from fancy typefaces and colored paper. You're wasting money, and nobody will be impressed.

Keep it simple and professional and adhere to standard letter form with 1-inch margins top and bottom and ½-inch margins on the sides. Use block format, like the letters above, and stay consistent.

Letter-Writing Checklist

Before you mail your letter, here's a quick checklist to make sure it's "letter" perfect.

1. Do your opening sentences capture the reader's attention?
2. Does the letter sell you by highlighting important accomplishments?
3. Is it a fast, easy read?
4. Is it professional and businesslike?
5. Is it grammatically correct?

6. Are there spelling errors? Be careful, it's easy for one to slip through the cracks. If you use a computer, take advantage of your software's spell-check feature. It is an excellent tool, ultimately saving you embarrassment and grief.

7. Are there unnecessary spaces or awkwardly hyphenated words?

8. Are names butchered?

9. Is it clean? One tiny smudge is too many.

Letter-Writing Dos and Don'ts

Finally, consider these all-purpose letter-writing guidelines:

Do:

1. Tailor your experience to the employer's needs.

2. Be brief and focused. Don't wander off on aimless tangents. A page and a half, single-spaced, should do it. If it runs longer, you risk losing your reader.

3. Present facts and figures to back up your accomplishments. "When I started, I coordinated projects up to $500,000. Two years later I was promoted to project coordinator, supervising projects with budgets ranging from $1 to $5 million."

4. Always personalize the letter. Never send a letter addressed to a title (Human Resources Director) or, worse yet, To Whom It May Concern.

Don't:

1. Be shy about your accomplishments, but do avoid hollow claims and outrageous statements. ("I'm the best salesperson on the East Coast." "I'll write copy guaranteed to impress your clients.")

2. Include irrelevant information about college, hobbies or personal insights. Save it for the interview. Stick to the issue at hand—selling yourself.

3. Repeat yourself. It's very easy to use the same adjectives over and over. Words such as *implemented, supervised, organized, accomplished, conceived, impacted* and others are used to death. Often, it's hard to find synonyms for many of these action words. At least, be con-

scious of repeating yourself and, when possible, find new descriptive words.

4. Give references in a letter. It's inappropriate and in bad taste. The employer will conclude you have stock references who will recommend you for anything, even high-paying mercenary work in a third-world country. References are to be provided later when an employer is considering you and wants to check to see if you're as good as you say you are.

5. Give your age. In the past it was common to include your age. Today, it is illegal. Many employers get around it in want ads, "Looking for senior person with 15 years experience" or "Ideal opportunity for recent college grad" and by simply asking it during interviews. If an employer asks how old you are during an interview, you can courageously say it's illegal. But chances are you'll give your age because you need the job and you can't afford to be a martyr, at least not with rent and a stack of bills to pay.

6. Say disparaging things about a past employer. It's bad form and not to be discussed either in a letter or during the interview. (More on this in Myth 9: "Interviewers Are Sadists in Business Suits.") Just stick to facts; don't get into personality differences.

7. Offer personal or nonpertinent information. Don't mention that you're married or have children. The same goes for listing hobbies, religious affiliations or your contributions to a string of charities and nonprofit organizations. This stuff regularly appears on résumés, for what reason I've never understood. If employers are more than casually interested in whether you're married, divorced, childless or an active member of your church or synagogue, maybe you ought not to work for them. Ideally, employers shouldn't care whether you're married, single, divorced, gay, Catholic, Protestant, Jew, Hindu, Seventh Day Adventist, agnostic or atheist. It all comes under the banner heading of *irrelevant*.

Now, let's hone our interview skills.

Myth 9: Interviewers Are Sadists in Business Suits.

Reality: *Don't let your imagination get carried away. Fear of interviewers and the interviewing process are unnecessary and counterproductive.*

Chapter Snapshot

- □ What Are You Really Afraid Of?
- □ The Performance of Your Life—The Interview Is Your Platform
- □ Each Job Interview Is a Learning Experience
- □ The Interview Goal—Sell! Sell! Sell!
- □ Build Rapport and Make Connections
- □ Getting in Shape—Rehearsing for the Event
- □ Control the Interview by Learning Everything You Can
- □ Make Your Voice Count—Watch Your Posture—Look the Part
- □ Dissecting the Interview—The Human Factor
- □ A Three-Part Play
- □ Don't Blow It! Ten Sure Ways to Turn Off an Interviewer
- □ Evaluating Your Performance
- □ The Coda Sales Pitch
- □ Interview Dos and Don'ts

****

It's mind-boggling when you think about how many job searchers actually have nightmares before a job interview. Some of them are real horror stories, the stuff of Hollywood thrillers. Wait till you hear one dream a job searcher told me. Hold on to your seat.

Seconds after he walked through the austere, cavernous halls of the large corporation, the young man was greeted by two Arnold Schwarzenegger look-alikes dressed in matching black business suits and ties. They led him by the arm into an enormous room that resembled a courtroom. His heart pounded as his voice reverberated throughout the wood-panelled chamber. Waiting for him were 10 similarly built stern-faced executives sitting behind a long table. In front of them was a high-backed thick wooden chair that looked like an electric chair without wires.

The two men sat him in the chair, pinioned his arms to the chair with leather straps and took positions on either side of him. They stood there, stone-faced while the 10 men, in turn, fired questions at him at machine gun speed. He barely had time to answer one question when the next was hurled at him.

Each time he answered incorrectly the goons slammed him in the face with the back of their hands. As the questions became harder, the blows intensified because he could barely answer them. An hour later he was a bloody mess barely able to keep his head up. As he slipped into an unconscious stupor, he was lifted from the chair by the two men, dragged to the door leading outside and thrown in an unconscious heap into the street. As his body hit the ground, he awoke in a cold, shivering sweat.

Not everyone's dreams are as graphic and scary, but it's safe to say no one sleeps like a baby before a job interview. At this very second, thousands of job hunters around the world are tossing and turning in their sleep, anxiety-stricken about the ordeal before them. Job interviews have been compared to going to war, running a marathon race, even going to the dentist—the ultimate fear.

Unfortunately, most job seekers spend more time worrying about interviews than preparing for them. Just reading a book about interview techniques is enough to terrify anyone. After all, the interview is your walk on hot coals. Blow it and you don't get the job. Runners-up don't get half a job for turning in an almost brilliant performance. Like they say, it's all or nothing.

No wonder we transfer all our anxiety to the people interrogating, I mean, interviewing us. They are in control, holding our fate in their hands.

What Are You Really Afraid Of?

Job searchers have always been terrified of interviews. The core of the myth is a fear of authority, which can be traced to childhood. We've all been brought up to listen and obey. Be polite and answer people when they speak to you, we're told. When a job and all that it implies is in question, healthy respect for authority escalates into irrational fear, even terror.

Rather than seeing interviewers as little more than screeners and professional information gatherers, we equate them with stormtroopers. When you think about it rationally, you discover interviewers are not demons or monsters out to demoralize, embarrass and humiliate you into a blabbering piece of degraded flesh. They're not "Terminators" in business suits. Like you and me, they're just people holding down jobs. They've also got bills, mortgages, annoying kids, ex-wives and ex-husbands and alimony payments.

Unless you're applying for a job in a small company where the employer does all the interviewing and hiring, count on corporate middlepeople to screen applicants. It doesn't matter who asks the questions, they're just people playing parts in the real-life drama we're living. Digest all that, and 20 percent of the fear evaporates immediately.

Along with an irrational fear of authority, we're also afraid of screwing up, making fools of ourselves and not being prepared. Put it all together and we're afraid of losing by not getting the job.

The best way to deal with that fear is by channeling nervous energy into preparing for the event.

The Performance of Your Life—The Interview Is Your Platform

Interview preparation starts with a positive mindset and attitude. Most job searchers fail to realize that the interview is a chance of a lifetime. It's not you against them (the company), but a chance to shine, perform, do your thing and swing from the rafters. See it as a platform.

Just as actors audition for parts, you are, in a sense, auditioning for your interviewer. If he or she likes the way you perform, you're called back for a second audition, or callback. This time you may be performing for new people. Often, you'll have to undergo two or three interviews before a job offer is made.

Does it sound nerve-wracking? Actually it is, but it's also exciting because you're dealing with the unknown and learning in the process. Instead of chewing your nails to the bone worrying, see it as a positive experience. If you fumble your lines or spill coffee on yourself and your interviewer, don't sprint for the door. Like the well-disciplined actor, get yourself together and go on with the show. Your interviewer will respect you for having the guts and cool to continue. (More on analyzing your performance later on.)

Each Job Interview Is a Learning Experience

Whether you're walking into utopia or a mine field, welcome each interview as an opportunity to learn about yourself. No interview, no matter how badly it goes, is a waste of time. If nothing else, a bad interview is preparation for the next one.

You don't become an expert interviewee after just one interview. Like mastering a sport, it takes dozens of interviews before you become comfortable with the process. Each one will be different. Some will be grueling, tense and formal; others will be relaxed and informal. And still others will be inane. They'll vary in length from 20-minute conversations to 90-minute distillations of your life.

The Interview Goal—Sell! Sell! Sell!

See the interview as an opportunity to make your big play by proving you're the greatest thing to hit the planet since the wheel.

Approach the interview with an open mind. Think of the interview as the equivalent of a salesperson's cold call. Salespeople have no idea what to expect once they cross the prospect's threshold. A sale might happen instantly, or the bewildered salesperson may find the door slammed in his or her face before the attaché case is even opened. There is no predicting the outcome. Similarly, there is no gauging the outcome of an interview. Your interviewer may seem like a cross between the marharishi and Santa Claus, yet you have no idea how this person is actually reading you. Don't misconstrue smiles, laughter and ingratiating small talk. A sea of difference separates appearance and reality.

Like the salesperson's cold call, the very unpredictability of the event makes it challenging. Because of the unknowns, you ought to work 10 times as hard to give more than your best. If that isn't enough of a motivator, remember that if you don't impress the interviewer, the next nervous, quaking person sitting in the reception area clutching her or his attaché case will.

Build Rapport and Make Connections

The goal is to sell yourself. The best way to do it is by building a rapport and making connections with interviewers. Let them set the stage so you get a sense of where they're coming from. Follow their lead and don't jump ahead. Pay attention and you'll discover that certain nuances, thoughts and opinions make stronger impressions than others. This is what you ought to play on.

When the interview is over, it's those subtle connections, as much as right answers, that interviewers remember. A sales manager working for a national computer chain told me that one of the things that helped him ace a job interview was discovering he and the interviewer shared the same hobby. They both were avid comic book collectors. He discovered it by carefully listening and working toward building meaningful connections. For close to 15 minutes they talked about the current market value of *Superman, Batman,* and *Wonder Woman* first editions.

It doesn't take a Freudian analyst to figure this out. When the interviewer weighed the 20 to 30 applicants for the job, the applicant comics collector jumped to the head of the line. He might have been no better or maybe even mediocre compared to other applicants, yet he was vividly remembered and thus stood a better chance.

So stay loose and play it as you go along. Whatever you do, don't prejudge the situation or the interviewer. You never know how things may work out. Be a chameleon and adjust your rhythms and strategies to the moment.

Getting in Shape—Rehearsing for the Event

Would an actor choose not to memorize his lines before going onstage? Ridiculous question. Yet, thousands of job seekers fail to prepare for interviews. And it's only because they're lazy. They reason charm will carry the day and they can get away with passing off generic pap instead of hard facts and information.

It's easy to adopt that attitude when you're constantly going on interviews and being turned down. You arrive at a negative state of mind at which you're saying to yourself: "Why bother? Why spend time preparing for interviews when I'm only going to be rejected?" Yet they fail to consider how self-defeating that rationalization is.

Assume that attitude and I guarantee you'll be out of work a long time. What's more, the defeatist attitude will permeate your life. It will be your excuse for never trying anything new or taking risks. You'll be on the outside looking in because you're afraid to gamble on yourself. You'll be a lifetime complainer saying, "If you don't have someone on the inside pulling for you, you're a goner. You can't beat the system."

Make sure you're not humming the defeatist's dirge. It's crippling. Instead, start saying you'll do whatever it takes to turn in a brilliant performance. Then success is inevitably guaranteed.

Control the Interview by Learning Everything You Can

The only way to give an Academy Award–caliber performance is by trying to control the interview. There is no way to predict how things will work out, but you ought to start by going in prepared.

The first step is answering the three Ws: where, what, and who. Where is the company and what does it do are easy to answer. Who will be interviewing you is another story. Concentrate on the company by getting answers to these questions:

1. *Where is the company located and what does it do?* Twenty years ago, these were easy questions to answer. More likely than not, the office you reported to was the home office. A quick call to the personnel office, and you were showered with information. Not so today. Companies have spread out, diversified and consolidated. It's shocking how many employees have no idea who actually pays their salaries. They don't have the foggiest idea that a multibillion-dollar Hong Kong conglomerate thousands of miles away owns their company and 30 others.

Suggested sources for the where and what are:

- *Funk & Scott Index (Predicasts Inc.).* This work is a respected guide to published articles, corporate news and developments. Excellent for finding out about acquisitions and mergers, products, technology, forecasts and business analysis.
- *Standard & Poor's Register of Corporations, Directors and Educators.* This work consists of three volumes. Volume 1, *Corporations*, is an alphabetical listing of corporations, plus addresses, phone numbers, names and titles of key officers and directors, subsidiaries, number of employees and financial data. Volume 2, *Directors and Executives*, lists officers, directors, trustees and partners. It also includes some interesting executive personal statistics—date and place of birth,

colleges attended and professional affiliations. Volume 3 provides indexes.

- *Dun & Bradstreet's Million Dollar Directory.* This directory is a popular source for business and financial journalists. It consists of five volumes of information on companies with net worth in excess of $500,000. It offers an alphabetical listing of company names, subsidiaries, headquarters, phone numbers, addresses, sales, etc.
- *Thomas Register of American Manufacturers.* The three-volume set lists manufacturers' addresses, phone numbers, products, asset listings, and other information.
- *Corporate Technology Directory.* Updated yearly, the four-volume directory offers data on 35,000 U.S. high-technology companies (products, key executives, phone numbers, etc.).

With such sources, there is no excuse for not knowing a lot about the company prior to the interview. A few well-spent hours in the library ought to tell you what you need to know.

2. *Who will be interviewing you?* If you luck out, you may find out who is interviewing you. It's almost impossible to do in large companies employing dozens of human resources interviewers, but there is a chance with small- and mid-size companies, especially if they're nearby. If possible, try.

Tap your network to see what you can learn. You may luck out and find someone who interviewed with the company who, in turn, may hook you up with someone working there.

If you make the connection, you have an opportunity to get priceless inside information. What are the interviewers like? What kind of questions do they ask? Are they routine, or do they try to surprise you with curveball stumpers? In general, what kind of people do they hire, and what do they look for?

Find answers to the above questions and you have a toe in the door. Now let's rev up for the interview.

Make Your Voice Count—Watch Your Posture—Look the Part

Remember, you're not just a bunch of job skills, but a package, a multipurpose product. Every part of the product must be right—voice, posture and clothing.

First, voice. Here are six suggestions to avoid vocal mishaps:

1. *Think before speaking.* Don't blurt out the first thought that pops into your head. The interview is not a race. Think first, speak second. Formulate your answer in your head before vocalizing it. Keep your answers brief and terse. Avoid long, involved answers. Even the most complicated questions can be answered simply. If the interviewer constantly has to ask you to elaborate or simplify your answers, you're not answering directly and succinctly.

2. *Your voice must convey confidence and clarity.* Some people, especially first-time job seekers, have a bad habit of making declarative sentences sound like questions. They do it unconsciously because they're nervous and unsure of themselves. It's almost as if they fear the sound of their voice will offend the interviewer. If you do this, work at stopping it.

3. *It's normal to be nervous.* But don't let it get in your way. Nervousness often causes an adrenaline rush which makes you sound like a professional speed-talker or a 33⅓ record played on 78 rpm speed. A fast way to slow down and relax is by taking a few deep breaths.

4. *Maintain an enthusiastic tone.* Regardless of the interviewer's tone, try to be enthusiastic and energetic. The interviewer may be expressionless and his or her tone monotonal, but your voice ought to express excitement and curiosity. Remember why you are there. This is the place you want to work, and you can't wait to prove what you can do.

5. *Enunciate and don't mumble.* Most people don't realize they mumble or slur words, but it's something you must be conscious of. Unconsciously, we bridge thoughts or sentences with "Umms" and "You knows," or worse yet, "Ya knows," which is very common among New Yorkers. Rather than working compulsively to keep the conversation going, you're better off lapsing into an occasional silence rather than filling it with an awkward barrage of umms.

6. *Avoid jargon, buzzwords, slang and sloppy phrasing.* That means no computer, sports or corporate terminology. Interviewers don't appreciate it, and using this language makes you look like you don't have a mind of your own. Answer in grammatical sentences using your own words. If you enjoy working with people, whatever you do, don't say you're a "team player" or a firm believer in "self-empowered work teams." The interviewer may vomit or lunge at you with the closest sharp object. If you want to tell the interviewer you're a tireless, energetic worker, simply say so, rather than saying, "I'm the kind of person who gives 100 percent and enjoys carrying the ball all the way to

the end zone." An answer like this could give the interviewer a stroke. Then you certainly wouldn't get the job.

The following is a useful exercise for working on "voice." If you don't have a tape recorder, borrow one and have a friend conduct a mock interview so you can hear what you sound like. This is an excellent tool for whipping your voice and performance into shape. Like everyone hearing their voice for the first time, you'll be horrified. But you'll get over it. The idea is to critically listen to your voice, paying close attention to tone, pitch and enunciation. Ask yourself these questions: Is every word spoken clearly? Do I slur words? Is my voice too loud or too soft? Are questions answered with simple, yet precise sentences? Do I lapse into a regional dialect when I get nervous?

As for posture, whether you're standing or sitting, keep your back and spine straight. Most people have bad posture. Unconsciously we let ourselves sag, droop and list to one side like sinking ships. But once you are conscious of posture problems, they are easily correctable. You certainly don't need an image consultant to teach you how to sit in a chair properly. Remember not to slump over or slide into the chair. Not only will you look horrendous; slouching makes your voice sound breathy and weak.

Look the part. I'm not going to make a big deal about dress, because it doesn't warrant it. Nevertheless, it's critical to look great. You don't have to go out and buy *Dress for Success* to learn how to put together a presentable outfit. It's common sense.

The guiding word in dress is "conservative." That means tasteful and simple. It doesn't mean buying a $1,000 business suit, $300 pair of shoes and custom-made shirts, blouses or ties. Don't try and knock out interviewers with your Sunday finest. They won't be impressed. In fact, you might even draw negative attention to yourself. "Who does this guy (or woman) think he (or she) is?" You're not going to a wedding, so don't try to look like you stepped out of the pages of *Cosmopolitan* or *Gentlemen's Quarterly*.

The key to looking good is avoiding extremes. Stay away from bright or clashing colors or inappropriate outfits. Men and women should wear business suits, preferably in dark, tan or muted colors. Ties ought to be stylish and appropriately trendy. Avoid outrageous colors. Men should stick to single-color shirts, preferably white or blue, rather than striped or patterned.

Once you are hired, you can come to work in pants and jackets or maybe anything that suits you. Many companies, especially those in the computer, fashion or communications industries have loose or no dress codes. Silicon Valley's high-tech companies, for instance, are legendary for not caring what employees wear to work. It doesn't matter whether they wear shorts and tee shirts or three-piece business suits, as long as they get their work done. It's a refreshing far cry from the constipated dark suits, starched white shirts and spit-polished shoes IBMers were traditionally required to wear.

Whatever the dress code, look neat, clean and presentable. Wear conservative business shoes. No sneakers, sandals or spike heels. And make sure your shoes are polished. Don't underestimate interviewers: They notice everything, even minute details like whether your nails are cut and groomed.

Dissecting the Interview—The Human Factor

You've done your homework by boning up on the company. The next step is dissecting the interview to find out how it works. Once you see it's a fairly logical process, you won't be terrified. You'll have a good idea what to expect. Twenty-five percent of the mystery has been solved.

Unless you have inside information about your interviewer, the rest is up to you. Let's call that vast gray area the human factor.

Human interaction is complex. Put two or more people in one room, and anything can happen. There could be a magical harmony, a mystical meeting of minds, or it could be likened to musical cacophony or running your fingernails down a chalkboard. In short, a disastrous meeting of people planets apart. They speak the same language, yet not even an axe could penetrate the tension.

As we said above, interviewing for a job is like auditioning for a part. The interviewer is your audience. This is the person you must play to and impress. Once again, even though interviewers are in charge, *they are not gunning for you.* Turn in a winning performance, and you've made their jobs easier. They can drop the curtain on the interview process, send the rest of the applicants home and get on to other business. Interviewers don't have an easy job. Screening applicants all day is exhausting work. With an enormous applicant pool compounded by competitive job standards, interviewers have the tedious job of interviewing dozens, sometimes hundreds, of applicants to find one that is right. The challenge you face is meeting those criteria.

Let's carve the interview into its component parts.

A Three-Part Play

Surprisingly, an interview is a logical progression of events. Think of it as a three-act play. Each act calls for a deft performance. The goal is to capture the role and give the interviewer exactly what he or she wants. Don't worry about fancy footwork; just convince the interviewer you're the person needed. It's that simple.

Let's look at each act closely.

Act One—Small Talk

This section takes 5 to 15 minutes and is an introduction of characters. This is the get-to-know-you stage when the tone, mood and pacing of the interview is set. Veteran interviewers say these early moments are accurate predictors of things to come. When you are battle-worn with a couple of dozen interviews under your belt, this stage will give you an indication of what's ahead.

Typically, considerate, easygoing interviewers will welcome you warmly as soon as you walk through the door. They'll get up to greet you, shake your hand firmly, seat you and ask if you'd like coffee or a cold drink before beginning.

A more rigid interviewer presents a colder reception. She or he will offer a limp, half-hearted handshake and bypass comforting amenities to get to the business at hand. Don't jump to conclusions. Just because the interviewer is not the warmest or most gracious person you ever met doesn't mean he or she is going to chop you into little pieces with mind-bending questions. Like yourself, he could be nervous or uncomfortable. Or maybe he has 15 more applicants to interview and wants to get you out of the way. Either way, take it in stride, and *don't take anything the interviewer does or says personally.*

Whatever the greeting, expect a light, chatty exchange before the interview gets seriously underway. But don't think these introductory moments are not important. They are as important as the guts of the interview. *The interview begins as soon as you walk through the door.*

Are you relaxed and comfortable and are introductions easy for you? How quickly do you adjust to new situations? These are just a couple of the traits indicating whether you're right for the job.

Expect small talk as an icebreaker. The interviewer may start off with some observations about the weather, ball scores, politics or traffic. Go with it and get involved with the conversations. Interviewers set the pace. They're orchestrating the show and will let you know when they're ready to change the subject.

Just as interviewers size you up in these early moments, it's an opportunity to get a reading on them as well. Adjust your rhythm to theirs. If they move at a leisurely pace or suddenly quicken the tempo, do the same. Whatever the conversational rhythm, keep your answers brief and tight.

Act Two—The Interrogation

This part of the interview lasts 40 minutes to one hour. Accounting for the bulk of the interview, this is where the interviewer gathers most of the information. If the introductory act went well, the interviewer will agilely downshift you into Act Two without your realizing it. Sit back and just answer the questions. Don't try to second-guess interviewers. They have an agenda, a battery of questions and issues they plan to cover.

Interviewers have their own styles. Some have a laundry list of questions in front of them. Others ad-lib. Some take notes during an interview, others don't. Whatever their technique, as soon you exit, a crisp summation of your performance will be put on paper or filed in a computer. If the summation is favorable, you'll be called back within a week. If you flunked, you'll get a form rejection letter two to three weeks later.

Here are some classic tough questions that will help you bone up for your next interview.

"Tell Me about Yourself" and 16 Other Killer Questions

What kind of questions will interviewers ask? Absolutely anything they want from the pertinent to the ridiculous. They're asking the questions; your job is to fire answers back. Here are some killer questions plus tips for answering them correctly.

1. *Tell me about yourself.* This is the crown prince of tough questions. I rank it as the popular favorite because it's usually the first question, setting the tone for the rest of the interview. Answer this one brilliantly, and you're off to a great start.

One career counselor compared this question to an attorney's opening statement because it permits you to set the stage by saying anything you want. Yet that leverage can also make or break you. The interviewer is not looking for a five-minute biography, complete with childhood stories or information about your spouse or siblings. Your response should focus on job-related strengths. The interviewer is testing you to see how well you communicate—how fast you think on your feet.

Since you can count on being asked this or a similar question, prepare for it beforehand. Your answer should run between four and five minutes and should include a brief description of your career, professional and personal skills, goals and something innocuously personal. I call it a "full-circle" answer. Start with a childhood experience, if career related, or possibly your degree and summer work experience if you're a recent college grad, and work toward the future. Here are some highlights of a good answer:

> Ever since I was a teenager, I tinkered with computers. It was my hobby, my passion. Like most kids I enjoyed computer games. When my folks gave me a computer as a gift, I mastered it within six months and went on to teach myself programming basics. By the time I graduated from high school, I knew I wanted to study programming. From that point on, everything fell into place. My life has revolved around computing. By my sophomore year, I decided I wanted to work for a major software manufacturer. That's why I applied for a job at Skoobedoo Software. I wanted to work for a major player so I could be at the forefront of breaking trends and new technology.

A great answer doesn't wander. "Tell me about yourself" means "Tell me how motivated, skilled and special you are and why we should hire you." It doesn't mean going off on tangents and spilling personal facts unrelated to the job you're applying for. Personal insights are fine—as long as they're job-related.

2. *What are your weaknesses?* Say you have none and you'll lose points for being inhuman or dishonest. The real meaning of the question is: "Tell me about weaknesses that are actually positives within the work setting." For example, "Once I'm involved in a project, I find it hard to stop before it is satisfactorily completed." You're telling an interviewer that you enjoy getting things done and take pride in your job.

3. *What are your strengths?* The flip side to the previous question, this one doesn't mean you should spell out all your assets. Employers are interested in those assets that demonstrate your ability to do your job well. A possible answer: "I'm fast and accurate and I pride myself on enlisting the cooperation of people around me."

4. *Why do you think you fit the job?* The trick to answering this off-putting question is combining your strengths with an understanding

of the company or industry. Let's say you're applying for a job as a researcher or administrative assistant in a criminal law firm. A smart answer would be: "I'm confident I can do the job because I have the word processing and stenographic skills you are looking for."

5. *Where do you see yourself in five years?* Don't say "as a manager of a department" or "in a supervisory position." Your interviewer may be the person you will be reporting to and could be threatened by your answer. Don't assume that his or her job is secure either. The interviewer wants to know you have a realistic career plan. You can say you want to master your job, refine your skills (learn new word processing or desktop publishing programs, for instance) and find out how other divisions work. In other words, you're saying you're open-minded and want to learn as much as you can.

6. *Why did you decide to leave your last job?* Nothing negative, please! Don't say you left your last job because your ex-boss was a creep and a low-life who turned the entire department against you because you wouldn't support him. Or that he was a letch and couldn't keep his hands off you. Even if you worked for a tyrannical megalomaniac, present a neutral answer that doesn't paint you as someone who might have problems getting on with management or coworkers. Stress the positive and discuss limitations in objective terms. For example: "I learned a great deal about the widget industry but because it was such a small firm, I could only go so far. I want to learn more so I can undertake bigger projects."

7. *How long have you been looking for a job?* This is only tough if you make it so. Ten years ago, being out of work six months meant there was something wrong with you. Maybe you were chronically unemployable, an interview screw-up or just plain unstable. Today, you've got the economy and a tough job market on your side. A direct honest answer should do it: "I've been looking for a job for almost six months. As you know, because of all the layoffs and consolidations, it takes a while to find openings in this field." The interviewer will nod in agreement and move on to the next question.

8. *You've had five jobs in the last 10 years? Can you explain why?* Like the previous question, this one also destroyed applicants in the past. Job-hoppers were one step away from lepers. No loyalty, team spirit, direction, goals and all that stuff. Today, job-hopping is a survival tactic, and employers know it. Don't be ashamed of it. But watch your answer and avoid political traps. Like the answer to number 6, don't get into personalities or corporate politics. If you left a job because of a tyrannical boss who ran your department like a military

battalion, alter the facts and say you had gone about as far as you could in the job and were ready to move to better things. Or if it was a consolidation, bankruptcy, leveraged buyout or reorganization, just outline the facts.

9. *Would you call yourself a risk taker?* This is a sneaky one. The obvious answer implies an unequivocal yes, complete with flag waving, drumrolls and fife and drum accompaniments. What kind of a stupid question is that? Haven't all the movers and shakers in this great land of ours been risk takers? Absolutely! But watch how you answer this one. Employers don't always want far-out, headstrong risk takers who can't follow rules. Instead, they want controlled, moderate risk takers who respect the system—team-playing risk takers, if you will. In research companies, for example, uncontrolled risk takers have been known to go way over budget, adding months, even years, to projects. You ought to say you are challenged and motivated by risk but are also sensitive to the fact that risk has to be tempered to strict budgets and organization rules.

10. *What would you consider an ideal job?* Another beauty. Most applicants go off on tangents saying the ideal job is one that challenges, motivates and has enormous potential for reaching their career goals. Their answers are chock full of $50 buzzwords. I don't recommend that tack. Surprise the interviewer by saying you don't think there is such a thing as an ideal job. And that it's up to the applicant to make something meaningful of the job. You might even say high-visibility, glamor jobs have a downside. The interviewer will think, "Wow, this person has a mind. The first original thinker this month. He (or she) is not trying to feed me factory pap memorized from some awful career book."

It's not always easy being original, but when you see an opening, bolt for it. It could be an important victory.

11. *What does success mean to you?* Be careful, this one could be a veritable elephant trap if you're not careful. Don't lead off with anything that sounds remotely like you want to make a lot of money: "My goal is to be a millionaire before I'm 35 so I can collect Corvettes, have a modest house in Malibu, surf at least two hours every day and enjoy three superdry martinis by my pool before dinner every evening."

An interviewer would not deem this an appropriate answer. The canned correct answer combines professional and personal goals. Interviewers want to hear that your personal life is an extension of your professional one. In other words, you are doing something intellectually rewarding that also gives you the financial latitude to pursue a compatible lifestyle. That's a subtle way of saying you want a job that pays you enough to live decently without having to squirrel away money in a cookie jar to pay the weekly laundry bill. In other words, you can mention money, just don't make a big deal of it.

12. *What aspect of the work do you think you'll enjoy most?* Be careful. This can be treacherous too. It could be an explosive booby trap if you're not prepared. Make sure you know enough about the job so you can describe its important parts intelligently. The interviewer wants to know you will be motivated and stimulated by your job. Discuss the crucial meat-and-potatoes elements of the position. If it's a research job, for example, you might say:

> I will enjoy the problem-solving parts of the job. I'm the type of person who needs to be challenged. That's why I enjoy immersing myself in research projects. I can work by myself, unsupervised, from morning till night. It's very exciting starting with nothing and finding answers to difficult questions.

Whatever job you apply for, be specific about what you think you'll enjoy most. If you're a chemical engineer applying for a job with a pollution control company, for example, highlight only essential job functions, such as field or lab work, or research and development, etc. You'll come across as a well-informed engineer who knows exactly what you want.

13. *What aspect of the work do you think you will enjoy least?* Flip side of the previous question. Watch out for this one too. Honesty is fine to a point, but whatever you do, don't tell an interviewer you expect to enjoy 100 percent of the job. No one likes every part of her or his job. So don't make yourself look like a fool by saying so. However, making too much of a job's deficits could toss you out of the race.

The key to answering the question correctly is to cite an insignificant aspect of the job you think you won't enjoy. Even though you're introducing a negative thought, stick to the positive parts of the job. For example:

> I find that once I become involved in a project, I have little patience with small details, such as filling out forms and similar paperwork. I realize it has to be done, but I can't wait to get it over with so I can get back to the most important aspects of the job.

The above answer turns a deficit into an asset. It demonstrates you'll do the boring, tedious parts of the job, yet you're most concerned with concentrating on the crucial, productive/creative parts of the job.

14. *Where do you see yourself 10 years from now?* An answer that immediately pops into your head might sound something like: "Judging by this rotten job market, just holding down a job will be a major accomplishment." It's an honest, heartfelt answer, but I guarantee it will draw bad reviews.

Obviously, you don't know where you're going to be 10 years from now. But if you want to be considered for the job, you ought to have a tight answer worked out beforehand. By now you know what companies want. Ideally, they'd like slaves who'd work for nothing. They don't want job holders, but career builders. Craft an answer that says in a decade or so you hope to be well on your way, in terms of mastering skills and moving up several notches, on the career ladder. Junior copywriters ought to be senior copywriters. Fledgling assistant sales representatives ought to be sales managers or coordinators.

15. *How would you describe yourself?* "I'm just a little under 6'1", I'm built like Sylvester Stallone, women can't keep their hands off me but I also happen to be a nice guy." Maybe you'd make a fine movie extra but corporate America isn't ready for you.

Interviewers don't want to hear about your physical characteristics, they want to know about personality characteristics making you right for the job. Don't overload the interviewer with too many flattering, overzealous adjectives. That's overkill. You may be deemed too good to be real. You might say, "I consider myself a curious, hard-working person who loves what she does and wants the opportunity to learn more." Or, "I enjoy searching and finding solutions to problems. I see myself as a careful person who doesn't give up on a problem until answers are found. That's why I enjoy analyzing statistical data."

16. *What are some memorable college experiences?* Occasionally, they'll toss this one in somewhere near the end. Don't talk about the time you stayed up for 48 straight hours, drank a case of beer by yourself or biked from Buffalo to Manhattan on a dare. The nut to this one is relaying an experience or insight that is job-related. For example, you had a telling insight, i.e., the thrill of problem solving, or had a job experience that put you on the right career path. Often, college students stumble on careers by taking internships or cooperative work/study programs. This is the kind of stuff interviewers want to hear about. For example, a project engineer employed by an international food company discovered he wanted a career in the food industry after he did an internship at a food company during his junior

year. Until then, he thought he wanted to work for a large defense company. The experience proved to be a career lesson, driving home the importance of having an open mind, being flexible and jumping on an opportunity when it occurs.

17. *Why should we hire you?* This question, often saved for last, is your chance to pull everything together. It's a variation on many of the above. The idea is to toot your horn so you sound not like a braggart but like someone who will be valuable to the organization. If you consider your two prior jobs excellent preparation for the job you're applying for, for example, talk about what you learned and what it will mean to this employer.

If this is your first job out of college, you might talk about how the courses you took helped make you an excellent candidate. This is an excellent tack if you graduated with impressive grades. "I worked very hard to graduate with a B average. I learned a lot about my field, and now I want to apply it." As we said earlier, companies want contributors, not paycheck collectors.

If you're passionate about your field and have been following it closely for many years, let your interviewer know it. Or if you had to work your way through school by holding down two part-time jobs, spare none of the details. Interviewers won't know how dedicated and committed you are unless you tell them.

Score high on these questions and you'll be well on your way.

But, no matter how well an interview is going, be prepared for some inappropriate—and illegal—questions as well.

Illegal Questions

You don't have to be a labor attorney to know when a question is inappropriate. It's simple: If the question has no bearing on work performance, the interviewer is out of line and breaking the law.

Employers cannot ask you about the following:

1. *Creed, Religion or Race.* Employers are not permitted to ask about your religious affiliation or the holidays you observe. You can worship pagan idols or the devil, it's your right. You also can't be asked questions about your lineage, ancestry or nationality. A question like, "Dostoyevski, why that's a Russian name isn't it?" is absolutely forbidden. The same goes for race, "So you're a full-blooded Apache, are you? You look like everyone else."

2. *Age.* If you're 85 and fit to hold a job, you're entitled to the same

consideration a 25-year-old gets. "You look about 35, am I right?" may be a sneaky way to get you to reveal your age. It all falls under the heading of age discrimination.

3. *Sex or Marital Status.* "Are you married?" "What does your husband do?" "Do you have kids?" More no-nos.

4. *Military Service.* Employers can ask you what branch of the service you were in, but they can't ask what kind of discharge you received.

Think Twice about Filing Charges

What do you do when an employer asks an illegal question? Unfortunately, there is no pat answer. More often than not, employers don't realize they are asking questions forbidden by the Equal Employment Opportunity Commission (EEOC) laws. This is particularly true of small companies where either owners or their managers are doing the interviewing. Large companies using professional human resource professionals, however, are well-versed in EEOC regulations.

Don't be too quick to threaten employers with a lawsuit for asking illegal questions, advises Ilene Lainer, a well-known New Jersey labor and employment attorney. More likely than not, they have no ulterior motive; they're asking the questions simply because they're curious. You must decide that by the way questions are asked. If it's a random question, don't give it a second thought. You could do more harm than good by trying to straighten them out. But if you find yourself confronted with a barrage of inappropriate questions, you could diplomatically say, "I don't understand why you are asking these questions, Mr. Birch. They have nothing to do with the job I'm applying for." Resort to this tactic as an avenue of last resort.

Attorney Lainer waves a cautionary red flag about filing charges. If you are in a close, competitive field like advertising or public relations, for example, word could get out you're a troublemaker. If that happens, you could be blackballed and no firm within 100 miles will consider you. Also, consider the fact that proceeding with legal action is a lengthy process taking several months, even years, before resolution. Unless you've got a trust fund to support you while you're building your case, you'll go right on pounding the pavement searching for a job.

But if you're convinced that you are a victim of blatant discrimination, don't hesitate to exercise your rights and simultaneously file complaints with the federal government's EEOC and your state's

Department of Human Rights or Fair Employment Practice
Commission. These agencies go under different names, so check your
telephone book.

Now let's wind down and move on to the final curtain.

Act Three—Your Turn

Your chance to ask intelligent questions and read between the lines
will last 15 to 30 minutes. Just as introductory small talk was important, the final moments of the interview are equally important. The
interviewer controls acts one and two, but it's up to you to direct the
final act by asking intelligent questions. Score impressively here and
you'll be called back for an encore—another interview or possibly a
job offer.

Interviewers expect applicants to ask questions. It's unwritten interview protocol. If you don't ask questions, it indicates no interest or
that you'll take any job offered. Equally important, it gives you a
chance to read between the lines and find out what the job and company is really like.

Below are some suggested questions interviewers like to hear:

1. *Will you describe a typical day?* This is one of the most important
questions you can ask. After you hear what a typical day is like, you
may not want to work there. If you didn't ask the question, you'd
never know you are required to start at 8 a.m. and work to 6:30 p.m.
That's not to mention an occasional Saturday here and there. When
you hear phrases like "We put our company first, Mr. Lazybones,"
you might think twice about working there. Or you may consider taking it if you're desperate with nothing else in the offing.

2. *Whom will I be reporting to?* It's nice to know what the power
structure is like. If your boss is way down in the corporate hierarchy,
your promotional opportunities may be limited.

3. *Could you describe my responsibilities?* Often interviewers briefly
cover this, but if your job isn't clearly laid out, this is the time to find
out exactly what you're going to be doing eight or more hours a day.

4. *What happened to my predecessor?* This could be an eye-opener.
Maybe your predecessor was axed or left on his own accord because
the job is a revolving door. Or maybe she had a nervous breakdown
because the on-the-job pressures were insufferable. If five people held
the job over the past six years, it doesn't take Perry Mason to know
something is wrong. The job may be stressful, unpleasant or just

impossible. Or if your predecessor held the job for 15 years, it's clearly no fast-track opportunity.

5. *Are there performance reviews?* This tells you what your chances of advancement are like. A policy of regular performance reviews, every six months or yearly, demonstrates the company intends to reward exceptional performers.

6. *What are the possibilities for advancement?* An extension of the prior question, but no less important. You want to know if your good work will be rewarded.

7. *Can you tell me a little about the people I will be working with?* Try to find out about their backgrounds, jobs and how long they've been with the company. This will give you a valuable, capsulized picture of your work environment. It's safe to conclude that if your coworkers are bright and motivated, it's a high-energy, stimulating environment in which you stand to learn a lot.

8. *Can you tell me about profit sharing, health insurance, vacations and bonuses?* Don't assume the company will provide you with an excellent benefits package. Get specifics.

9. *What learning opportunities are available?* Training possibilities make a job offer all the more attractive because it makes you more valuable not only to your present employer but to others if you leave.

Don't Blow It! Ten Sure Ways to Turn Off an Interviewer

Books have been written about how to score high points on job interviews. But little has been said about screwing up—committing the dirty negatives that can eliminate you from the race faster than a missile in take-off.

It's easier to fail an interview than it is to pass one. You'd be surprised how effortless it is to make an interviewer loathe you. Following are eight faux pas that can hurl you to the sideline.

1. *Knowing Little (or Nothing) about the Company.* This is the number-one eliminator. This was mentioned above when we discussed poor attitude and the importance of "controlling the interview by learning everything you can." Yet it's amazing to think applicants still have the chutzpah to walk into a job interview knowing practically nothing about the company they'd like to work for.

Face it, if you owned a company, would you hire someone who knows nothing about your company or industry? Wouldn't you interpret it as disinterest, apathy or just sheer stupidity and assume that the only thing this person wants is a steady paycheck and a place to hang out for the next couple of years?

2. *Negative Attitude.* A negative attitude is like a pall hanging over an interview. Interviewers pick it up immediately. Companies don't want downers, whiners, chronic complainers, career victims or end-of-the-worlders convinced Armageddon lies ahead. If you're a chronic pessimist, your chances of getting the job or being called back for a second interview are scant. Don't gripe about crowded trains or airports, the high cost of living, a prior boss or how you can't beat the system and get ahead. If you're miserable or angry about something, a job interview is not the place to vent. That's what spouses, lovers and shrinks are for. The guiding tenet is if you don't have anything good to say, shut up.

Companies want upbeat, positive souls who, like Dr. Pangloss in Voltaire's classic *Candide,* think anything is possible "in this best of all possible worlds." They want team players, outgoing extroverts ready to work around the clock and go without meals to get the job done. Incredible as it seems, many brainwashed corporate types actually believe all this.

3. *Poor Communication Skills.* If you can't communicate, stay home, find a patron or join a networking group. Better yet, ask a rich relative to support you until you master the fine art of mixing chitchat with intelligent conversation. Companies want talkers and mixers, not loners or misanthropes. Even engineers, scientists and computer programmers have to get their points across and express themselves. Employers want people who can sell their product or service. Look at the careers of dozens of top CEOs and you'll find that most came up based on sales skills. Maybe they were brilliant strategists or financial wizards, but they were also gifted schmoozers who could sell ice in the Antarctic if necessary.

Company recruiters commonly complain about applicants who can't form a simple declarative sentence without relying on buzzwords, clichés and jargon. Example: "How would you describe the ideal job, Ms. Marpel?" Answer: "The ideal job gives me the opportunity to work to maximum capacity while plugged into cutting-edge technology in order to find effective solutions to challenging problems." It's scary, but actual applicants are vomiting gobbledygook like this. Avoid tired jargon like "plugged-in," "cutting edge," "input" and "effective." Find your own words so you sound original. Don't sound like you memorized canned answers from a how-to-get-a-job book.

4. *Rambling, Disconnected Answers.* Job applicants readily blurt out answers without thinking. The result is confused, wordy, discombobulated answers. Recruiters shouldn't have to decipher answers. Don't try and impress interviewers with "power" words and expansive answers. Shoot for succinct, simple answers. No one cares that you got a near perfect English score on the SAT (Scholastic Aptitude Test).

5. *Inappropriate Behavior.* An interview is not the place to chew, smoke, fidget or fumble. While it's polite for interviewers to ask if you want to smoke, you're better off restraining yourself until the interview is over. Keep your vices in check until you're hired. Avoid cutesy behavior; overfamiliarity with your interviewer will kill your chances immediately. Arrogance, cockiness and egotism aren't appreciated either.

6. *Failure to Make Eye Contact.* Although much has been made of the importance of body language (holding head and shoulders a certain way, arching back menacingly or slumping in a chair), most of the published stuff on the subject has been debunked. Let's give credit where credit is due: Job recruiters are not Freudian scholars. Obviously, staring angrily at your interviewer for 60 minutes straight is not a good idea. However, making eye contact most of the time, especially when speaking, is recommended.

7. *No Career Direction / Not Knowing Self / Unassertive or Passive.* Most entry-level job seekers don't have the foggiest idea where they want to be in 10 years, and many seasoned workers are still trying to "find themselves." Nevertheless, when you're in the hot seat, you must come across as a walking amalgam of perfect traits, sharing attributes of both Clark Kent and Mother Teresa. Be assertive and tactfully aggressive.

8. *Canceling or Showing Up Late.* Unless you're seriously ill—like on death's door—or in the midst of a real catastrophe, don't cancel an interview. Even if it's for legitimate reasons, it's a strike against you. If you must do so, try to give the recruiter enough warning to slot someone else in and reschedule your appointment. Another no-no is showing up late or even seconds before the interview. The interviewer may brand you as a person who is chronically late. If the job in question entails countless meetings or the wining and dining of clients, lateness is a most undesirable trait. Play it safe and get to interviews at least 15 minutes early.

Evaluating Your Performance

Wouldn't it be incredible if you could peruse the interviewer's notes evaluating your performance? That priceless information could save you time and grief. In minutes, you'd find out where you excelled and screwed up. Forget it; you'll never see it. The next best thing is devoting 15 to 20 minutes to evaluating your performance. Ideally, you ought to do it immediately after the interview or while the experience is still fresh.

An easy way to do it is to create a checklist of questions. For example:

1. How did the interviewer react to me?
2. Were there any awkward moments?
3. Were answers tight and to the point?
4. Did I give any weak answers?
5. Were there any surprise questions?
6. How did I speak?
7. What was the rapport like?
8. How was I dressed?

It may be too late to do anything about the interview you're evaluating, but the process can serve you well on subsequent ones.

The Coda Sales Pitch

One last chore before you start biting your nails waiting for the company to contact you. Dash off a fast thank-you note to your interviewer. Of course you don't want to. Who does? Even though you deem it a waste of time, do it anyway.

The reason for writing the thank-you note is that many interviewers expect it. If you don't perform this last annoying chore, you risk being branded lazy or rude. "I liked Mr. Ripper a lot, but I'm disappointed he didn't have the courtesy to follow up with a thank-you note." Chalk it all up to postinterview protocol. If a dumb note is the icing on the cake deciding whether you get the job, do you want to sabotage your hard work by not doing it?

Here's how to construct it: Three brief paragraphs will do. The first ought to thank the interviewer for seeing you. The second quickly summarizes your background, driving home your qualifications. And the third tells the interviewer you will be following up and look forward to hearing from her or him.

Consider this sample letter:

> Dear Ms. Dillinger:
>
> I appreciate your taking the time to see me on Friday, August 18. I enjoyed learning about Mercenaries Anonymous and once again would like to express my enthusiasm about working for the company.
>
> I'd like to emphasize that my five years' experience as a terrorist in Latin America and a smuggler of light arms makes me an ideal candidate for coordinating covert arms operations in Venezuela. I fully support the company's mission and am prepared to devote myself to its pursuit.
>
> I will call you on August 29 to see how the search is going. I look forward to speaking with you again.
>
> Sincerely,
>
> Candy Zoomboolakas

Don't overdue it. Like the résumé replacement letter, keep it tight, brief and to the point. The reader should be able to digest its contents in 30 seconds or less.

The letter's goal is to tactfully explain why you're qualified for the job and to drive home the fact that you're very interested. Nothing more. No hard sell.

Finally, like your initial selling letter, tell the interviewer you'll be calling on a specific date. Never say you're awaiting their call. Be gently, but appropriately, aggressive.

That's it. You ought to feel good knowing you did everything you can.

Interview Dos and Don'ts

To summarize, here are some fast interview tips to remember.

Do:

1. Learn everything you can about the company.
2. Keep answers tight, brief and direct.
3. Maintain eye contact.
4. Be optimistic and confident.

Don't:

1. Interrupt the interviewer.
2. Dominate the interview.
3. Be late.
4. Introduce negative ideas or thoughts.
5. Chew gum or smoke.
6. Bad-mouth past employers or supervisors.
7. Use nauseating buzzwords or phrases like "I'm a team player" or "results" or "action-oriented." (Do find your own words.)
8. Fidget, play with your hands or move around in your seat.

Myth 10: *Employers Are Autocratic Powerlords Who Know Exactly What They're Looking For: Ergo, They Hold All the Negotiating Cards.*

Reality: *Don't give employers that much credit. They're just people like you and me. More often than they'd like to admit, they don't know what they want, and many make poor hiring decisions. Welcome to Oz.*

Chapter Snapshot

- ☐ You're Expendable
- ☐ Watch Out or I'll Sue You!
- ☐ We Won't Take It Any More
- ☐ The Emancipation of the U.S. Worker
- ☐ Followers Are More Important Than Leaders
- ☐ I Can't Believe My Boss Is So Young
- ☐ Smart Employers Question Conventional Thinking
- ☐ Employers Want Human Machines
- ☐ Employers Only Think They Know What They Want
- ☐ Talking Your Way into a Job
- ☐ Sell Value

✳ ✳ ✳ ✳ ✳ ✳ ✳ ✳

We've all been brought up to think all employers are smart and powerful. Our parents told us that, just as it had been drummed into them by their parents. It's easy to understand, especially if you came from an immigrant background in which a job meant survival. What could be more basic?

Your survival rested in the hands of those who paid your salary and thereby fed, clothed and protected your family. If they liked and treated you well, you were on easy street. It paid to work hard and get in their good graces. Their power was all the more impressive when jobs were hard to come by. When the boss spoke, you listened. And when the boss said something with certainty, you took it as gospel. After all, she or he was the *boss,* the person who paid your salary and, therefore, smarter than you.

The image of the omniscient boss still exists, yet it's rapidly fading in the shadow of an economy dominated by giant conglomerates with tentacles extending around the globe. When you work for a sprawling corporation, you're not working for one person, but an amorphous legal entity. It has no face, no soul; decisions are not made by one person but by pockets of authority. You report to one person, yet he or she is one of thousands of soldiers. Your check is generated in another part of the country by payroll department workers who don't have the slightest idea who you are or what you look like. Nor do they care. You're a file number, a mathematical formula that's entitled to a certain amount of money minus deductions every week. You are a computer entry, a tiny, insignificant speck of information in an enormous database. As long as you work for the company, you are part of the system. The day you're terminated, your records are stored in an inactive file with thousands of others rendered redundant. Think of it as the company graveyard visited only when old records have to be retrieved for references or legal purposes.

You're Expendable

Everything and everyone is expendable in our throwaway society. Corporate bookkeepers and number crunchers don't think about people; they think data, random access memory, bytes, kilobytes and networks. You could be a cyborg or a two-headed, five-armed alien from another planet and the folks who guard the databases wouldn't care less. If you have an employee identification number, you'll be paid.

Watch Out or I'll Sue You!

The more layers a company has, the more removed you are from the people making decisions. Hence, the more desensitized you become. When there are problems or frustrations, it's often hard to figure out the culprit. If you don't know who to blame, there is no one to confront. If it's a big issue that affects the entire company, you blame the system for being too big and out of control. If the problem is more immediate and affects your daily work routines, you blame your boss for being an insensitive cog in an inefficient machine.

One thing is certain, whoever is to blame for problems, workers are fast realizing they don't have to take it. They can open their mouths and complain. Even though it's a tough job market, there are other jobs out there.

If your immediate supervisor gives you grief, you can protest, argue and make his or her life miserable. You may not keep your job, but at least you'll feel good knowing you are fighting back. You can start by going above your supervisor's head and complaining to her or his boss. If you've got the nerve, you can go all the way to the big person at the helm and cry your eyes out.

If none of the above works, there are plenty of options. You can sue your employer if you have what the legal beavers call "protective status." This means you're a minority, a female or over 40 and can prove your civil rights were violated, or you're a majority worker who was mistreated or wrongfully terminated. Suing doesn't cost a farthing and it's surprisingly easy to do. You can start with the Equal Employment Opportunity Commission (EEOC), a federal agency, or you can file charges with your state's civil or human rights department. Every state has one in major cities. They'll take your case with excellent odds in favor of an out-of-court settlement.

Or you can contact your local affiliate of the American Civil Liberties Union (ACLU). If your civil rights are violated, they'll review the facts and possibly take your case at no charge. According to an ACLU spokesperson, there has been a marked increase in cases involving telephone, video and computer monitoring, lifestyle discrimination and especially, wrongful termination.

Whatever legal avenue you take, few employers can afford the time or the expense of a messy court battle. The fastest and cheapest way to handle the situation is by finding a middle ground, an amount of money that will quietly send the complainant away for good.

A labor attorney employed by a prestigious New York law firm told me the average amount of money won in a wrongful termination case is about $732,000. In some cases, angry employees walked away millionaires. Since the mid-1980s, there has been a raft of new laws to protect workers' rights.

I'm not suggesting you threaten to sue your employer every time you have a disagreement. That tactic is bound to backfire. Like the boy who cried wolf, sooner or later people will be on to you.

We Won't Take It Any More

It's reassuring to know there is machinery that can protect you. If you have a good case, that is, solid evidence your boss mistreated you or violated your rights, you stand an excellent chance of coming out ahead.

Just as in the Oscar-winning film *Network*, when the late Peter Finch screamed from an open window, "We won't take it any more!", workers have more control over their destiny than they realize.

Even if the employer is right, crafty employees know full well the system can be manipulated in their favor. The laws were made to protect the worker, not the employer.

Fifty years ago, none of these options existed. Employers were part of the power elite. If you belonged to a strong blue-collar union, you stood a chance. Even then, if management stuck to its guns, you could have a long expensive battle. For everyone else, workplace injustice meant either swallowing your pride and sticking it out or quitting to find another job. If you tried to sue, you were stamped a prime candidate for the funny farm.

The Emancipation of the U.S. Worker

Time changes, heals and improves. It took a century of wars, financial upheaval and major global developments to change the way we work and think.

Despite a tough job market, you have options and leverage our ancestors didn't have. If wronged, you can cry injustice and build a case for yourself. You have the power to improve your lot.

The U.S. worker has never enjoyed more freedom. Just as working conditions have changed, so have employers' attitudes.

Humanistic Companies and Enlightened Management—"My Boss Actually Listens to Me!"

The corporate shakeups of the '80s, accompanied by a raft of management theories and books screaming for change, helped dispel the archetypal vision of the boss as demon. As corporate America changed, so did management styles and the way work is performed.

We were in trouble, and change was the only remedy. The United States was no longer the towering industrial giant of the past. We were losing our grip. Japan was overtaking us, and we had to act quickly. Stripping organizations of deadweight was only part of the solution. The other part was figuring out how to better manage the survivors. A tall order for sure.

The mid-1980s was the era of the management consultant. Every business school of any notoriety had a few management experts pulling down hefty consulting fees far surpassing their salaries. When they weren't teaching and consulting, they were writing books telling companies how to revamp their organizations.

Publishing houses couldn't crank out management books fast enough. Meanwhile, superstar management consultants—such as Tom Peters (author of *In Search of Excellence* and *Thriving on Chaos*), who has the charismatic charm of a television evangelist—were getting rich traveling the country motivating managers and workers. In the mid-1980s, Peters was to the management community what hard rockers were to pubescent fans. When *In Search of Excellence* was the hot new management anthem, Peters was giving close to 200 speeches a year at $25,000 a pop.

Peters is not capturing headlines the way he used to, but he's still at it—as determined as ever to drive his message home. He's not making as many public appearances, but his fees on the lecture circuit have jumped to about $60,000 a performance. And he's got a new book for the '90s, *Liberation Management: Necessary Disorganization for the Nanosecond Nineties.*

Although many of the management experts of the '80s have turned to teaching, their cumulative message did not fall on deaf ears. When you boil down the jargon and the buzzwords and the call for self-directed or self-empowered work teams, you have progress: better management, happier workers, improved products and higher profit margins. Management is more willing to listen, bend the rules, even create new systems.

If employers merely digested by osmosis bits and pieces from the truckloads of management theories, they'd conclude they're fallible and, like the people they hire, have a lot to learn. You and I can teach them a thing or two. Given half a chance, we can do far more than we were hired to do.

Question the hard-working drones on the lobster shift, and they'll tell you a thing or two. Rather than bristling, thinking their authority has been questioned, smart employers are listening.

Thank You, Boss, for Empowering Me

Employers are giving more than lip service to change. Many actually care about their workers—or at least pretend to. They're concerned about team building, rapport, positive interaction, creativity, developing leadership skills, motivation levels and managing change. Soft-spoken management consultant Robert H. Waterman, Jr. covered all these heady management issues in his lengthy treatise, *The Renewal Factor*, published in 1988. He talked at great length about empowering others and encouraging worker creativity. Waterman contends that by empowering workers, employers give up tight control in order to achieve better results. As for creativity, he says it's a fallacy thinking only top management can be creative. Waterman insists each person is a wellspring of renewal.

By the early '90s, Waterman's theories were old hat. A newer, more outspoken breed of management consultants calling for radical change have joined veteran motivator Tom Peters on the lecture circuit. They've written books on their newfangled theories accompanied by the latest lingo for management students to bat around at cocktail parties. A few of the hot "$200 an hour" buzzwords are "reengineering," "core competencies," "organizational architecture," "time-based competition" and "the learning organization." Even the reasoning behind downsizing is being debunked. Downsizing, says Michael Hammer, a former Massachusetts Institute of Technology computer science professor, is like a Band-Aid over a sore. Companies must totally redesign, or reengineer, their organizations and how work gets done.

Enough on trendy management theories. This is not a management book, and I'm not a management expert, so there is no point explaining all the above terms and the dozens of others that have surfaced. Suffice it to say, the organization, the old-style corporation of bosses and workers, is in the throes of being torn down and rebuilt. The result will be better organizations. That means more profitable, efficient and democratic.

Followers Are More Important Than Leaders

For you, the job searcher soon to join corporate ranks, all this equals a better deal. It means more power, more say and a chance to be a star. Consider this: One outspoken management consultant has overturned the common notion of leadership. He estimates leaders contribute about 20 percent to an organization; the followers are responsible for the remaining 80 percent. (More on new organizations and their leaders in Myth 13: "Big Companies Offer Better Advancement Opportunities and Greater Job Security.")

You can't put a gun to employers' heads and force them to hire you. But you're a fool if you don't try to persuade, cajole, argue and convince them to hire you. Let's be realistic. Don't credit employers with more than they deserve. Seeing a scorching beam of radiant white light in the wee morning hours didn't turn them into benevolent saviors. It's not altruism that opened their minds, but dollars and cents. And why not? Employers are not your parents. They're not responsible for you. All they owe you is fair, ethical treatment, which is, of course, subject to interpretation.

With thousands of companies running with skeleton staffs to cut overhead and boost profits, every person is important. So it pays to find great people and keep them happy. Employers want quality, not quantity. Rather than hire three adequate workers, they figure they'd save money and get more mileage from one smart superachiever who desperately wants the job.

Employers are a finicky bunch. You'd be the same way if you were about to shell out $25,000 to $60,000 a year (without benefits) to an untried person. No wonder employers want perfection. Unconsciously, they know it's a mythical goal; nevertheless they can't help trying. It's up to you to get on your platform and do some high-powered selling and convince them there is no one in the galaxy better qualified for the job than you.

I Can't Believe My Boss Is So Young

The good news is employers can be sold. It may not be easy, but it can be done thanks to the emergence of the new breed of manager who is willing to listen to smart applicants with something to sell. Remember, their minds have been opened.

As companies fold and others break up, thousands of entrepreneurially minded corporate refugees are launching their own companies. They're listening to the new management gurus and building democratic rather than autocratic organizations. They reason anything is better than being lost in a clumsy bureaucracy bloated with layers of ineffectual decision makers.

Similarly, talented younger managers are taking the helm of their family's businesses, intent on building and improving the organizations. Where their elders focused on growth and expansion, the younger generation is all about improving worker conditions by letting workers tell them how they think work should be performed. Once again, empowerment rears its altruistic head.

Perdue Farms, Inc., the fourth-largest chicken processor in the

United States, is a good example. When its deadpan founder and spokesperson Frank Perdue stepped down, relinquishing power to son James, the company's management philosophy took a new turn. James is just as committed as his dad, yet he has a different agenda. Frank was demanding and riveted to the bottom line. James, on the other hand, is conciliatory and concerned about the quality improvement process by making plants safer and involving workers in decision making. James subscribes to a more progressive management school.

In the best of circumstances, young, novice entrepreneurs are open to criticism and willing to learn. Loyal employees say they're great to work for because they don't think they walk on water. They have the courage and maturity to admit when they're wrong. Or they simply have the street smarts to know they've got to tread gently and listen to the people around them.

Most important, the goal of many young and enlightened bosses is to involve their new hires in their mission. Hard times and the driving compulsion to make it are drawing employees and employers closer together. They've never needed each other more.

Smart Employers Question Conventional Thinking

Employers are fast learning that superstars are not always wrapped in conventional packages. Most of the mavericks who built household-name companies don't have MBAs. Many never completed college, and a generous handful, including fast-food titans R. David Thomas (Wendy's founder), Al Copeland of Copeland Enterprises (Popeye's and Church's Chicken) and Truitt Cathy (Chick-fil-A restaurant chain) never completed high school.

Some entrepreneurs lack the very social skills employers insist are the bedrock for success. Apple Computer founder Stephen Jobs is remembered by colleagues and associates as being smug and abrasive, a man who repelled just as many people as he attracted. And Bill Gates, the brilliant founder of Microsoft, has been called reclusive, introverted, secretive and unsophisticated. Clearly, not the life of the party at the annual Palm Beach sales bash.

Yet an employer would have to be insane not to hire a potential Jobs or Gates. So what if they're oddball misfits who come to work in torn jeans, sandals and tee shirts? And what if they alienate all their workers and wind up quitting two months later? Think about what they might contribute during their brief stay. They might turn the company around in one day by creating a new product or service or by coming up with a snappy way to promote the company. I know what I'd do if it were my company—hire them in a minute. I'd reason I have nothing to lose, everything to gain.

That's why insightful employers are more inclined to look beneath the surface to find out what the person is actually like. They'd be making an expensive mistake by not doing so, reason enough not to take amorphous job descriptions as gospel.

Employers Want Human Machines

Twenty years ago, a three- or four-line description pretty much described most jobs. Not so today. Despite automation, jobs are more complicated and demanding. Even on factory floors where computers do everything short of taking coffee breaks, workers who hope to keep their jobs better be multiskilled. They should know something about how the machinery works so they can fix it or at least know who to call when it stops working. Workers ought to be tuned into the whole process.

As cutbacks and consolidations continue, employers are searching for energetic workers willing to do more than they were hired to do. The 9-to-5 mentality went out with long-playing records. If you're not willing to put in 10- or even 12-hour days, you're considered a slacker with a bad attitude.

Juliet B. Schor blasted the perception of the U.S. worker as lazy in her well-researched *The Overworked American* by concluding that Americans are working harder and longer and enjoying less leisure time than at any time since World War II. She points out that U.S. manufacturing workers, for example, work 320 hours longer a year than their counterparts in France and Germany. There is no abatement in site. As the United States works around-the-clock to regain its position as an industrial leader, expect your children to have to work as hard as you do.

Employers Only Think They Know What They Want

Don't Take Want Ads at Face Value

With most workers doing more than either they or their bosses anticipated, job descriptions are little more than threadbare explanations of daily responsibilities. No matter what a job description says, count on doing at least 25 percent more.

Despite that reality, if you're not a carbon copy of what employers want, the challenge you face is convincing them you are. The problem starts with want ads, which are often little more than watered-down job descriptions full of platitudes.

The problem is compounded by human resource departments who write catchy come-on want ads based on job descriptions. It can be likened to the game "telephone," where a large group of people pass along a message, which is whispered in each player's ear. By the time the message reaches the last person, it's a complete distortion of the original message.

It's pretty much the same story when job descriptions are translated to want ads. You get real excited when you read them: "Wow, this job is incredible. It's just what I've been waiting for. Great salary, responsibility, benefits, incredible people. It's got my name on it." When you go back and read it again, you have only a vague idea what you'll be doing 40 hours a week.

The following ad that appeared in a trade magazine searching for a young cable television professional is a good example:

ASSISTANT MANAGER
ADVERTISING AND
PROMOTION

You've been in advertising for two or three years now and you figure it's time you were given more responsibility. Well here you go. In this position, you will be joining the 30 people in our corporate marketing department. You will assist in project management (and manage some projects yourself) for one of the nation's largest TV cable distributors. And while you are busy putting your considerable skills and talents (including PC literacy) to work, you'll be enjoying a very competitive salary and a terrific benefits package.

What does it all mean? Got me. All we can conclude is someone gave the ad a lot of thought. For openers, they got around the age discrimination thing by saying they're looking for someone with two or three years experience. In other words, if you're over 26, they don't want to hear from you. It's a junior position, but you can count on plenty of people looking over your shoulder. Competitive salary doesn't say anything either. The cable industry is notorious for paying appreciably less than the broadcast industry. So the salary may be no better than any other company in the industry is paying. If you're looking for $35,000 a year, you may have to kidnap the CEO and hold him or her ransom.

But don't be upset by all this confusion. Use it to your advantage as a bargaining wedge. If the ad is bloated with hype, just imagine how the job description reads! Several years ago, a veteran headhunter gave me some precious advice. He said, "Read a job description and then find out what they want you to do." How right he was. It's your job to find out what the job entails so you can fit yourself into it snugly—like a hand in a custom-made glove.

The problem with job descriptions is that they usually describe only part of a job, seldom all responsibilities. A computer programmer for a well-known San Francisco software company said his job description was packed into one line. "Update and develop software packages for consumer line." It mentioned nothing about spending 30 percent of the time working with clients, either selling or teaching them how to use software. Or about the countless meetings, reporting levels and endless deadlines that often keep him glued to his computer until 9 p.m.

And a salesperson for a New Jersey apparel maker said his job description said: "Develop new accounts in the tri-state area, concentrating on New York and Connecticut." It failed to tell him he'd have to develop his own leads by constant cold-calling. That means investing at least 20 hours a week making telephone calls to people who can't wait to slam the phone down in your ear.

Are Employers Out to Dupe Us?

Job descriptions, however, are not traps. They aren't written to dupe or confuse you. They're not purposely evasive so employers can pay you less than you deserve.

Many employers simply don't give job descriptions that much thought. As important as they are, only key responsibilities are mentioned. Everything else is a matter of interpretation. Entrepreneurs, especially, do it all the time. They hire people to do jobs they once did, yet don't take the time to break a job into its parts. What they did by rote may be a series of tasks that could keep two people busy sunrise to sunset. What's automatic to them could give someone else a coronary.

Don't give employers that much credit. Yes, they know what has to be done, yet they only have a vague idea about the type of person best suited to do it. Whether they or someone else did the job, it never crosses their minds that candidates with very different qualifications are capable of doing the job as well or even better. Simply, their perception of the most qualified person may be dead wrong. It's up to you to straighten them out.

Employers Are Pressured to Fill Jobs

Don't blame employers for not fully understanding all the responsibilities of a job. Often they're too close to it or they're panicked to fill the slot because they got a large order or new client. Often, all they care about is hiring a body so they can get on with business. They take the easiest and fastest route. They slam down on paper what they think the job entails and hope for the best.

The faster you realize employers don't hold all the cards, the sooner you'll be able to manipulate the system in your favor. In short: create a job opening for yourself.

Talking Your Way into a Job

Since for every job there are at least a dozen skill sets that can execute it perfectly, prepare to sell yourself aggressively. The time to do it is during the second or third interview. This is when you've passed muster. You have impressed the human resource people enough to be called back. Now the weeding out process begins. They're considering a few candidates: Your job is to prove you're the best.

There Are More Ways to Skin a Cat—What Are You Looking For?

If your qualifications perfectly match what the employer is looking for, you've got it made. In a buyer's market with employers having to choose one supercandidate from among hundreds or thousands, most employers are overwhelmed with talent, making decision making almost painful.

Go a level deeper than your competitors. Find out precisely what's expected of you. During the first interview, you politely asked basic questions about the job and company. Now is your opportunity to go further and get down to nitty-gritty details.

Rather than curiously asking who you will be working with, find out precisely who they are, what they do and what their qualifications are. Ask employers about their goals and mission. Don't talk in generalities. Be specific and show real concern. Think of yourself as a physician trying to diagnose a sick patient. Your job is to find the disease and cure it. "When you launched Laundromats Anonymous, what was your vision for the company?" To make America's two billion tons of laundry the whitest in the galaxy? "Did you have a five-year plan? How did things work out?" Don't stop there. "Do you have lots of competition? Have you lost market share because of it? What makes your company different? What is your strategy for the '90s?"

All the while, you can interject intelligent observations, opinions, even suggestions, if you have any. See your role as an intelligent, concerned observer. Gather this information tactfully and diplomatically and the employer will be impressed.

Demonstrate Sincere Interest and Be an Attentive Listener

Asking intelligent questions is not enough. You must also listen attentively and demonstrate sincere interest in what your interviewer is saying. Once again, empathize with the person questioning you. Sure you want the job, but also understand how important this decision is to this person. If you were in his or her shoes, would you want to go through this tedious process every few months? All the more reason that choosing the right person is so important. The manager or employer is under pressure. As we said, it may be imperative to hire someone immediately. Say the person who held the job unexpectedly quit for a better job. Suddenly, the overwhelmed employer finds she or he has a leak in the corporate hull that must be patched immediately so deadlines and production quotas can be met. You get the idea.

Sell Value

Link Your Career Goals to Those of the Employer's

But when you're selling, know your strong and weak points so you offer value rather than smoke and mirrors. Go in knowing the people interviewing you may not be as smart as you are. They may not have a college education or have your intellectual capabilities. They may even be total bores. *But* they know how to run their business. So don't embarrass yourself by trying to snow them.

Rather than making unrealistic claims and promises, sell value. In corporate lingo, that's impact on the bottom line. In simple language, it's dollars. Most employers aren't impressed with big words. But show them how they can make money, and their ears perk up. See yourself as a money-making tool employers need. Sell value.

Without mincing words, explain what you can do for their business. Before you climb into the hot seat for what could be *the* deciding interview, think about your unique talents you feel they need. And it's not just the stuff you learned in school. It's a lot more. Remember what we said in Myth 7: "The Candidate with the Highest Qualifications Always Gets the Job." Technical skills are only 50 percent of the equation. The other half is your ability to persuade, convince, reason and schmooze. In one word, sell!

This is not the time to be modest. Employers are not going to know how good you are unless you tell them. Explain why your work style is compatible with that of the company's and how you have a knack for picking up the beat and falling into step.

Like people, companies have personalities. Drive home the fact that you're in sync with the organization. If the company has a reputation as a no-nonsense organization that gets things done, make it clear it's also your work style. As they say, you're a "hands-on" person. You don't wait to be told something. Like one of entrepreneur Ross Perot's favorite rallying cries in the 1992 presidential race, "If there is a problem, fix it." That self-propelling attitude helped make Perot a billionaire.

In building a case for yourself, look for ways to link your career goals with those of the organization. Be ready to talk about the employer's industry and the company's role within it. Offer intelligent insights and, if nothing else, well-framed opinions.

Be Prepared for Objections

But don't expect an easy sale either, especially if you're not quite sure what the employer is looking for. As we said, if the person who held the job before you had a very different background, the employer may be looking for ways to weed you out. Employers have been conditioned to think only one set of skills can do the job. Your mission is to deprogram them and prove them wrong. In the process, expect to be showered with objections.

What will you reply when the employer says, "But Ms. Hogwash, how can you expect to sell our new gourmet food line when you've never sold food before?" Your response should be:

> You're right Mr. Goofball, I've never sold food before. But I don't see that as the main issue. I'm a professional salesperson. I've had five years' experience selling a trendy upscale shoe line to high-end department stores. Yes, the products are very different, but the selling strategies are the same or similar. Both are niche products sold to educated consumers willing to spend more for quality. Your expensive food line fits those parameters. You need a good professional salesperson, and I'm that person. My track record on my prior job proves it. I'm a fast study and can learn the gourmet food industry in no time. Equally important, it's an industry I'm fascinated with and follow. I'm familiar with a few of the industry's important publications such as *Modern Grocer, Food Distribution Magazine* and *Food Business.*

An answer like the above could change an employer's mind in seconds. The above applicant made some excellent points that will unfailingly hit home. She made it clear that skilled salespeople can sell anything if they're interested and motivated. The final brilliant touch was mentioning trade magazines only insiders know about. Our hard-working applicant went to the trouble to learn something about the industry and the publications covering it. Nice touch.

In building your case, draw on experiences the employer can relate to. Mention accomplishments on prior jobs. If relevant, cite college work experiences, even projects. Rather than mentioning them merely to impress the employer, draw insights and lessons from them so you're perceived as thoughtful, intuitive and most important, potentially productive.

Ask Why

Don't stop with one good reason that you should be hired. Eliminate all the objections. Get your interviewer to put all the *whys* on the table so you answer what Frank Bettger in *How I Raised Myself from Failure to Success in Selling* calls the hidden objections. He quotes J. Pierpont Morgan, who said a person has two reasons for doing or not doing something—one that sounds good and a real one.

Finding objections is all about getting employers to put all their cards on the table. Don't look for logic. Some objections may be off-the-wall; others may be well-founded. Regardless, find out what they are and do your best to allay them. Otherwise, hidden objections could knock you out of the race.

Typically, employers reject applicants because they lack experience (like the gourmet food company owner cited earlier who thought he needed someone with a food sales background). It's an easy and uncomplicated reason for not dealing with the real objection: fear of taking a chance on someone who doesn't fit the conventional mold and who hasn't played by the book. Once again, many employers think they can find perfect candidates. Your job is to tell them you're worth gambling on.

Think on Your Feet

Finally, be prepared to think on your feet. Even though you've rehearsed, prepared and psyched yourself for the event, there is no telling how it will go. Anything can happen. It could be a pleasant, warm exchange or it could be strained, tense or awkward. The challenge you face is building a pleasant rapport with all interviewers— even tough, icy, distant ones who have all the charm of Attila the Hun.

There you have it. If you've changed an employer's mind, redefined and reevaluated the job so you fit it like a glove, you've written your own job description and opened the employer's mind. In short, you've created an opportunity for yourself. Congratulations. Now let's negotiate the salary you deserve.

Myth 11: *In a Competitive Market, Job Seekers Have Little Negotiating Power. They Should Take the First Salary Offered and Be Happy They Got It.*

Reality: *The rules of the game have changed. A more open-minded job market has created relaxed salary-negotiating opportunities that past generations never had. Job applicants have more power than they realize if they choose to exercise it. A new corporate environment has toppled traditional salary-negotiating rules.*

Chapter Snapshot

☐ You Take What I Give You and Be Happy You Got It!

☐ So What's the Big Deal about Money?

☐ How Salaries Are Determined

☐ Salary Isn't the Whole Story

☐ What Kind of Money Are You Looking For?

☐ The Fine Points of Salary Negotiation

☐ Get It in Writing

☐ Summary

❈ ❈ ❈ ❈ ❈ ❈ ❈ ❈

Money is one of those dirty subjects everyone thinks about but nobody discusses. Didn't your folks ever tell you to never ask how much someone is earning? It's the height of bad taste. Etiquette expert Letitia Baldridge would have you publicly flogged if you broached the ugly subject.

Most people can only guess what their friends are earning. And children have only a vague idea what Mom and Dad bring home each week. I didn't find out what my father earned until I was 43.

Is it any wonder we have problems negotiating salaries? Most job applicants are squeamish when it comes to money. They don't know when to talk about it or how to do so. Colleges ought to make a course in salary negotiation mandatory for graduation. Not only would a course help young people get decent salaries; it would boost their confidence and sophistication level.

You Take What I Give You and Be Happy You Got It!

The irony is that money is casually mentioned throughout the hiring process, yet it's only seriously discussed just prior to the actual job offer. It's another tired carry-over from days past when autocratic bosses set salaries and no one dared question them. The thinking on the employer's part was: "If you don't like what I'm paying, I'll find somebody who will." And the applicant thought: "I better take what's offered. I can't risk going another week without any money coming in." There you have it. The boss is in the saddle leading the charge, and the poor job applicant can't do anything but take what's offered. It was a simple process based on an unwritten rule: Keep your mouth shut, take what's handed to you and be happy.

Most job applicants aren't aware of it, but those days are long gone. Even though it is a tough and demanding job market with employers holding most of the cards, applicants can and ought to negotiate for the highest possible salary. By the time you complete this chapter, you'll understand why.

You have more negotiating power than you realize. You don't have to accept the first offer made. If you play the game well, you can wheel and deal for more money. The command words are tact and strategy. Ignore them and you lose.

Welcome to the new age of 1990s-style Darwinism. Don't accept a "fair" salary. If you don't stand up and fight for the salary you think you command, no one else will. Don't expect an employer to pay you what you want or deserve. You've got to ask first and then negotiate for it. It's a simple game. If people want what you have to sell, they will try to get you as cheaply as possible. The question of "fair" salary isn't an issue, since fair is relative. Some employers may consider 20 to 30 percent over current minimum wage standards fair. I call it starvation wages. We all don't share the same standard of living. A necessity to me may be a luxury for someone else or vice versa.

So What's the Big Deal about Money?

In an earlier chapter we talked about emancipated organizations run by fair-minded bosses. Now let's deal with our money hang-ups so we get the salary we deserve.

After all, isn't money one of the most important reasons we're working? It's been drummed into all of us that money should be a means to an end, a reward for doing something you love. Terrific. Idealism is fine, but don't get twisted out of shape over it. We're also working to pay the mountain of bills that accumulates every month—student and car loans, rent and electric, gas and telephone bills. Eating three meals a day isn't a bad idea either. And what about wanting frivolous luxuries like expensive clothes, boats and exotic vacations? Command a high enough salary and you can actually have all these things one day.

Yet, there will be plenty of times you'll take jobs just to keep the wolves from the door. Whatever your needs, money is crucial. So don't shelve the issue of salary; talk about it and, when you have the opportunity, negotiate it so you get what you want and need.

"I Hate Money!"—We're All Hung Up on the Green Stuff

Our lives revolve around money. The average person invests 40 to 60 hours a week working for it, others scheme and cheat for it, and a dangerous few kill for it. Yet, we don't talk about it. You figure this out. A prominent New York psychiatrist told me that for a lot of people, it's easier to discuss their sex lives than it is to talk about how much money they earn and what money means to them. But as my Dad used to say, "Try and get along without it."

Whatever your feelings about money, one thing is certain: your salary determines your lifestyle. The more you make, the better your standard of living. For many, how much they make is a measure of self-worth. For others, it's a scorecard. Some of us have to make more than our friends, fathers, even our spouses. The more we make, the better we feel about ourselves and the more toys we can buy and flaunt.

Don't push the uncomfortable subject of money under the covers. Deal with it. As for being reluctant to discuss it, think about how you will feel if you take a job and settle for a lower salary than you think you deserve. You may not get precisely what you want, but you must try. Six months into the job, you don't want to beat yourself up thinking: "I can't believe I'm working for these slave wages."

Money Is What It's All About

When you get down to the wire, money is what business is all about. For a business to survive, compete and endure, it must sell enough products or services to record a profit to pay for plant, equipment, raw materials, and yes, even your piddling salary. So you see, both company and individual are out to increase their wealth. Remember that no matter how complex the organization, employer and employee are in the game together. In fact, they're on the same side. They need and depend upon each other. They're just playing on different parts of the field.

Think about these fundamentals and you'll have no qualms about negotiating your salary. To pervert the old cliché, money is what makes the world go round.

How Salaries Are Determined

Most large companies have compensation plans. Human resource managers often say they're cast in stone, yet applicants negotiate salaries every day. On the executive level, it's practically sport. It's not just salaries they're negotiating but mouth-watering perks—cars to country club memberships—totalling thousands of dollars a year.

Salary negotiation amounts to an enormous game. Sadly, most job seekers fail to play because they don't think they can. Career writer Marilyn Moats Kennedy talks about the myth surrounding salary negotiating in her book *Salary Strategies.* Kennedy says job searchers are under the impression some gigantic, mysterious, all-knowing corporate force determines salary levels for workers. She refers to this bureaucratic force as the mysterious "they."

To allay fears and blow the myth to smithereens, there is no omnipotent "they." Don't believe employers when they say the salary is firm, or "this is our final offer." If they want you, they'll negotiate.

Salary Negotiation, Then and Now

Corporations are like giant ocean liners. Only first-class passengers get to schmooze with the captain. Everyone else pays homage to their immediate supervisor, a lowly cog in a towering machine. Within sprawling conglomerates, it's easy to see how salary negotiation was reduced to a pretty limp process. Many potential achievers didn't have that much negotiating power because they weren't given the chance to strut their stuff and prove what they could do. Most were one-function workers who were easily replaced. So they shut their mouths and accepted whatever was doled out—"If I get too pushy, I'll be replaced."

All that changed in the early to mid-1980s when intense pressure from foreign competition, particularly the Japanese, forced U.S. corporations to slim down to fighting weight because U.S. industry had lost its edge. It was industrial warfare as international powers fought for world markets. The rule was fight back or perish. The result was radical change with companies eliminating unnecessary layers at a frightening clip. Thousands of companies went bankrupt; others systematically laid off workers like sinking ships lightening their load to stay afloat. It hasn't stopped yet. More on this in Myth 13: "Big Companies Offer Better Advancement Opportunities and Greater Job Security."

As I said, the name of the game is survival. What's different today is, unlike the recessions of 1973 to 1975 and the early-1980s, the layoffs are permanent. Companies are discarding people because they don't need or can't afford them.

It is scary only if you're looking to snuggle on a big daddy company's lap for the next 20 years. The flip side, however, is *opportunity.*

I Have More Bargaining Power Than I Realized!

The survivors of corporate shake-ups are discovering options they never imagined. Not only do they keep their jobs, they also inherit other jobs as well. They're working harder and longer than they ever worked before. They don't have the security they enjoyed a decade ago, yet opportunity awaits them like the parting of the Red Sea—if they take advantage of it. Suddenly they're more valuable. They are worth more because they are doing more. They can negotiate fatter salaries and more extras, opening the door to bigger jobs and more raises later on.

Corporate consolidations have rendered conventional ranking and classification systems obsolete. They were great when you slotted people into neatly defined jobs with explicit job functions. But those jobs are fast disappearing, making salary negotiation all the more important. Employers don't want one- or two-function drones. They want people who can do the work of two, maybe three people and understand other functions as well.

What does it all mean? You have more bargaining power than you realize. *Use it!* Don't let it slip through your fingers. Also keep in mind that salary isn't everything.

Salary Isn't the Whole Story

The idea is get the best salary you can, but in the long run it ought to be leveraged against a long-term career objective.

Taking a job for salary alone can be a tactical error. Yet remember, we're only human. No matter how principled we think we are, most of us can be seduced by a high salary. But if it throws you off your career course, think twice. You could be wasting precious time.

Many fields, especially highly competitive ones, such as television or radio broadcasting, cable, public relations, advertising, journalism, publishing or fashion, for example, have the equivalent of long apprenticeship periods. If you survive them, your pay can jump dramatically.

In many fields, starting salaries are little more than starvation wages. Until you earn your stripes, you're working against long-term dividends. Regardless of the field, get ready for the big question.

What Kind of Money Are You Looking For?

Early in the salary-negotiating process, a placement manager, human resource person, low-level manager or even the employer will offhandedly pop the question, "What kind of money are you looking for?"

What do you say? First, here is what you don't say: "I'm looking for $45,000, Mr. Cheapskate." Worse still, "As much money as I can possibly make."

You've tied your own noose by locking yourself into a firm figure in the initial stages of salary negotiation. If it's lower than the employer planned on paying, he or she has gotten a bargain without having to haggle over money. If the figure is too high, you've presented yourself as inflexible and unwilling to negotiate. Either way, you're up against a wall.

The second answer is worse and will probably knock you out of the race. Saying you want as much as you can get makes you look like a rank amateur. It's an inappropriate answer lacking tact and thought. Of course, you want as much money as you can get. But you don't say it, you negotiate it!

At this stage of the game—before a concrete offer is made—mention only a salary range, which ought to be the very lowest amount of money you'd accept to the highest, the outermost limit of an acceptable range. (More on this soon.) Employers know exactly how much they want to pay you. Whether they can be budged is up to you. This is why a salary range ought to be presented in early discussions; doing so gives flexibility and bargaining leverage.

Your answer ought to sound something like, "Ms. Marple, an acceptable salary range is $50,000 to $55,000." Her answer might be, "That's pretty much the range we had in mind, Mr. Gehring." Stop! End conversation. That's as far as you have to go now. No more blabbering about money until later on when the negotiations get serious.

Do not negotiate salary until an employer demonstrates sincere interest or actually makes you an offer. Prior to that point, all you can do is present salary parameters as mentioned above.

As soon as an offer is made, your position suddenly becomes rock solid. Because you've impressed this person, you stand an excellent chance of going to the outer limits of the salary range.

Now we're ready for the negotiating process.

The Fine Points of Salary Negotiation

Get Ready to Sweat a Little

See the game for what it is and understand the respective positions of the players. If you were an employer heading a multimillion-dollar business you built from the ground up, would you willingly give a new worker anything he or she wants? It stands to reason you'll try to get that person as cheaply as you can. That doesn't mean you won't discuss terms and kick offers back and forth. Nevertheless, you'll do everything you can to keep the new worker's starting salary down to the lower end of the range.

There lies the rationale for the tug-of-war between the two parties in the negotiating process. Each one is out to protect her or his own interests.

Why Negotiate?

By negotiating, you're strengthening your future position with the company. If you shoot for the highest possible salary, you capture immediate points as being a potentially valuable employee. They conclude you're a cut above the average, the type of worker who is not about to accept anything offered.

As soon as you speak up for yourself, you're considered an individualist, someone who will fight for his or her beliefs. You're not a rank-and-file person, but someone with a clear sense of your self-worth. Your willingness to negotiate could mean gifted selling or even managerial abilities. In short, you have the potential to boost profits.

Negotiating serves a dual purpose: You stand a chance of capturing a higher salary, and you create a favorable impression. Let's negotiate.

Eight Salary Negotiating Strategies

Strategy 1: Confidently Sell Yourself. So far you've managed to chalk up an impressive track record on all your interviews. Just because you're at the wire and about to close the deal, don't let that burning fire of confidence dissipate. It's just as crucial in the negotiating process as it is on interviews.

Picking up where we left off in Myth 7: "The Candidate with the Highest Qualifications Always Gets the Job," think of yourself as a super salesperson during this nerve-racking negotiating phase. You're selling yourself, and, in order to do that, you have to believe in your-self 150 percent. You must appear confident, in control and secure. This doesn't mean bragging or climbing on a podium and grandstanding your talents.

If you hope to conquer the higher end of the salary range, the best position is one of quiet, understated confidence. So far, your prior career record and flawless interview techniques have propelled you to this advanced stage in the hiring process. Now you must win the employer over to your position by demonstrating that you have total confidence in your abilities and that you have not the slightest element of doubt that you're the only person on this planet who can do the job right.

Even though you're at the finish line and understandably nervous about finalizing the deal as quickly as possible, try not to show apprehension. Walk into your prospective employer's office as if you have all the time in the world. Make up your mind that you're going to deal from a position of strength.

Strategy 2: Let the Employer Set the Pace. Sit back and relax and let the employer set the rhythm and pace of the conversation. Like the first interview, some employers may insist upon your joining them for a cup of coffee. If they really want to see how you react under fire, there may be some aimless small talk before the conversation turns serious.

Play it by ear and go with it. Even though you had 10 cups of coffee, smoked half a pack of cigarettes and chewed your fingernails down to the bone before walking into the negotiating chamber, play the game. It's going to be a long day.

Strategy 3: Define Negotiating Parameters. Just as generals know their strengths and weaknesses before launching all-out frontal attacks on their enemies, you need to know your position well before negotiating with an employer. Your basic negotiating position is based upon three important factors: (1) salary on prior job, (2) industry salary ranges and (3) your individual strengths.

Let's look at each one closely. Like it or not, your salary on your prior job has a great deal to do with determining what you'll earn on your next job. I'm not saying it's impossible to snare a job at a dramatic increase. It just takes clever negotiating. If you earned $25,000 on your last job, prospective employers may reason they can get you at a 20 percent increase or $30,000, which means that if the agreed-upon salary range is $28,000 to $38,000, employers will try to buy you at the lower end of the range.

To negotiate higher, you must build a solid case. If you have an exceptional track record, you can push for the higher end of the salary range. If employers deem you a necessity, they'll pay the price. If your track record speaks for itself and you have the credentials and references to back it up, go for a 25 or 30 percent increase, even more.

The second factor has to do with broad industry salary parameters. If you did your homework, you know what your industry pays at all levels and the prime locations. If not, find out by checking out the following:

- *Want Ads.* Your reliable daily newspaper is the place to start. Follow the want ads daily and you'll have a pretty good idea what salaries are like in your industry.

- *Employment Agencies.* Visit employment agencies and speak to placement managers specializing in your field. They'll candidly tell you what salary levels are like and may even pass on some negotiating tips as well. Since they talk to companies daily, the information couldn't be more timely.

- *Trade Associations and Professional Groups.* As with job leads, trade associations and professional groups can give you an excellent idea of what the salary ranges are in your industry. Many of these organizations publish charts and surveys, providing a panoramic picture of industry salary levels throughout the country. An electrical or chemical engineer with three to five years' experience will probably earn more money working in a large city like New York or Los

Angeles than in Mansfield, Ohio, or Boise, Idaho. The same rationale applies to hundreds of professional and skilled jobs.

- *U.S. Department of Labor's Bureau of Labor Statistics.* The Bureau publishes a truckload of information. There are special reports and the
  yearly edition of the *Occupational Outlook Yearbook.* Caution! The
  information is reliable, yet the salary information is a year old,
  maybe more. In high-demand jobs, like computer programming, for
  example, salaries can change dramatically from year to year. Don't
  follow government salary figures as gospel. You could wind up taking last year's salary rate. For updated salary information, call your
  state's labor department. They may have current numbers.

- *Consulting Firms, Organizations and Companies.* Through your industry association, you may stumble on consulting firms, organizations
  and companies that prepare their own research and publish it.
  Some is free, some costs money. The American Management
  Association and the Administrative Management Society, for example, prepare lengthy surveys, which they sell to companies and
  interested parties. If you're clever, you can save money by obtain-
  ing these surveys through contacts or friends or possibly a public
  library.

If you're fortunate enough to have a high-demand skill, your bargaining position is all the more secure. If you're a computer programmer, systems analyst, medical technician or occupational therapist,
you already have a leg up on your employer in the negotiating
process. You and the employer know full well that the demand for
your particular skill outpaces the supply of workers, putting you in a
strong negotiating position. If a company wants you badly enough, it
will pay more than the competition.

Strategy 4: Stress Accomplishments.   Keep in mind that employers are practical people who see no reason to pay for anything they don't
need. Knowing that, you must solve their problems and meet their
needs. Cold-hearted as it seems, employers are not all that concerned
about your needs. They know they have to pay you a decent wage,
whatever that is, but they see no reason to gild the lily and pay you
more—unless you make a sound case for yourself. That case revolves
around making it absolutely clear that they need you and that you'll do
more than you're hired to do.

Just as you did in your correspondence and prior interviews, drive
home your accomplishments. This is no time for false modesty. Like a
veteran actor bringing a packed house to tears with a brilliant solilo-

quy, this is your chance to bring the house down with brilliant insights and persuasive arguments.

Strategy 5: Be Flexible and Argue Logically. If the moon is in the right place, the salary discussion will go smoothly and you'll be celebrating 45 minutes later. As we said earlier, there is no predicting human behavior. However, the person you're meeting may be a world-class negotiator, which means you have a hard sell on your hands.

No matter what arguments you present justifying the money you're asking for, this person is going to shoot you down. So guide yourself accordingly. If you find yourself facing a brick wall, back off and try another strategy.

No matter how tense it gets, don't try to snow or bluff a potential employer. Be honest, direct and respectful of the employer's position.

Strategy 6: Demonstrate Understanding of the Company and Its Problems. When highlighting your accomplishments, make it clear you understand the company's problems and goals. If the company is trying to revive a dying product line, break into a new territory, overtake a competitor or turn around an unprofitable division, address these problems. You talked about these issues during the interview, here is an opportunity to do it again. "For the past five years your company has been experimenting with new sales programs to overtake Soupy Sales, Inc. Having created direct selling campaigns, I know I can design a program that can boost sales."

How can employers turn a deaf ear to arguments that could mean new business? It also doesn't hurt to mention that the company's goals are not very different from yours, another irresistible bargaining tactic. It sounds hokey, but employers like hearing sentiments like: "Tokey toothpicks are the most innovative toothpicks on the market; I want to work for an industry leader."

Strategy 7: State Salary Demands Tactfully and Diplomatically.
Now it's time to get serious and talk money. Employers present either narrow or broad ranges. A broad range usually means employers are flexible and not quite sure what they're looking for. In other words, depending upon who applies, they'll either consider a very experienced person at the upper end of the range or a moderately experienced person at the lower end of the range.

When negotiating with a broad range, pursue the salary matching your background and experience. Naturally, try to get as much money as you can, but don't be unreasonable and naive and think you can walk away with the high end of the range when you don't have the credentials to support the higher salary.

If a narrow range is offered—$18,000 to $20,000, $25,000 to $28,000, $38,000 to $40,000, for example—employers usually know exactly what they want and are not about to compromise and consider an inexperienced person. They left little room for negotiating leeway so they can try to get the applicant at the lower end of the scale.

Say you're faced with a broad salary range of $25,000 to $30,000 and, since you're moderately experienced and have good credentials, you feel you're well worth $28,000. What should you ask for? If you said $28,000, you're wrong. Remember, negotiating takes strategy.

Since your target salary is $28,000, you must shoot for the high end of the salary range and ask for $30,000. The negotiating bell will ring when the employer smiles, looks you dead in the eye and says that the company is prepared to offer you $25,000 as if it was the greatest gift since God handed Moses the Ten Commandments.

Prepared for the offer, you didn't fall off your seat, have a temper tantrum or storm out of the office when the offer was made. No matter how disagreeable the offered salary, don't reply with negative statements such as: "That figure is just *not* acceptable," or "With my background, I don't understand how you could offer me the bottom end of the salary range," or "I'm *really* disappointed. I thought for sure you'd offer me a higher starting salary."

That's not going to get you far, since you've already put a damper on the negotiations by dropping a negative attitude like a lead balloon. No matter how insulting the offered salary, don't blow your cool. Be positive and upbeat. If you hope to get more money, you must present facts supporting the salary you're asking for.

Your answer should sound like: "I'm very flattered you want me to work for your company, Mr. Tightwad, but I have to be honest and say I'm disappointed with the salary you're offering. I would, however, consider a salary of $30,000 acceptable."

Expect a long silence, maintain eye contact and wait for the employer to come back with a counteroffer. Just as tactfully as you declined the stated offer, he or she will probably say that $30,000 is just out of the question, that the company is not prepared to pay that much money, that it's beyond budget limitations or that the salary you're demanding is more than veteran workers are getting.

This last move shouldn't surprise you. Obviously, he's not going to pay you $30,000. The next move is yours. You might say, "If $30,000 is excessive, how much can you increase the offer?"

You've returned the ball, bringing the discussion to a new plateau. You didn't mention an amount, yet your salary parameters are more than clear. The employer now has to come back with a figure that is agreeable and that does not offend you. At this point, don't be alarmed if the employer backs off and asks for time to consider your proposal or possibly discuss the offer with associates. It doesn't mean the employer is not interested. Often, employers ask for time for two reasons: One, they legitimately want time to ponder the offer and discuss it with colleagues, and two, it's a cunning tactic forcing you to take the offered salary. When an employer asks for time, many applicants, fearful that they'll be replaced by someone willing to accept less money, lose their cool and reluctantly agree to the offered salary—even though they're seriously compromising their position. As uncertain as the situation is, you must play it out and wait. Salary negotiations often require nerves of steel.

Another tactic is to reason respectfully with the employer by adding: "Thirty thousand dollars sounds like a lot of money, Mr. Tightwad, but I'd like to remind you that it's less than 20 percent over what I earned at Krypto Loons, Ltd."

With that last statement, you're reasoning intelligently. What pragmatic businessperson can deny irrefutable logic? After all, aren't most qualified applicants entitled to anywhere from between 15 to 20 percent more when they change jobs?

All the while, you're tactfully driving home your accomplishments. If you play your cards right, your employer will probably wind up offering you $28,000, the salary you wanted. With your background, $30,000 will seem out of the question but $28,000 will seem a more than fair compromise. If it turns out this way—and there are no guarantees that it will—you can do a fast cartwheel as soon as you leave. There is nothing sweeter than victory.

Face facts. No matter how confident you are, the negotiation session may not come off as planned. As much as you want the high end of the salary range, this person is not going to hand it to you on a silver platter. You're going to have to work for it.

Consider this last tactic. Even after you have a presented a barrage of logical, irrefutable arguments, the employer may come back with, "I'm sorry, the offer is firm. I can't give you a penny more."

Naturally, you now want to lunge for the interviewer's jugular. Nevertheless, restrain such impulses. Throughout your negotiations you're going to have to demonstrate almost superhuman qualities.

For instance, the employer may say: "The best we can do is 5 percent better than the offered salary. Understand that I don't act alone. Salaries are set by a five-person committee. So this is the best we can do for the time being."

What do you say? If it's less than you wanted, but you really want the job, try this: "I understand you're in a difficult situation, Ms. Eichmann. Since salary is set by committee, couldn't we negotiate the salary up to the 15 percent level six months from now? That way, it doesn't put you in the hot seat, and you have plenty of time to discuss the matter with the salary committee. By then, you'll know me a lot better and you'll see that I do quality work. At that point, you and the committee will be convinced I deserve every penny of the increment." Smart answer. It shows you're a gracious person willing to compromise.

Even though you agreed upon a broad salary range earlier, employers may toss a flat salary at you and drop a trite line like: "I hope we're in the same ballpark."

Don't make the mistake of thinking you can't negotiate. Rarely is a stated salary cast in stone. You've got more leeway than you realize. If they want you badly enough, they'll up the ante.

If you feel you're worth more, say so:

EMPLOYER: I'm sorry, the salary is set. I can't do any better.

APPLICANT: The salary is very reasonable, Mr. Cheapskate, but taking into consideration my track record, I'm only earning 12 percent more than I made at Bombast Cannon. I don't feel I'm being paid what I'm worth. If you consider that within a three-year period I was single-handedly responsible for increasing profits in my ailing company by 45 percent, you'll agree I'm well worth a 20 percent increment. I hope you can understand my reasoning. If you put yourself in my position, Mr. Cheapskate, I'm sure you'd ask for the same salary.

Nice touch. This applicant is standing fast, hell-bent on getting what he wants. He's respectful, upbeat, positive, yet diplomatically assertive. To drive home his point, he cushions his plea for more money by stressing his accomplishments. He also asks the employer to put himself in his shoes, a good tactic appealing to this person's sense of reason and justice.

Most important, while presenting logical arguments, he's doing it in a positive and confident way. He's not offering ultimatums, just irrefutable reasons.

Negotiations can go any number of ways. If you're lucky, everything will be worked out in one meeting. However, if you have a great deal to negotiate, it could take longer. Although waiting plays havoc with your nervous system, it may be unavoidable if you hope to hold out for the salary you're shooting for.

Strategy 8: Negotiate Fringe Benefits and Perks.   Rest easy, because the last leg of the negotiations should go as smooth as silk. The biggest obstacle was agreeing on a salary figure. All we have to do now is determine fringe benefits and perks—issues second to salary in importance.

Just as employers try to commit you to a salary before you're hired, they may similarly try to entice you with benefits and perks before you know how much your weekly paycheck will be. Conversations about fringe benefits and perks, however, are premature until you've agreed upon a salary.

Don't be surprised if employers mention the fantastic fringe benefits their company offers before a salary is nailed down. "Let me tell you about the fabulous benefits package our company has to offer. You may not be aware of it, but it's probably the most lucrative in the industry. Our comprehensive medical, dental, life insurance and pension plans are worth an incalculable amount in the long run. And our perks are fantastic."

Don't interrupt, but understand the strategy being used. You may not know it, but you're being softened for the kill. If you get excited about the company's liberal benefits package, you're making it easier for employers to lock you into a salary that may be less than you wanted. The employer's reasoning goes something like this: "You're not getting the salary you anticipated, but look at the benefits package you're walking away with. Tack it on to your salary and you've got an additional several thousand dollars worth of important extras."

That's true to a point. Benefits are important, but on a priority scale, salary heads the list. Your salary, not your benefits, pays rent and grocery bills. Benefits and perks are separate issues, above and beyond salary.

If the employer launches into a diatribe on benefits and perks before you've agreed on a salary, wait for the right moment and steer her or him back to reality: "The benefits sound great, Mr. Conman, but I think we should seriously discuss them later when we arrive at a compatible salary. In fact, I have a lot of questions concerning benefits which I'd like to discuss with you."

That wasn't so hard. Without being abrasive, you gently turned the conversation to the issues at hand. With that cautionary note out of the way, here's some general information on benefits and perks. Whether you work for a large company or a two-person shop, you can expect some type of fringe benefits. Generally, the larger the company, the more fringe benefits provided. However, many small companies are going out of their way to provide generous fringe benefits as well.

The more you give a worker, the more you'll get in return. The credo is that a contented worker is a productive worker. Most of us will spend our careers working for others; only a tiny percentage will go off on their own. If it makes you happy, there is nothing wrong with a 9-to-5 lifestyle, weekly paychecks, regular vacations. Not everyone has the stomach or constitution for the nonstop seven-day-a-week aggravation of running a company.

Knowing this, smart employers go out of their way to create appetizing, secure havens for prized workers. In a tense environment of corporate upheaval, many humanistic employers consider good benefits packages more important than ever. But be sure to find out exactly what you'll get. Typically, benefits include some kind of medical coverage for yourself and family, a flexible pension plan, two weeks of paid vacation, a number of major holidays and a specified number of sick days. Some companies also provide life insurance coverage and options to buy company stock.

For instance, there are different types of medical coverage, parceled out by rank. Top executives get the best coverage; everyone else brings up the rear. A growing number of companies, small and large, are offering lower-level workers flexible benefits packages where they get to tailor a package to their needs by choosing from a menu of benefits. Common benefits are term life, medical and accidental death insurance. In addition to insurance benefits, flex plans commonly offer reimbursement accounts in which employer and employee contribute and the employee receives tax reimbursements for unused medical, dental and optical expenses. A popular account is a before-tax reimbursement account for reimbursement of dependent care or baby-sitting expenses.

Perquisites, or perks, as they're called, are something else entirely. A perk is a privilege or extra beyond salary parcelled out according to rank. For most companies you won't find many perks beneath the middle-management level. The higher you go, the more exclusive and incredible the perks get. Presidents of large companies, for example, have Lear jets, limousines, apartments and servants at their disposal. In the '60s and '70s, many middle- and senior-level workers perks' exceeded their salaries. The rest of us have to be content with a modest expense account and maybe a company car if traveling is part of the job.

Typical perks include:

- Company car
- First-class travel
- Stock-option plan
- Extended vacations and bonus vacations
- Large office
- Special medical and insurance coverage

Get It in Writing

Before you shake hands with your employer consummating the deal and head to your favorite watering hole to celebrate, get your employment agreement in writing. It's a professional touch, benefiting you and employer so there is no misunderstanding about the fine points of your employment. Before you begin work, everything will be clearly spelled out—responsibilities, salary, benefits, perks. Any disagreement can be resolved before you start your first day on the job.

It's also good to have a letter of agreement on record should there be a corporate shakeup, a takeover, merger or radical reorganization and you have to renegotiate your employment agreement. If there is a takeover and consolidation, for example, it's to your advantage to present the letter to your new boss to negotiate the best deal.

The letter may also come in handy if you think you are being unlawfully fired. There is no guaranteed legal benefit to having the letter, but it can't hurt. Its value is subject to interpretation according to each state's employment laws.

Summary

The following is a salary-negotiating summary:

1. Be yourself.
2. Don't try to snow employer.
3. Stress accomplishments.
4. Be flexible.
5. Argue logically.
6. Demonstrate understanding of company problems and goals.
7. Define negotiating parameters. Your negotiating position is based upon salary on prior job, industry ranges and your individual strengths.
8. Don't discuss money until a job offer is made.
9. State demands tactfully and diplomatically.
10. Be patient. Negotiations can take days, sometimes weeks.
11. Don't forget to negotiate fringe benefits and perks.
12. Get the terms of your agreement in writing.

Myth 12: *A Perfect Job Means a 35-Hour Paycheck, Great Benefits and a Fat Pension.*

Reality: *There is no such thing as a perfect job. The best you can hope for is a great job which is a short-term play leading to a better job.*

Chapter Snapshot

□ A Perfect Job Was Any Job

□ Prosperity and the Perfect Job

□ The Perfect Job Ain't a Guaranteed Paycheck

□ A Secure Job Is Not a Perfect Job

□ The Meaning of Work after 100 Years of Change

□ What Do You Want? A Job or a Career?

□ I'm Gonna Get Me a Great Job!

□ Promises! Promises!—Listen to Your Gut

□ When to Move On

＊＊＊＊＊＊＊＊

It took about a century to change our traditional thinking, but we're fast learning that the perfect job doesn't exist. It's 100 percent myth.

Since childhood, we've been primed to search for the perfect job. There was nothing complicated about it. The perfect job would give us more than enough to live on, plus health benefits, pension, bonuses and plenty of perks. It was a giant security blanket for all or at least the better part of our careers. On paper, it sounds positively utopian. But as we said in the introduction, it often meant boredom, inertia and apathy.

A Perfect Job Was Any Job

Like other myths discussed in this book, this one's roots also lie at the turn of the century, when the United States emerged as a melting-pot nation as immigrants from central and eastern Europe flocked to its shores. A perfect job to an impoverished immigrant was any job, no matter how menial, that offered enough money to meet essential needs.

Then there was the Depression, a period which made this current job market seem tame in comparison. With millions begging and sleeping in doorways, no one cared what kind of job he or she took. It didn't matter whether it was brutal physical labor or the mind-numbing tedium of adding or subtracting numbers 10 hours a day. If it was a day's pay, workers were delighted. A perfect job was any job.

Prosperity and the Perfect Job

But even when things got better, we still clung to the myth of the perfect job. Even in the questioning '60s, we secretly believed it existed. For a half decade or so the world seemed like it was coming apart at the seams. The Vietnam war raged; vocal students protested everything from civil inequities to big business to pollution, you name it. Some dropped out to return to the land to grow their own food and reinvent the world; others became full-time protesters. Yet, by the early '70s, it was back to normal again as the "me" decade blossomed. All the former protesters had shaved their beards, cut their hair, discarded their hand-me-down clothing, bathed and re-entered society. Some joined their parents' successful businesses and others went on to launch companies of their own.

Even prior to that we all knew we'd have to get serious and find a way to earn a living. Many of my friends had 12- to 24-month bouts of rebellion, then it was back to the real world to settle down to a paycheck and adulthood.

By the late '60s, after conquering degrees and sowing some oats, we, as every prior generation, back-pocketed our idealism and looked for jobs. There was nothing complicated about it. We were broke and had no choice. When our folks stopped taking care of us, idealism and rebellion gave way to practical thinking. Like it or not, we had to get serious. We didn't want any job, we wanted the mythical perfect one. We deemed it salvation, the mystical key to a great life.

We weren't sure what that perfect job was, but we thought it would put us on easy street. Employers could be likened to surrogate parents. They would nurture, feed and protect us. Why, they would even educate us and, if we did really well, would provide for our children as well.

Until pretty recently, many companies did just that. They actually took care of their workers. Two and three generations of entire families have worked for big companies.

We clung to the fantasy that the perfect job, like the Garden of Eden, Fountain of Youth and Atlantis, existed. What a reassuring fantasy. I remember two college profs going on about the metaphysical qualities of a great job. Somehow they tied philosophy, psychology and employment and drew eye-crossing connections about how work ought to tap our spiritual and creative natures. Maybe there was some truth to that, but I've yet to find it. They rambled about the cleansing quality of work and the pure satisfaction that comes from doing something you love.

Let's get real. Yes, you ought to love what you do and take heartfelt satisfaction from it. But don't forget we're talking about work, jobs, the stuff you do from 9 to 5, not sainthood or enlightenment. I never got around to asking these wise men where they worked before they became omnipotent pundits, but I never believed they spent any real time working for companies. What did they know about the harsh working world when they were protected by a security blanket of lifetime tenure?

The Perfect Job Ain't a Guaranteed Paycheck

Nevertheless, many of my friends believed the myth of the perfect job. For five years after graduating from college, a half-dozen of us got together every Friday night to play poker, drink beer, eat sandwiches and speculate about the meaning of life and work. Since we all held full-time jobs and felt flush, we thought we knew how the world worked. With enough money to make our car payments, pay rent and feed ourselves, we had it made. By 1 a.m., drunk and babbling, we solved all life's problems and answered questions even Socrates, Descartes, and Schopenhauer never got straight. One question was the meaning of work and the essence of the perfect job.

One of my buddies who worked for the New York City Welfare Department told me he had found the "working man's nirvana." "This job is incredible," he said. "You're out in the field three days a week, and by 4 p.m. you're on the court playing basketball. There is nobody looking over your shoulder, you don't kill yourself, salary and benefits are great, yearly raises are guaranteed and in 20-odd years, you can retire on a full pension."

My friend is still working for the welfare department, but he doesn't think it's perfect any longer. He's a reluctant company person, a bureaucrat, bored, disgruntled and frustrated. The very thing that attracted him to the job—the chance to rip off the system and have fun—now bores him to tears. In his mid-40s with 20 years' experience behind him, he's become a victim of his routines. Looking back, he says he made a mistake playing it safe and not taking chances. Frightened, hopelessly stuck, and shoulder-deep in organizational quicksand, he's turned into a living corpse who doesn't know how to change his life. And he knew it 10 years into his job. By then he had made supervisor. He was trapped and didn't have the guts or initiative to try something else.

In short, my friend threw in the towel too soon. Maybe he thought the search for meaningful work wasn't worth the effort. Like millions of others, he learned the hard way that the perfect job was not a guaranteed paycheck.

A Secure Job Is Not a Perfect Job

I had other friends who managed to find more pleasurable jobs. Some held jobs for 10 or more years; others held many. In time, most radically changed their views of work. They became either angry, disillusioned, cynical or, most often, all the above. Ultimately, they arrived at the startling conclusion that the perfect job was pure myth. A perfect job is not a secure job. Job security, even in the worst of times, is no replacement for motivation and happiness.

Richard H. Stansfield, in *The Best Ever How-to-Get-a-Job Book*, said that the only real security is the security you create yourself. Sound advice. If we've learned anything from the past 100 years, it is that we must be autonomous, tough and flexible. We must learn to take care of ourselves. That doesn't mean building a bomb shelter in your basement along with two years' worth of canned C rations, but it does mean being primed for the unexpected. Adaptability and resilience are critical career skills.

Suffice it to say no company, large or small, can promise career-long paychecks. If the once towering Rocks of Gibraltar of U.S. business can no longer guarantee it, no one can.

In the long run, security is a suffocating substitute for happiness. I can't tell you how many times I've heard people say, "I'm just biding my time till I'm fully vested and I can retire on a full pension."

Most did nothing. A few hearty souls mustered the energy to change their lives.

The Meaning of Work after 100 Years of Change

What the Heck Is a Perfect Job?

What changed the minds of these brave souls? Growth, maturity, routines and a crazy world. If we learned anything from the past 30 years, it's that no one is going to take care of us. Unlike our ancestors who had few job options, even in today's toughest job markets, there are jobs to be had. There will be times when we have to take any job just to get by. But, ultimately, we have options. Believe it or not, we're not stuck.

Here we are in the '90s, and the mythical perfect job has mushroomed into something even more intangible and out of reach. By the late '80s, the ideal job was no longer a steady paycheck, a 35-hour workweek and a fat pension, but something more amorphous. A job also had to be meaningful, pleasurable and fulfilling. And it ought to require commitment and creativity. These were attributes our grandparents never considered because most of the available jobs were menial. When you're living at survival levels, you're hardly thinking about job fulfillment.

But just as quickly as an enlightened new generation of job searchers realized the ideal job ought to have the above attributes, they quickly concluded no single job could possibly provide all of them, especially in light of unabated firings. Nothing like an unexpected pink slip to make you an instant cynic.

Let's Bury the Perfect Job Once and For All

Here we are in the present, the right time to end the search for the mystical perfect job once and for all. With companies struggling for survival, the only people they're making promises to are venture capitalists and stockholders, the folks funding their growth. Everyone else is dispensable. If the corporate machine falters, you're history. And once you're let go, the chances of being rehired are slim indeed. As we said in Myth 11, the days of temporary layoffs are gone forever.

No wonder companies like the words *downsizing* or *rightsizing*. These are the new euphemisms for permanent housecleaning. Traditionally you were fired for screwing up; now you're fired because you're not needed. Either way, you're on the street.

It's little consolation to a veteran worker who grew up in the shadow of company smokestacks and whose father and grandfather worked the assembly lines that technology, global competition or shrinking profits were the reasons they were axed. Who cares? They're finished and must start over. That's a bitter reality pill to swallow.

That's a down-and-dirty summary of a half century of change. Companies can no longer make lifelong promises or guarantees. In light of unabated corporate upheaval, even the fantasy of a perfect job has been shattered forever. But let's be realistic, the perfect job never really existed. It was no more than a mirage, an illusion—plain, old-fashioned wish fulfillment.

What Do You Want? A Job or a Career?

Let's take this knowledge and create something special for ourselves. If the perfect job doesn't exist, what should we aim for? The answer is *meaningful jobs that build a career.*

Once again, let's make a clear distinction between job and career, an issue briefly touched on in Myth 2. As we said, a sea of difference separates them.

A job is a short-term play leading to a better job. A career is a string of related jobs in one field, all of which are aimed at achieving mastery, knowledge and experience. Rather than jump from one unrelated job to another, a career is all about mastering one skill or profession. More complicated still, many of us will have two or three careers throughout our lifetime. The mysterious part is that we have no idea when disillusionment will set in and we're once again on that uncertain path searching for meaningful work. It could happen next year or never.

Even in the best of times, it's unreasonable to assume one job will blossom into a full-blown career and consume 20-plus years of our lives. Think about it. Can a company and its workers grow at the same pace? With new career options tempting us every day, topped by a job market as uncertain as the wind, chances are you'll tire of the job first.

As you learn more and build new contacts, you'll crave change. Don't assume all job changes will be upward. Lateral moves can be just as constructive as vertical ones.

I'm Gonna Get Me a Great Job!

Now that we've capsized the notion of a perfect job, let's get realistic and settle for a great one. A great job is a stepping-stone to a better job. Yet there is more to a great job than most people realize.

In *The Right Move, How to Find the Perfect Job,* Michael Zey talks about interim or stepping-stone jobs leading to bigger and better jobs. The stepping-stone job fulfills a short-term function, such as teaching a skill or offering immediate opportunity. He calls it a bridge or temporary job because it's flawed. A stepping-stone job is one of possibly several jobs en route to the perfect job, he says. Zey's entire book is about the quest for the perfect job. Like so many career writers, he dangles the perfect job in front of job seekers. It's like a delicious lollipop off in the distance. But like a desert mirage, it's an illusion.

Think of every job as a stepping-stone job. Certainly, we take jobs for different reasons. For example, a company has a great reputation; it is well known as a launching pad for budding superstars; its products are household names; its acquisition tactics are legendary, etc.

Don't put time limits on jobs. "I'll get what I need and move on in two years." You never know how things will work out. A so-called stepping-stone job may be the best job you ever had. One day you might say, "I can't believe I love this place. They said it was a jungle that burns engineers out in two years." Five years later, you've moved up four notches and have no intention of leaving.

Play it loose and find out for yourself. Jobs, like people, are unpredictable. There is no telling how things will work out. You could shock yourself and wind up staying at a stepping-stone job for the rest of your career. Avoid preconceived notions. Do your homework and have a plan, yet be open-minded and ready to abort if things should work out unexpectedly.

Let's take a look at eight components of a great job.

Eight Components of a Great Job

1. Company Is High-Profile, an Industry Leader.   If the company has a great name and reputation, by association you have immediate recognition by merely working there. It's analogous to going to a high-profile college such as Harvard, Yale, Radcliffe, Wellsley and the like. It doesn't matter whether you graduated with an A or C average, the fact that you graduated is worth immediate points. The same goes for working for well-known companies respected as industry leaders. In the computer industry, for instance, companies like IBM, Apple, Microsoft, Digital Equipment Corporation and Sun Microsystems, to name a few, command immediate respect. It doesn't necessarily have to be a large company either. Many smaller players have incredible reputations as well. If it's respected as an innovator, you profit as well.

2. Excellent People.   Combine a high-profile company with the opportunity to work with talented people and you have a chance to learn and contribute to a stimulating environment.

Put five brilliant people together on a project and the results could be spectacular. It's like being part of an Olympic team or playing with gifted musicians in a world-renowned symphony orchestra. Creativity is contagious when you're working with the best. But it could also be a ferociously competitive environment with in-fighting, a place where powerful egos fight for dominance. Either way, it's the place to be, an experience not to be missed. Not only will it be an incredible learning experience; it's something you can market for the rest of your career.

3. Training Opportunities.   Training, whether on or off the job, amounts to a powerful incentive for taking a job. The American Society of Training and Development's executive vice president Curtis Plott insists training is more critical than capital resources. A company's survival depends upon it. Not too long ago, only large companies invested heavily in training programs. Small to mid-size companies either didn't bother or made half-hearted attempts to update their workers' skills. Facing rampant competition, now they're singing a different tune. More than an altruistic move, training is a critical survival tactic.

Many small companies throughout the United States are investing heavily in training. Shepard Poorman Communication Corporation in Indianapolis, for example, a commercial printer, invests over $200,000 a year in structured training programs that teach its 400-person work force new technology. President Bob Shepard says technology is changing so fast, he has no choice but to train and retrain just to stay alive.

Then there are maverick entrepreneurs such as Mike Muth, who is so committed to the idea of an educated work force that he pays for full-time employees' continuing education classes in almost any subject they want—glassblowing to remedial math. Muth heads K. W. Muth Company, Inc., an automobile-parts manufacturer in Sheboygan, Wisconsin. But Muth seldom uses the word *training*. *Education*, he says, is a better word because it is the essence of training. He vehemently believes the only way to create the ideal workplace is through education. And it doesn't matter what you study: It is the incentive to learn that broadens workers' horizons. The results are improved communication and decision-making skills. Before long you have motivated and confident workers with high self-esteem.

Muth puts his money where his mouth is. His employees are reimbursed for up to $1,000 for tuition and books per semester, as long as they earn at least a "C" in the course. They can take courses at the company training facility or at a nearby college.

Oddly, Muth isn't upset when workers who have taken advantage of his free tuition plan quit for better jobs. He feels good knowing he's enriched their lives by giving them the knowledge and incentive to further their careers. Because of his pro-worker philosophy, Muth is somewhat of a local hero with a waiting list of applicants anxious to work for him. They consider K. W. Muth Company a springboard to a better life. Muth is unusual, yet he's not alone. He's part of a growing army of idealistic employers who go out of their way to give workers excellent training and educational opportunities.

It makes sense taking a job for its training opportunities. Some companies offer sophisticated in-house facilities; others provide training at a nearby training facility or university. Companies either pay for or reimburse workers for education or training courses. Many companies actually pay, in part or full, for a bachelor's, master's or even a doctoral degree. You'll have to commit to a couple of years with the company—nobody is giving anything away—but it's clearly worth it.

Translate that training or education into dollars and you have an irrefutable reason to stick around to learn as much as you can.

4. Good Pay and Benefits. We've already explored this subject in great detail in Myth 11. As we said, salary isn't the whole picture, but it is certainly important, especially if you're burdened with debt. If you're overwhelmed with student loans, don't think twice about taking a high-paying interim job just to get out of deep water. Combine that with an excellent benefits programs paying 80 to 100 percent of your medical expenses and the chance to get a master's degree on the company (mentioned above) and you're out of your mind not taking advantage of it. When you add up all the extras, you may be shocked to discover they almost equal your salary.

5. Enlightened Management. Every company thinks it has an incredible management team, especially companies run by new-breed entrepreneurs in their 30s and 40s. Autocratic, tyrannical management styles were out by the late '60s, and by the mid-1980s, enlightened and altruistic theories were the rage. There are a slew of them, yet they're all about creating the perfect workspace where management and workers coexist in happy union.

Many companies worked hard to build new images for themselves by radically improving the way they manage workers. Instead of aristocratic hierarchies of officers and enlisted people with dozens of gradations in between, they tried to join the traditionally antagonistic forces to build democratic organizations that work for a common good. The battle cry was "We're in this war together. So let's find out how we can help each other."

That's the essence of hundreds, maybe thousands, of management books published during the '80s. There were dozens of theories from esteemed management consultants, each one purporting to hold the secrets of brilliant management. Psychologist Charles Garfield invested years studying successful businesspeople. He wrote several books, one of the most popular being *Peak Performers, the New Heroes of American Business.* From studying the men who participated in the Apollo 11, the first space mission to put a person on the moon, he uncovered common attributes shared by peak performers. Garfield's insights and conclusions were translated to managers across the globe. Since peak performance characteristics can be isolated and understood, managers can encourage those talents in their workers. Garfield discovered that all of us have peak performance characteristics. The idea is to create the right environment so they flourish.

Garfield and other scholarly management experts devoted their lives to telling U.S. managers how to make better use of their most productive natural resource—people. The result is that management and workers have joined together in a loose partnership with unwritten rules. They're participating, communicating, and forever redefining their relationship. They're talking about shared missions and goals through team-building, self-management and empowerment, to name a few.

The conclusions of all this canned rhetoric are obvious. It's just smart business for management to perk up its ears and listen to what workers have to say. Even the lowly person staffing the lobster shift on a Detroit automotive assembly line may have a brilliant idea that could mean millions, even billions, for a company. After all, innovation exists everywhere, and it often has nothing to do with someone's education or training.

Enlightened management that recognizes, supports and encourages workers can elevate a job to a 24-hour high. In *Think Twice before You Accept That Job,* Richard J. Thain advises job seekers to find an organization that both needs and values their skills or talents. It may take a while, but it's worth the effort.

For example, computer professionals from all corners of the planet would practically sell their souls to work for Microsoft. Recognized as a living legend, Bill Gates revolutionized the computer industry. We're only years away from Gates's vision of a PC in every home. It's no wonder Microsoft receives thousands of résumés each month from programmers and systems engineers who share the same passions of its founder.

Gates has joined the U.S. elite billionaire club, yet money has never distracted him from creating more breakthrough products. In fact, as the market becomes increasingly competitive, Gates is more determined than ever to hold on to his title as one of the personal computer's foremost architects. Yet with all his money and power, he's still the reclusive computer nerd who eats pizza, drinks Coca-Cola at his desk and puts in 15-hour days.

Microsoft's programmers work as hard as their boss because they share Gates's vision. For a computer professional, working at Microsoft is as close to heaven as you can get. Knowing that creativity is rewarded, Microsoft's offices never shut down. Twenty-four hours a day, seven days a week, you'll find programmers hunched over terminals. Many of the tee-shirted, bearded techies in torn jeans and dirty sneakers who have been with Gates from the beginning are multimillionaires in their own right.

Like Microsoft, dozens of other companies give workers the breathing space to do their own thing. That spells a high-powered—but not perfect—job.

Great management encourages creativity. It recognizes talent and is willing to go to bat for you. In large organizations especially, supportive management ranks high as a reason that fast-trackers stick around. If workers can get things done without being frustrated by bureaucracy, red tape and organizational politics, why leave?

6. Hooking Up with a Mentor. A subheading of supportive management is the possibility of establishing a mentor relationship with a corporate veteran at the supervisory or management level. Like networking, the word *mentoring*, the concept of taking a younger protégé under your wing to show him or her the ropes, has been around a long time. The origin of the word *mentor* can be traced to Homer's epic poem, *The Odyssey*, recounting the long wanderings of its hero Odysseus. Mentor was a friend of Odysseus entrusted with the education of Odysseus' son Telemachus. Thus, mentor has come to mean tutor, coach and counselor.

Mentor relationships can be formed anywhere—in families, at school and athletic teams, to name three. They've always existed in companies on an informal basis. The new twist is that over the past decade, many companies have instituted formal mentor programs and, on a lesser scale, have encouraged informal mentor relationships. Michael Zey, for example, explored the mentoring process in great detail in his books *The Mentor Connection* and *The Right Move*. In the latter, he says companies such as Merrill Lynch, AT&T and many others have created programs whereby new recruits are linked to senior managers who act as their mentors. Some of these relationships are loose and informal; others have rules concerning where and how mentors and protégés meet and interact.

Zey points out that mentoring has its good and bad parts. On the plus side, protégés gain both a coach and inside source. They learn to master their jobs alone and tap into the inner workings of the company. They also learn how the grapevine and political structure works and how decisions are made. Put it all together, they learn how to do the tricky corporate hustle.

Another plus is that the mentor-protégé relationship can be a career-long association. As the mentor moves up, so does the protégé. Or, when the mentor takes a bigger job in another organization, she or he takes the protégé along. They become a team.

The mentor-protégé relationship often means the difference between organizational success or failure. However, the downside is that the protégé's organizational strength is often uncomfortably tied to the mentor. This can be a blessing if the mentor is powerful and well-connected. If the mentor is on a fast track headed right for the top, the protégé will be right alongside. But if the mentor is disliked, or on the outs with the power elite or on a lower rung of the management ladder, the relationship could ultimately do more harm than good. The protégé masters organizational survival tactics, but his or her chances of advancement may be limited. You could be an organizational jewel, but your association with your mentor could obliterate any chance of going very far. The age-old clichés "you're judged by the company you keep" and "guilt by association" can present insurmountable roadblocks.

If you form any type of mentor relationship, formal or informal, stay alert. Build your own contacts and view the corporate world through your own eyes. Don't be totally dependent on your mentor. If you enjoy your job and find that your mentor is out of favor or about to be given the boot, find a way to gently sever the relationship so you can fend for yourself. It's a tricky process involving building new alliances, hopefully in high places.

7. Excellent Promotional Opportunities and Regular Performance Appraisals. Typically, large and mid-size companies with human resource departments have clearly defined promotion programs based upon yearly performance appraisals. Most small companies don't have formal performance appraisal programs. Promotions are based upon merit or need.

It doesn't matter what the system is as long as it's committed to recognizing and promoting talent rather than letting employees languish.

In many small family-run companies, for example, promotional possibilities are severely limited because of nepotism. Regardless of ability, family members get the best jobs, and, no matter how capable you are, you'll never capture a job at the top. This is an excellent reason to bail out when a better opportunity presents itself. More on this important issue in the next chapter, Myth 13: "Big Companies Offer Better Advancement Opportunities and Greater Job Security."

8. Compatible Corporate Culture.   Like the people who work for them, companies have personalities. Some are like slow, languishing turtles; others, high-performing race cars. Some companies espouse traditional, conservative values; others are freewheeling and radical. A company's philosophy and mission determine its culture.

If possible, try and find a company which has a philosophy similar to yours. Often, but not always, enlightened management (discussed above) and compatible corporate culture go hand in hand. In *Think Twice before You Accept That Job,* Richard Thain advises job seekers to match their personal style to the organization they hope to join.

If you're an informal person who rebels against mindless rules, you won't be happy working for IBM or a large bank where conservative suits and adherence to strict corporate dogma are mandatory. You'll need a company that considers dress codes silly and unnecessary. As we said earlier, most Silicon Valley computer companies deem dress codes a waste of time, even a hindrance. Some of these progressive companies wouldn't care if programmers worked in their bathing suits. The idea is to get the work done.

Many progressive companies feel the same way about how and where work is performed. Hence, the advent of flex-place and flex-time arrangements. Like dress, it often doesn't matter where or when work is performed, as long as it's done on schedule. If it takes you four hours, rather than seven to do the job, why should you stick around till 5 p.m.? Similarly, if you can do the same high-quality work at home, why not?

However, many traditional companies have militaristic cultures with strict adherence to rules, regulations and bureaucratic lines of authority. Senior management is off-limits to the rank-and-file. If you want an audience with a senior executive, it's protocol to make an appointment. Casually stopping by is considered bad taste. When in Rome, would you just pop in unannounced for a quick audience with the Pope? No wonder rank-and-file workers at *Fortune* 500 companies wouldn't know their CEO if they bumped into her or him in a crowded airport.

Other companies pride themselves on open-door policies. Their philosophy is everyone ought to be accessible, even the top honcho. Not only are the CEO and top management accessible, they're visible as well, routinely strolling company corridors and schmoozing with everyone from secretaries to the tattooed bruisers working the loading dock.

Rus Solomon, president and founder of Tower Records, the growing international chain of record stores, is a good example. Solomon seldom closes his office door; anyone can amble into his office to discuss work or even personal problems. The powerful figure of Solomon, who looks like a cross between an aging hippie and Santa Claus, symbolizes Tower's laid-back corporate culture. The white-bearded maverick wouldn't ask an underling to do anything he wouldn't do himself.

As for a dress code at Tower, Solomon doesn't know what the term means. His usual attire is jeans, short-sleeve shirts and tennis sneakers. Tower employees swear their boss doesn't own a suit or tie.

Finally, some companies' cultures are strongly influenced by religious and moral tenets. A company cannot show religious bias in hiring, yet companies like Chick-fil-A, Inc., ranked as the third largest fast-food chicken company in the United States, openly supports religious doctrines. Self-made man Truitt Cathy, Chick-fil-A's founder, is a God-fearing, churchgoing person who actually built his life around biblical principles. A man of his word, Cathy insists that all his chains close on Sunday in respect for the Christian Sabbath—despite the fact that it is one of the busiest days of the week.

Don't get the wrong idea. Cathy is no Bible-toting evangelist hell-bent on converting the world to Christianity. He's the first to say he respects people's differences. Yet, he insists upon running his business according to ethical and moral principles. And, as he always says, you're not going to find those rules in any business plan but rather in the Good Book itself, the Holy Bible. The message for job seekers couldn't be clearer. If you don't hold up to Cathy's religious ideals or are a vocal atheist or militant Shiite Muslim, you'd be smart looking for a company that has no religious bias.

There is something to be said for corporate culture. Yes, you can do your job anywhere. But don't think for a moment a company's vibes and philosophy can't get in your way. They are the heart of corporate culture, its very pulse.

We've covered the pluses of a great job. But there are also some compelling negatives that could teach you a lot.

High-Wattage Negatives That Might Be
Turned Around

1. High-Pressure Environment.   Some companies are like pressure cookers or time bombs waiting to go off. There are constant deadlines and high-strung bosses breathing down your neck waiting for you to get the work done. Each day amounts to a test of your ability to withstand what feels like lethal doses of stress.

It sounds horrible, but the experience can be priceless. Hang in there more than a year and you can last anywhere. You've gained a priceless survival skill, adaptability, making you more marketable. "Wow, I can't believe you lasted 14 months at Killer Bongos. Most people don't last 6 months. How did you do it?"

2. Revolving Doors and Political Instability.   Some companies are political hotbeds with new senior management taking the helm every couple of years. No sooner is a CEO given the boot than a new management team marches in.

Sounds like another bad deal. But consider the B-side of this scratchy record. Look what you can learn from being there. It's like watching a streetfight firsthand. You witness the intrigue and get to hang out with the players; the trick is keeping your nose clean and staying neutral. No small feat. It amounts to quite an exciting education. If you have a sense of adventure and a strong stomach, you might say to yourself: "Wouldn't it be incredible to break a record and wind up staying a few years?"

The experience will pay off when you command immediate respect with a prospective employer. "After spending three years at Conquest Panels this person has to have the tact and political savvy of a ranking diplomat."

3. Financial Chaos.   Finally, there is the company in serious financial trouble. It could be on the verge of bankruptcy, in bankruptcy or about to be sold, merged or closed for good.

The reasons for working for a company in financial deep water are similar to the ones mentioned above. It too could be a priceless real-life lesson. You read about companies going under every day, but experiencing it is another matter. Firsthand, you witness people working under numbing daily tension and uncertainty. Each evening, they leave anxious about whether their checks will clear on payday and whether they'll have a job when they return in the morning.

With heightening tensions, each day people bail out for better jobs.

Many don't even care what kind of jobs they get as long as it's more certain than the one they left. They fail to see the virtues of staying.

It's smart to be a level-headed cynic. But there is an excellent chance the company will turn itself around. The second that happens, you assume a new identity. You become a survivor. Management, new or old, sees you in a new light. Unlike the disloyal workers who jumped ship, you had the guts and pride in your company to stick it out so you could try to salvage the badly listing boat. Suddenly, the drums are rolling, the trumpets blaring and you're a local hero.

Nobody cares that you stuck around because you were simply curious or had no place else to go. The fact is *you're there.* Whatever your motives, you're in an excellent position to move up to bigger and better jobs.

And even if the company perishes, you're still ahead because you can market that experience. Prospective employers will view you as reliable and ethical, someone who can be counted on when the going gets rough.

In short, the above situations teach critical skills, scoring priceless negotiating points when you're hondling over salaries.

Promises! Promises!—Listen to Your Gut

Okay, those are the components of a great job. Before we move on to Myth 13, a few final thoughts about jobs and people. Hopefully, the more jobs you hold, the smarter you get, making you better able to separate facts from double-talk and hype.

If it sounds too good to be true, it probably is. It's a variation on the old, "Your check is in the mail" scam. Beware of glib promises from tin men like employers who promise you the world.

Let your gut guide you. If the situation feels like it's not going to work out, chances are it won't. You can't expect guarantees, but you can demand honesty. Ethical employers outline the facts, no matter how harrowing. If the company is on the verge of disaster, for example, they will graphically outline the risks. If they don't do it, it's up to you to ask pointed questions. How else will you make a decision?

Summing up, a combination of factors make for a great job. Simply put, it is a balance of good and bad. It can be both stressful and relaxing. It's up to you to find the balance that lets you sleep nights.

We're all different. Some of us have high stress tolerance, others can take only limited doses, and still others crumble under excruciating pressure. There is no right or wrong. It's only a matter of temperament.

We don't all want the same things either. A great job may be an entree to the fast track, leading to the executive suite. Down the road it means money and power and Rolls-Royces, Lear jets and yachts. Or it might be something more modest. Maybe an unstressful job that pays you a decent salary and that gets you home at 6:30 p.m. so you can have dinner with the family and play with your kids before bedtime. The entire world doesn't appeal to you, just a tiny secure piece of it giving you the freedom and security to live moderately well. It's up to you.

Thankfully, we all don't share the same drives, motivations and aspirations. Self-knowledge is priceless.

When to Move On

You'll know when it's time to move on down that long lonesome highway in search of greener pastures. The signposts are easy to read.

More important than the obvious ones—hard to get up in the morning, boredom and apathy—when the adrenaline high that energized and fired you for several hours at a time disappears, it's time to look elsewhere. More on moving on in the Epilogue.

Myth 13: Big Companies Offer Better Advancement Opportunities and Greater Job Security.

Reality: *Small companies offer the best action. Welcome to the entrepreneurial age.*

Chapter Snapshot

- Economists Warned Us
- A 40-Year Aberration
- What the Heck Is a Small Company?
- Rapid Growth Forecasted for Small Companies
- Women Are Starting More Businesses Than Men
- Industries Offering Best Career Options
- The Fastest-Growing Small Business–Dominated Industries, 1990–2005
- Pros and Cons of Working for a Small Company
- Take Your Pick—There Are Plenty of Small Companies to Choose From
- Big Companies Are Starting to Think Small

❊ ❊ ❊ ❊ ❊ ❊ ❊ ❊

Working for a big corporation used to be an impressive status symbol. You were a big deal if you conquered a job at a *Fortune* 500 company. You found a place to hang out for your entire career. If you worked hard, there was no telling how far you could go. You stood a chance of sprinting up the corporate ladder to a management job or maybe being transferred to an exciting location. With plenty of time off, bonuses, benefits packages and pensions, you had it made. Once you built some seniority, you stood an excellent chance of getting your kids jobs at the company.

For many, working for a big company was more than a job, it was a lifestyle. It was like signing up with the military. Instead of Uncle Sam meeting your every need, your organizational mommy was a sprawling legal entity called a corporation.

If the company was a town's major or only employer, life revolved around the company. Parents took real delight in letting their kids know the company was going to take care of them. It was a comfortable feeling knowing a powerful company, whose tentacles extended around the globe, would always provide for them—or so they thought. When the kids finished high school or college, they knew there was a job waiting with their name on it. They would shop at the same supermarkets their coworkers frequented, attend the same churches, bowl together on Wednesday night and eventually marry other workers. And when they died, they'd wind up in the local cemetery where generations of company workers were buried.

Like owning a house with a garden and raising two healthy kids, working for a household-name company was part of the American dream. It was worth waiting for. If you were offered similar jobs with both a small and large company, you were a fool if you went with the small one. And if you had any intention of building a career with a small company, smart thinking dictated you get some big company experience first and take advantage of its impressive training options before taking a job with a small company.

In the past, you weren't wrong if you thought big companies offered better career opportunities and were more stable than small ones. Now it's myth. The tables have turned. Small is in, big is out. Small companies, once considered runners-up and second choices, are the job seekers' best hope.

Economists Warned Us

And it's not like we weren't warned. Economists saw it coming years before U.S. corporations decided they had to go on a permanent diet to shed unnecessary fat or perish. These economists predicted a radical shake-up, yet few heeded their warning. It started in the late '70s when steel mills pared staffs and eventually closed down all over the country. The railroads followed suit.

In 1979, approximately 21 million people worked in manufacturing in the United States; by 1992 that number dropped to a little over 18 million people. Pacific Rim countries were flooding the market with comparable but cheaper exports. The United States was losing its grip. The solution was simple: U.S. companies had to retrench. The big old bastions of U.S. industry were no match for tighter, fitter and more advanced foreign competitors. Line up all the nasty variables: the soaring cost of advanced technology, rampant corporate takeovers plus outdated inefficient management, and it was batten down the hatches, lighten the load or sink.

A 40-Year Aberration

Big Blue—How Could You Be So Cruel?

The big company as safe harbor was nothing more than a 40-year blip, according to the late Dan Lacey, editor and publisher of the bimonthly management newsletter *Workplace Trends* in Rocky River, Ohio, and author of *The Paycheck Disruption.* Lacey says long-term security working for large *Fortune* 500 companies was a post–World War II phenomenon, an aberration, as he calls it. The concept of lifetime security is a statistical accident.

We will never return to that kind of a paternalistic worker-company relationship. As one economist described it, work has become a business relationship rather than a de facto social program. That's the way it ought to be.

In the '60s and '70s, 22 percent of the population was employed by *Fortune* 500 companies. Lacey points out that in the period from 1989 to 1992, one in every 100 people in the U.S. work force has been directly hit by a corporate staff cut.

Within a 60-day period in 1992, for example, five major U.S. companies cut their payrolls significantly. Amoco Corporation, the nation's fifth-largest oil company, eliminated 8,500 jobs; Hughes Aircraft, 9,000; Alcoa, 2,100; Aetna, 4,800; Exxon U.S.A., 1,000; Chevron, 2,300; and Digital Equipment Corp, 4,000. But these are piddling cuts compared to IBM, once considered the perfect U.S. company. Between 1986 and 1993, IBM cut its work force from 407,000 to 275,000.

In *Horse Sense,* marketing gurus Al Ries and Jack Trout point out that *Fortune* 500 companies employ fewer than 12 million people, or 10 percent of the population. Your chances of working for one of these companies, say Ries and Trout, are only 1 in 10. Not great odds. By the year 2000, Lacey projects that employment in *Fortune* 500 companies will be cut in half to 8 million, down from 16 million in 1980.

The sick irony is that although companies have perfected machinelike procedures for firing people, these companies still are embarrassed by the word *firing.* It's like being uptight about explaining the facts of life to your kids. Babies are born every day, yet parents turn crimson when they attempt to explain the process.

The same goes for firing workers. We have a problem with the naked truth. So corporate bureaucrats skirt the issue by resorting to doublespeak. When Bank of America informed the press it was conducting a "release of resources," it wasn't talking about giving workers a surprise bonus. It was permanently canning 14,000 workers. Imagine using that phrase with your kids when they ask why you're still hanging around the house at 10 a.m. on a Monday morning. "Oh no, Larry, I wasn't fired. Nothing that extreme. I was just part of a resource release." Better yet, economists straightened everything out by calling job cutting "systemic efficiency." Feel better? William Lutz, a professor of English at Rutgers University and editor of the *Quarterly Review of Doublespeak,* unearthed still more terms for firing people. Try these: eliminate redundancies in the human resources area; enhance the efficiency of operations; take appropriate cost reduction actions; rationalization of marketing efforts; nonretained; and selected out. Finally, how about this mouthful? Volume-related production schedule adjustment.

Get beyond the icy jargon and you find many companies are embarrassed about permanent staff cuts because they lied to their workers. They promised them a permanent rose garden. Instead they got an uncertain stroll in a weed field.

As Michael Moore, director and writer of the 1992 documentary, *Roger and Me,* discovered on his obsessive search to interview former General Motors CEO Roger Smith after the company dumped 30,000 people from its Flint, Michigan, plant, profits are more important than people. The laid-back, yet powerful documentary was the film maker's quest to get GM's top official to explain why the company fired thousands of people. Cornering Smith was like trying to arrange a heart-to-heart with the Pope.

Smith avoided Moore like the plague. Even though doors were slammed in his face, and his calls went unanswered, Moore relentlessly stalked his prey. But to no avail. All Moore wanted were the answers to some simple questions. Uppermost, how the powerful leader felt about permanently altering people's lives, causing family disruption, not to mention sentencing thousands to the city's welfare system. Was Roger Smith upset about putting all those people out of work? Moore never found out.

Company Towns Become Ghost Towns

If the closing of the GM Flint, Michigan, plant wreaked havoc on the city's unemployment rate, imagine what plant closings did in small cities and towns throughout the United States.

Within the space of a decade, bustling one-company communities whose towering smokestacks belched fumes and black smoke that muddied the sky have become all but ghost towns. Thousands of once-healthy companies scattered about the United States have closed entire divisions, practically bankrupting these once-prosperous towns. Veteran employees whose lives revolved around the company are confronting a grueling reality: They must find new jobs and start over.

The big glamorous companies are still hiring, but they are doing so sparingly and differently. It's time to dump the old regime and replace it with fresh blood.

Change your thinking immediately. Let's debunk the myth that big companies offer better career opportunities than small ones. Rather than lifetime security, the best you can hope for is short-term employment. Big companies are no longer safer or better than small companies.

What the Heck Is a Small Company?

Economists and management experts have yet to agree on what *small* means. Most people think any company other than a *Fortune* 500 company is small. The U.S. Small Business Administration (SBA) defines a small company as any company with 100 or fewer employees. According to the Office of Economic Research (OER), a small company has fewer than 500 employees. William L. Haeberle, director of Indiana University's Center for Entrepreneurship and Innovation, says sales, not people, ought to be the barometer defining a company's size. A small company has sales of under $10 million, says Haeberle, compared to a mid-size company, which has sales under $100 million.

Rapid Growth Forecasted
for Small Companies

Currently, small businesses generate two-thirds of all new jobs in the United States as well as half the nation's economic output. Since 1980 *Fortune* 500 companies have slashed over 3.5 million jobs from payrolls. Approximately 28 percent of new hires are no longer with the company at the end of their first year of employment, according to the *Workforce 2000* report, published by the not-for-profit Hudson Institute in Indianapolis. However, small businesses generated 20 million new jobs during the same period.

The SBA reports that the small-company prognosis is excellent. In 1979, approximately 500,000 new companies were launched. Since then, that figure has jumped 40 percent and is accelerating. David Berch, president of an economics research firm, Cognetics, Inc., of Cambridge, Massachusetts, has identified 500,000 small and mid-sized companies that are hiring workers and growing at 20 percent a year. And according to a recent study by Chicago outplacement firm, Challenger, Gray & Christmas, more than 20 percent of all discharged managers want to become entrepreneurs.

Women Are Starting More Businesses Than Men

At the rate women are starting businesses, chances are good that you, and certainly your children, may work for a female-owned company. According to a 1990 study conducted by the Washington, D.C.–based National Foundation for Women Business Owners (NFWBO) and Cognetics, Inc., female-owned businesses employed close to 11 million people—90 percent as many as the *Fortune* 500 companies. Two years later, in 1992, the number of people employed by women-owned businesses surpassed those employed by the *Fortune* 500. NFWBO reports that approximately 9 percent of the women-owned businesses have annual sales over $1 million.

The study also found that approximately 30 percent of all businesses now are owned by women. In 1988, the House of Representatives' Committee on Small Business projected that by the year 2000, 50 percent of all businesses will be owned by women. And current SBA numbers conservatively project that 40 percent of all businesses will be women-owned by that year. Take your pick. I lean toward 50 percent and higher.

Many management experts contend there are advantages to working for a woman-owned company. NFWBO's executive director Sharon Hadary insists women-owned businesses are more stable because they tend to grow more slowly and cautiously. Hadary says women are less impetuous than men, bringing a holistic approach to management. Rather than seeing issues in one-dimensional terms, they're concerned with a whole galaxy of demands made on people. They're more adept and sensitive to building relationships and creating flexible, alternative working schedules.

Industries Offering Best Career Options

According to Office of Economic Research statistics, the best job prospects in small firms can be found in the following areas:

- Strong growth is forecasted for health and business services.

- Industries related to the aging population will grow the fastest. There will be an estimated 1.3 million new jobs in doctors' offices and 762,000 new opportunities in nursing and personal care facilities—both of which are small business–dominated industries.

- Jobs in small environmental firms will grow 3.3 percent annually until 2005, while opportunities in legal and other business service organizations will add another 600,000 new jobs.

- In the education field, libraries of private vocational schools and private elementary and secondary schools are expected to add over 350,000 new jobs.

The Fastest-Growing Small Business–Dominated Industries, 1990–2005

The following chart from the U.S. Department of Labor lists the fastest-growing small business industries through the year 2005.

Industry	Employment (thousands)	
	1990	2005
Residential care	469	911
Health services	697	1,262
Water and sanitation	184	299
Libraries, vocational and other schools	207	335
Offices of health practitioners	2,180	3,470
Passenger transportation arrangements	192	299
Individual and miscellaneous social services	638	991
Legal services	919	1,427
Nursing and personal care facilities	1,420	2,182
Miscellaneous equipment rental and leasing	211	324
Elementary and secondary schools	457	689
Business services	937	1,397
Photocopying, commercial art, photofinishing	200	293
Total	8,711	13,879

Pros and Cons of Working for a Small Company

Weighing Long-Term Opportunity against Short-Term Risk

The small-company outlook is excellent. The big decision is do you want to work for one? Beyond the obvious differences in size, people and profits, dramatic differences exist between small and large companies. What may be an advantage or opportunity to you may be a drawback to someone else.

Career Paths or Market Niches—Efficiency and Quantity versus Quality and Service

Ralph Kilmann, director of the University of Pittsburgh Katz Graduate School of Business program in corporate culture, says big functional organizations are designed to efficiently make products in quantity, whereas small companies are focused on market niches, effectiveness and quality.

Philosophically, large and small corporations have different attitudes, according to Cognetics's Berch. Large firms are concerned with career paths, bureaucracy and politics. In large companies, the whole focus is on the company; in small ones, focus is on the marketplace.

Many large companies have lost touch with the market. Successful small ones anguish over staying in touch.

The Thrill of Being on the Firing Line

Whether you're working for a small company employing 3 or 300 people, there will never be any doubt about your purpose. If you're a technical, administrative or sales employee, you can count on being close to the action. You'll be constantly reminded that the battlefield—the marketplace—is just outside. It's the quest for markets, the race to be better than your competition, that keeps workers motivated, say successful small company heads.

Small- versus Big-Company Politics

At the same time, small companies aren't perfect either. No organization is. Like large companies, you'll encounter office politics, albeit on a smaller scale.

The big difference is that small-company politics seldom slow down the organization. Because of their very size, large companies breed power pockets and fiefdoms which clog communication lines, stalling the business machine. The bigger a company gets, the more bureaucratic and political it becomes. The result is that lines of authority are unclear and decision making can be a hair-pulling process taking 10 times as long as it should.

Built for Speed, Faster and Nimbler

Successful small companies are lean, tightly managed and rooted to market realities. Small-company owners justifiably brag about how quickly and efficiently they can get things done. A snap decision by the owner can put the wheels in motion, sidestepping memos, meetings and decisions by consensus. Small companies can achieve the same results as a large company in less than half the time, spending significantly less money in the process.

Food giant Nabisco spends between $15 and $20 million to launch a single product and takes up to five years to get it on supermarket shelves, according to Richard Worth, president of R. W. Frookies, a New York cookie company. Worth boasts he can do it in as little as 5 to 6 months. If it weren't for printing and packaging delays, he could cut it to 2½ months.

Things get done faster in small companies because the business machines are built for speed. Comparing a small organization to a large company is like comparing a destroyer to an aircraft carrier. Both will reach the same destination; the difference is that the destroyer gets there faster.

No Dead Weight—Prima Donnas Stay Home!

Every person counts at a small company. There is no dead weight. If you can't do what you're hired to do and a lot more, you're useless.

Worth points out there are countless advantages to having a small staff of dedicated workers. Unlike large corporations where you can crawl into a cubicle for months on end, invisibility is impossible in small companies. Everyone's accountable.

It can take months to get to the bottom of a foul-up in a large company; in a small one, doing so only takes minutes. Depending upon your personality and career ambitions, this could be a blessing or a curse. If you're looking for an opportunity to shine and strut your stuff, getting your feet wet at a small company could be the opportunity of a lifetime.

They say everyone is expendable. This is true in large companies, but not in small ones. Big companies hire specialists, people who do one thing well. Small companies prefer to hire smart generalists who are jacks-of-many-trades and masters of all. You can always find another engineer, programmer or purchasing agent, but try and replace someone who fills all three slots. Today, valued workers have multiple skills.

Entrepreneurs heading tiny start-up companies, for example, pride themselves on hiring workers like themselves: renaissance people capable of wearing several hats. (More on working for entrepreneurs later.)

Unlike the one-function job of the archetypal large corporation, small companies expect you to roll up your sleeves and do whatever is called for to keep the ship afloat. That spells extraordinary opportunity if you're willing to sweat and put in long hours.

Once you prove your value in a small company, you're not so easily replaced. Small-company owners losing valuable workers can be likened to an assembly line failure. The operating machinery has been disturbed, and it could be months before a suitable replacement is found.

Rapid Advancement

Once you prove your value, the average small company can practically guarantee rapid advancement. Unless you're a fast-track political strategist like Lee Iacocca, advancement in large companies is slow. In small ones, superstars can literally leap into management slots.

In *Horse Sense,* Ries and Trout point out that in large companies you're promoted to better jobs. The promotion system, like all corporate processes, is weighted down in politics and bureaucracy. It means waiting your turn in line.

Superstars working for large corporations report frustration when advancement is stalled because they don't meet seniority or promotion requirements. They're often told they can't be promoted because they haven't been with the company long enough or scored high enough points on performance appraisals or because it breaks precedent.

But in small companies, you can actually work your way to the top, enjoying rapid promotions and pay raises. It's not because small company owners are being altruistic. It's just smart business. If you're a hotshot, they're going to do everything in their power to keep you. The faster you learn and the more you do, the more valuable you are. Your victory is a shared one. Everyone wins.

Learning How the Whole Machine Works

Finally, when working for a small company you learn how the whole machine works, not just one part of it. You rapidly learn an industry as well. New workers talk about the thrill of learning how everything fits together. More than mastering a job, workers learn what makes a business tick. Working in a small company amounts to a well-rounded education, especially if you're not sure what business niche you want to settle into.

Take Your Pick—There Are Plenty of Small Companies to Choose From

Working for Entrepreneurs—Gods, Dictators or Benevolent Despots

If you've got a sense of adventure, consider working for entrepreneurs, the gutsy folks launching companies throughout the country. If you live through the experience, you could have a brilliant career.

Most people think any company head is an entrepreneur. Technically, the entrepreneur is the person who launched the company. Henry Ford, Andrew Carnegie, Alfred E. Dupont, Thomas Watson, Steve Jobs, Bill Gates, William Sonoma, Al Copeland (Popeye's), Frank Purdue (Purdue Farms), Arland Sanders (Kentucky Fried Chicken), Sam Walton (Walmart's), to name a few, are true entrepreneurs. They started and built their companies.

Studies have been done on the entrepreneurial personality. Entrepreneurs have been described as fanatical, intelligent, creative and obsessive, with a driving passion to succeed and build something of their own. As managers, they rule as saviors, dictators or benevolent despots.

Regardless of industry, they're mavericks with the confidence and belief in themselves to absorb criticism and hurdle barriers to build their businesses. Tough, enterprising entrepreneurs have created entire industries.

In making their dreams happen, entrepreneurs can be compulsive, driven and controlling. Some can be megalomaniacal in their fear of relinquishing authority. This trait has led many to their downfall.

Working for an entrepreneur can be a brutal survival course or an opportunity of a lifetime. Measure up and you've got a permanent home. Positive or negative, it's a priceless training ground for anyone who wants to learn the ABCs of starting a company. Working for an entrepreneur amounts to an education no MBA program can offer. You're in the jungle; it's survive or perish.

Entrepreneurs are packaged myriad ways. Although some are easier to work with, the pride in ownership and the awesome mission of taking the infant company to adulthood is the obsessive goal all entrepreneurs share. Employees who buy into the entrepreneur's mission are the most successful. These hard-working chosen few become the inner circle, the trusted elite with whom the entrepreneur shares responsibility.

Behind most successful entrepreneurs are a couple of people who faithfully stood by them since the beginning. They're colleagues as well as friends. Their dedication, loyalty and friendship are usually rewarded with a piece of the action, an ownership position and a leadership role.

The allegiance of these loyal friends often borders on blind faith in the entrepreneur's abilities. They put their lives in the entrepreneur's hands, making the leader's mission their own.

Whether it's blind trust or a healthy respect for the entrepreneur's abilities, the relationship of entrepreneurs to their captains can be complex. In many small successful companies run by high-powered entrepreneurs, the organization becomes a personality cult dominated by the owners. The closest in command emerge as clones, displaying the same mannerisms and personality characteristics. The company resembles a tightly knit clique, very much like a fraternity or sorority. At its worst, it's a homogeneous community whose members' work and social lives revolve around each other.

The numbing awakening is when the company is either mismanaged or overtaken by competition and forced to pare staff and eventually fold. Loyal staffers find themselves suddenly lost without an individual identity and forced to strike off on their own. Yet, when the company thrives—and victories are shared by entrepreneurs and their tight inner circle—resilient, lifelong relationships are built.

Many entrepreneurs are cut off from the world, lonely recluses committed to putting their companies on the map. No one knows this better than trusted employees. These are the people reporters seek out to find out what makes them tick. These trusted employees are best able to describe their bosses' personality, inner strivings and conflicts and what it's like working closely with them. The employees are qualified to praise, criticize and analyze their bosses and draw compelling accounts of the hardships and frustrations of getting the company off the ground. Eventually, many go on to bigger jobs at other companies or launch companies of their own.

Working for an entrepreneur can prove to be both a memorable and priceless experience as well as a refreshing course in human psychology. Prove yourself indispensable by working your way into a valuable position and you could be set for life.

Beyond money and security, count on good times as well. Sharing and participating in the entrepreneur's successes and failures makes for an exciting career. If you've got the right stuff, it ain't a bad lifestyle.

Entrepreneurs are the mavericks who run the following three categories of companies.

Start-Up Company

According to SBA statistics, most companies fail within three to five years of launching. The first three years are the most traumatic. Like a premature baby's first few months of life, a business must be nurtured and cared for or it will cease.

Working for a start-up company is a gamble. You're in the entrepreneur's hands. If you can tolerate high-wattage risk, it's a valuable learning experience, whether the company succeeds or fails. If it fails, you have marketable knowledge. You were one of the jack-of-all-trades people who carted refuse, swept floors, answered phones, kept the books and sold product. Your diversity carries a high price tag.

If the company prospers, you face an exciting future. You were part of the original team, maybe the third or fifth person hired. Ten years later, that number holds great meaning to the entrepreneur. You were one of the people who helped design and promote the product, put the distribution machinery in place and hired staff. Unselfishly, you gave your time and energy with only the promise of future rewards. You worked alongside your boss till 9 or 10 p.m., and Saturdays as well. Like the entrepreneur, you also took a gamble. Most often, that devotion and loyalty are rewarded.

Consider the risk-reward ratio of working for a start-up company. Initially, salaries will be rock bottom and benefits negligible. Every day tests new survival skills for both owner and staff. Yet, if the company makes it, you have virtually unlimited career options you won't find in large companies.

Established Company

Beyond the life-and-death phase, the established company has a track record. It has survived. Whether it's 5 or 100 years old, the company has achieved a certain amount of stability. Working for one doesn't mean you found a permanent home either. It's just more secure than a start-up company. Like any company, its future rests on a handful of variables; uppermost is the skill of the management team running it.

The good part about working for established companies is that procedures and systems are already in place. In many of them, low-key bureaucracy actually enhances performance and seldom gets in the way. One thing is certain: Like start-ups, they're all about growing aggressively, rewarding talent and promoting from within.

Family-Run Company

Family-run companies come in all shapes and sizes. Some are run as efficiently as *Fortune* 500 companies, others are hotbeds of unrest and dissension and are coming apart at the seams.

The problem with thousands of these companies is intrigue; politics and jealousies among family members get in the way, often causing the breakup of the business, even the family. Money and family don't always mix. Depending on the quality of family relationships, working in the company can be either an opportunity or a war zone for outsiders.

The important questions for job seekers are: How healthy is the company and what kind of career prospects does it offer? Secure, highly profitable family-run companies suggest that solid, proven systems are in place and that family members are working cooperatively and productively with each other. Yet profitability alone doesn't mean strong career potential. If it's a relatively small company, 10 to 20 employees, for example, and half of them are family members, you'd be wise concluding that promotional opportunities are limited. No matter how talented and aggressive you are, the power jobs will go to family members. The unspoken commandment is "family comes first."

But if it's a large sprawling corporation like Quill Corporation in Lincolnshire, Illinois, you have nothing to worry about. Quill, the largest independent distributor of office products in the United States, founded by Jack Miller in 1956, is practically a textbook example of the well-run family company.

Employing over 1,000 people, Quill is efficiently run by Jack and brothers Harvey and Arnold. Each one does what he does best, and they don't get in each other's way. Jack oversees marketing and sales; Harvey is the operations person, running the company on a daily basis; and Arnold, a CPA, is the numbers person, keeping track of the finances. The Millers are unusual. They've managed to run a multimillion-dollar business and remain friends. That's no small accomplishment. Other family members are sprinkled throughout the organization; yet the company is large enough that outsiders have unlimited career potential. Family ties and loyalties are not a threat.

Not so in other family-run companies. Family differences can take a devastating toll, observes Leon A. Danco, president of The Center for Family Business in Cleveland, and author of *Beyond Survival*, often touted as the New Testament for family business owners.

Clouding career opportunities for outsiders is the problem of succession. Since many family businesses are like monarchies, the oldest sibling becomes president and succeeding siblings, children or spouses assume roles based on order of birth, says Danco. Ability is a secondary consideration. The oldest child may be a perpetual drunk and the youngest a mathematical wizard, but this doesn't change their positions in the company.

Keep this in mind when job hunting. As with start-up companies, know what you're getting into. Beyond shaky financials, family-run companies can be psychological mine fields. If you can tiptoe through the fields safely and get what you want, you've earned a career.

The best family-run companies are those that have tight internal controls and strategically plan for the future. They don't rely solely on family members but have the good sense to hire competent professionals capable of ensuring the company's future. You could be one of those professionals.

Big Companies Are Starting to Think Small

Ralph Kilmann points out that the giant dinosaurs of U.S. business are beginning to think small. AT&T, IBM and hundreds of other giant firms are carving their companies into smaller, more manageable, autonomous operating units. Big companies are starting to think small so they can get "lean and mean," as the management gurus say.

The past decade is dramatic proof that small, smartly managed firms are better able to cope with adversity. They can change direction according to market whims, getting products to market faster and cheaper than their bloated counterparts.

Keep your options open. Stay tuned to the marketplace and be a critical observer. The future holds exciting new options. Who's to say that a decade from now many of the inefficient giants of U.S. business won't be revamped and refitted with new management and systems, and be as eclectic, open-minded and efficient as the average small company?

One thing is certain, continued decentralization of big companies translates to greater career leverage. Rather than a central corporate office doing all the hiring, each unit will do its own. Each entity develops its own style and corporate culture. With a possibility of moving from one company unit to another, career builders could be blessed with a good deal of mobility.

It seems like a lot to ask for, but anything is possible. The world is moving faster than any of us realize.

Myth 14: *Success Is Guaranteed to Those Willing to Work Hard and Put in Long Hours.*

Reality: *The old put-your-back-to-the-wheel puritan work ethic won't take you the distance. There are other components to the success equation.*

Chapter Snapshot

☐ Successful People Are Overly Aggressive

☐ Creativity and Success Go Hand-in-Hand

☐ Ten Success Traits

☐ Success Takes Luck and Other Half-Myths

☐ Are You Sure You're Up for the Joust?—The Dark Side of Success

☐ Find Your Own Comfortable Stride

❋ ❋ ❋ ❋ ❋ ❋ ❋ ❋

Blame the puritan work ethic for planting the seeds of this myth. The Puritans believed in the sanctity of honest work. Hard work bears its own intrinsic virtues, they said. That's true to a point, but it certainly won't guarantee success.

Ask those who have made it and they'll tell you quite candidly that the route to the top requires more than hard work and long hours. After all, there are bricklayers and carpenters putting in 12-hour days, but they're not tooling around in Rolls-Royces. The majority of farmers across the country toil from sunrise to sunset just to stay afloat and meet their mortgage payments. Success to many means just breaking even.

It's time all the clichés you've been spoon-fed since you were a kid were blown to smithereens, like: "Put your heart and soul into your work," "Don't be lazy," "Only the strong survive," on and on. No matter what you were told, hard work alone won't make you rich and powerful.

We love stories about the taming of the frontier and how, around the turn of the century, powerful rugged individualists launched tiny companies that evolved into full-blown industries. Hollywood films and a slew of popular novels only portray the brawn side of the success equation, which actually accounts for only about 20 percent of the picture. The other success components are seldom mentioned.

A lot of mythology surrounds success. Let's look at it and then identify common attributes shared by many successful people.

First, two mini-myths about successful people.

Successful People Are Overly Aggressive

Immediately robber baron legends Andrew Carnegie and Henry Ford come to mind. Most people don't know that much about them, yet they've heard stories about how they ripped people off and robbed, cheated and manipulated in order to amass their fortunes. We eat these stories up because they confirm the myths about rich people we've heard since we were kids. "If ya wanna make it big, you've got to have a killer instinct so you can pounce on people to get ahead." Or, "Most people who went anywhere in life have lied and cheated."

The conclusion is that successful people elevate aggression to a blood sport. If you believe all this, you've found a safe harbor for your inadequacies. It's the perfect rationalization for never trying.

The reality is many successful people are aggressive. Face it, it takes *chutzpah* to get heard, especially if you're peddling something new. It takes energy and guts to scream louder than everyone else to get your point across. That's why successful people are perceived as pushy. Knowing full well the world isn't waiting for them, they realize if they don't push their product, nobody will.

And isn't it human nature to reject anything new? Poor Columbus had quite a time convincing the nobility that he wouldn't fall off the face of the earth on his voyage to the Indies. If he wasn't pushy, he wouldn't have discovered America and proved the world was round. And you wouldn't be curled up in an easy chair enjoying this book.

Then there is the stream of endless inventions that changed the way we live and work. When the Wright brothers said they built a machine that flies, most people thought they were nuts. A maxim of success: The weirder the idea or product, the more aggressive you have to be.

But don't confuse aggressiveness and underhandedness. They are continents apart. Aggression is tolerable to a point, but cutthroat, underhanded tactics are reprehensible—no matter what the mission. There are sharks and vipers out there who'd sell their kids to get ahead. They lack conscience, morals, ethics, you name it. They figure whatever it takes to get ahead, short of bodily harm (and sometimes including it), is okay. The longer you play the game, the faster you'll be able to spot these sharks.

Yet the majority of successful people play it straight. Some are painfully shy introverts; a few are idiot savants. They do one thing extremely well. Everything else in their lives is pretty conventional right down to the Wednesday night bowling outing with the "gang."

Creativity and Success Go Hand-in-Hand

Many successful people are wildly creative. Some designed inventions, systems or products that changed or improved our lives. Inventors such as Thomas Edison and Alexander Graham Bell come to mind or entrepreneurs such as Kentucky Fried Chicken's Colonel Arland Sanders, Apple Computer's Steve Jobs, Microsoft's Bill Gates and a slew of others. These men built something new.

But they represent only a small minority. Many successful people don't have a creative bone in their bodies. They became successful because they had special talents, abilities or skills which they perfected. Some stockbrokers I know fit this description to a tee. A few that come to mind are not the least bit creative, but became rich because they loved the market and had the good sense to listen to people smarter than themselves. Two brokers I know well work for major national brokerage houses. Both only recommend stocks endorsed by their brokerage houses. They work conventional 9-to-5 business hours, and their daily routines seldom vary. Their success rests on a large clientele which they built following conventional investment philosophies.

One man is a commodity expert, a specialist who spent most of his career watching and studying the frenetic and highly sensitive commodity market. Traditional brokers get fired up over high-potential stocks; this man is ecstatic when soybean calls rise one-eighth of a point because of torrid weather conditions in the Midwest. His life revolves around coffee, pork bellies, wheat and soybean investments, which he follows compulsively seven days a week. When he tries to explain the commodity market, hardly anyone understands what he's talking about, not even his wife.

In short, these are quiet, restrained, understated people who spend their vacations in Palm Beach and their weekends playing golf at posh country clubs.

Now that we've dusted off those mini-myths, let's look at 10 common traits shared by successful people. Keep in mind the traits outlined below are not shared by all successful people. As we said in

Myth 12, success is relative, holding different meanings depending upon your take on life. To one person, it means a secure job paying $75,000 a year; to someone else it's running a business and pulling down a million-dollar salary. Suffice it to say, many successful people will have three or four of the below traits; others who wield enormous power and run billion-dollar companies may have them all. You might want to do a rough check on which ones you share—and which you don't.

Ten Success Traits

1. A Love of the Game, the Thrill of Winning

Successful people and athletes have a lot in common. They both love to win. Some seem to need to win, which is a pretty strong propellant. It's not just with their work, it's with everything. Competing is food and drink for them. It's a thirst for the chase, which is practically a biological drive.

An owner of a small regional chain of sporting goods stores who bikes for recreation says he finds himself competing at biking as well. A Saturday morning, 30-mile bike ride often turns competitive when he encounters other bikers. As soon as younger bikers pass him, the entrepreneur suddenly thinks he's Greg Lemond in the heat of the Tour de France. The 45-year-old biker rarely overtakes a squadron of more athletic bikers in their twenties; nevertheless he gives it everything he has, enjoying every minute.

As far as he's concerned, winning is a self-instilled commandment. It doesn't matter what he's doing—running a business, biking, playing poker, or even casually walking down the street—he's consumed by getting there first.

Although all successful people are not as compulsive about winning as this sporting goods store owner, they all share a love of the game and a need to be the best at whatever they do. Whether they sell a product or service, they're consumed with constantly improving.

Many successful people say that street smarts and gut instinct guide them through the game. Yet, they're not quite sure how it works. They never know how they'll confront problems or how decisions will be made. It's like tennis players trying to forecast what strategies they'll use against opponents. The moment of truth comes when a ball is fired at them at 50 miles per hour. If they return the ball and win the set, they've made a good decision; if they miss it, they've blown it. Many successful people make these kinds of decisions all day long.

They relish every tense, sweaty moment. Stockbrokers certainly do. Forget about what technicians, analysts and economists say the market is going to do. They're making educated guesses. Brokers often have to be contrarians and act on their own instincts.

In fact, many successful people are so masterful at playing their particular game, they don't even know they are playing it. It's second nature, intuitive. Yet most admit it's not a trait they were born with but something they've been unconsciously polishing since childhood.

2. The Vision Thing Meets the Mission Thing

Like the cliché says, "Ideas are a dime a dozen." I can't tell you how many times I've heard people say, "Boy, do I have a great idea for a novel. Incredible! Right? Why, it could make millions!" Or "I have a brilliant idea for a product. No one has done it. The market is just waiting for it. This will turn the world upside down." On and on. That's where it stops. They'll talk about their idea to anyone who'll listen and yet never put any effort into its execution. That's the painful part.

Typically, great ideas for products, books, inventions or companies are seldom talked about by their creators. As the successful Nike ad says, "Just Do It!" Nike Inc.'s founder and CEO Phil Knight has a reputation for being a loner and a bit odd, a man who answers questions in monosyllables. Actually, Knight is not a loner, just a private person who'd rather listen than speak. He personifies the catchy trademark ad for his company, which helps explain why Nike is one of the world's largest sports and fitness companies. Like many successful people, Knight bridges vision and mission.

In *Peak Performers,* Charles Garfield talks about how peak performers have flashes of insight, or a vision, about achieving something before outlining a plan to make it happen. The challenge, says Garfield, is analyzing the insight and outlining the steps turning the vision into reality. He says the first move to building a powerful mission is exercising a vision.

The vision is an abstraction, lacking depth, breadth and shape. The challenge is taking a filmy, ghostlike abstraction and breathing life into it. It takes intricate manipulation of ideas and concepts, honing them through several stages until they become tangible. The goal is finding the bridge linking vision and mission. That bridge is what separates the leaders from the followers.

That's why business consultants drive home the importance of a business plan's mission statement. The mission statement defines the business's vision, spelling out how it will be realized. Some entrepreneurs' mission statements go into great depth describing when and how goals will be achieved, even projecting future sales 10 years ahead. One successful entrepreneur heading an international retail shoe chain said he religiously redefines his vision statement every 5 years so it adjusts to changing markets and economies.

Konosuke Matsushita, the late founder of Matsushita Electric Industrial Company, Ltd., one of the largest consumer and industrial electronics corporations in the world (launched in 1918), wrote a 250-year plan in 25-year segments. How's that for thinking ahead? The more precise the mission statement, the greater the likelihood of success.

The process of turning abstract visions into missions can be likened to envisioning a disassembled crossword puzzle in your head. You can see the pieces scattered around; the nerve-racking part is fitting them together. Yet this is how many companies start. First, entrepreneurs envision a product or service before mentally designing, building, promoting and distributing it. The uncanny thing is they're able to break the project down into enough pieces to limit trial-and-error fumbling. There will be setbacks and errors, but the vision is clear enough to take the amorphous skeleton and turn it into an achievable mission.

What's fascinating about this process is that it can't be packaged. You can teach someone how to run a business, but you can't tell someone how to design a product or service, write a book or invent something. All you can do is outline vague information-gathering steps. The kind of information needed and where to find it amount to a judgment call. There is no order or method to the process.

When a vision isn't clear, the mission falters. It often means going back to the drawing board to refine the vision and sand the rough edges until it's right. If you're lucky, the vision is radiantly clear with success dead ahead. But that's rare indeed. Often missions have to be aborted because the timing is wrong. No matter how brilliant your product, the world may not be ready for it. It may be too far-out. If compact disks were marketed in the '60s rather than the '80s, they would have died.

Finally, mission plays a role in career building as well. Some of us have a clear vision of our career goals. You may want to be a market analyst, brand manager, police officer, cowboy, safecracker, advertising copywriter, or you may want to own a software company, newspaper or work with inner-city kids through a nonprofit company. Others have to search for their mission; some never find it.

One thing is certain—it's an essential key to success. Keep this in mind when planning your career. Success isn't one-dimensional. It's not breaking your back, becoming a millionaire before you reach 35 and owning a convoy of expensive cars. It's being propelled to achieve something you believe in and love. Your entire life may be devoted to one mission, or there may be several as you experience job and career changes. Again, there are no rules.

3. Total Commitment to a Mission

Successful people aren't casually committed to their mission, they're passionately driven to achieve it. Libraries are filled with thousands of biographies about men and women who abandoned eating and sleeping to achieve a goal. Like inspired inventors, entrepreneurs totally dedicate their lives to achieving their missions. Everything else takes a back seat. Garfield singles out the founders of IBM (Thomas Watson, Sr.) and Apple Computer (Jobs) as inspired visionaries. Watson envisioned the intricate details of a computer 15 years before the word was used. Fifty years later, Jobs's vision was to build a computer that was simple and fun to use. People laughed at both men. Computers, who could have imagined they'd catch on? As for simplicity, there's no way computers could be made simple enough for children to use. The results speak for themselves. Today, IBM and Apple Computer are as well known as Corn Flakes and Hershey Bars.

It doesn't matter whether you're making computers, automobiles, fried chicken or rubber bands, there is no such thing as part-time commitment to a mission. It's an all-consuming obsession.

4. Thinking Big—The Benefits of Parallel Thinking

How do you make decisions? Do you think sequentially or multidimensionally? Do you see one answer or several? When you plan a course of action, do you consider how your actions affect just yourself or others as well?

If you chose the latter answer to the above questions, you have the potential to be successful. Generally speaking, successful people have the unique ability to see things on a large scale. They are not intimidated by the word *big*. They can see the whole picture, envisioning how all the parts work together. Corporate managers and entrepreneurs describe the thrill of building something from scratch, conquering tight deadlines, delegating authority and pulling together all the strings of a complex project.

Most successful people think along parallel lines. Rather than finding one solution to a problem, they see many with multiple benefits. When they encounter obstacles, they'll stay up nights seeking solutions. It all comes back to the insatiable need to win, conquer and be the best.

And successful people are all about furthering their careers. We all define ourselves by the work we do. To most successful people, a career is closer to an intimate reading of inner strivings and secret longings to conquer and acquire, rather than merely a job. Some identify so strongly with their careers, they're like lost children when removed from their work. Ask them what their work means to them and they'll shower you with explanations. It's not just momentary gratification and financial rewards, but a learning experience, an opportunity to meet people and the thrill of taking risks, leading and inspiring others. It's also the intense need to push themselves to the furthest possible point.

5. Unafraid of Success

Another mini-myth: Everyone wants to be successful. Wrong. Some people are terrified of success. The reasons are complex and varied. They don't feel they are worthy of responsibility, money and power. As kids, they were told success breeds greed and selfishness, a dangerous addiction. Once hooked, there is no turning back. You turn ugly. You're never satisfied. There is no such thing as enough power or money. If this is drummed into you since childhood, by the time you're an adult, you believe it. You actually think folks living in big houses on the right side of the tracks are corrupt. "You know what they had to do to get where they are? They lied, stole and stepped on all the little people to get there. Thankfully, your mom and dad have real values."

It's scary, but real people are actually saying the above. Fear of success is wedded to the money hang-ups discussed in Myth 11.

How do you feel about success? You don't have to thirst for it 24 hours a day, but if you're violently opposed or afraid of it, ask yourself why. Your answers could tell you a lot about yourself.

6. Set Achievable Goals

As grandiose as their missions, successful people see the playing field realistically enough to set bite-size goals. As much as they want to conquer the world within a single business day, they're disciplined enough to pull in the reins and take it one tiny step at a time. That's no simple feat to someone who wants to fly when forced to crawl.

Whether it's a new business or a career, success ultimately hinges on moving cautiously in the beginning so you make few mistakes and do not get sidetracked. If you're a business, it's never straying far from the goals outlined in the mission statement; for career builders, it's playing it day by day and being prepared for the unexpected.

7. Relish Responsibility

Would you like to manage a department, division or an entire company? Or command a multimillion-dollar budget? Or have hundreds of people depending upon your every decision? Think about it.

Not everyone can cope with massive doses of responsibility. And it's no personality deficit if you can't either. Just holding a job and keeping a family intact is enough responsibility for most of us.

Among the very successful, responsibility and power are inseparable. It's as important as fat paychecks and awesome perks. The successful are willing to delegate authority, yet they're ready to accept full responsibility if something goes awry. You're a hero if you make a good decision, yet fortunes are lost and empires are shattered by bad decisions. Not everyone has the stomach to make these judgment calls on a daily basis and still sleep nights.

8. Strong Belief in Self

Successful people are often called tough-skinned, callous or hard-nosed. That's another mini-myth. Some successful people are tough as nails; others are soft as butter. What most people see as toughness is actually self-confidence. They may be total wimps, but when it comes to their business, career, craft, sport or whatever made them successful, they're in total control. They know they're good at what they do and are not beyond letting you know it.

They're also secure enough to take criticism, a trait many of us have to improve. In the journey to self-betterment, they've learned criticism is vital to self-improvement. To perfect their product, they constantly ask other people's opinions and reactions. "Well, how did I do?" "Did you like the product?" "What's wrong with it?" "How could it be improved?"

Secure enough in their own abilities and strengths, they've learned to constructively deal with defeat and rejection. That's a tall order. Nobody likes to screw up. Recognizing and examining yourself to find explanations is the painful part. No matter how strong your ego, rejection and defeat smart.

Accompanying that strong belief in self is a sense of resiliency. Successful people love recounting all the doors slammed in their face. Each door pried open helped make their victory all the more enjoyable. The more resistance they met, the more determined they became. It's reminiscent of the mythical Hollywood prizefighter, pummeled and bleeding on the canvas, who miraculously finds the energy to muster enough strength in the last seconds of the fifteenth round to knock out his opponent. Can't you hear Sylvester Stallone shouting "Adrianne" (*Rocky*, 1976) as thousands of fans applaud? It may not be all that dramatic, but successful people often say there is something cleansing about defeat. Overcoming it takes an epiphany, a mental, physical and even a spiritual awakening. As your folks said, nobody said it would be easy.

9. Astute Selling Abilities

As we said in Myth 7, just try to rise to the top without finely honed selling abilities. It's as basic as the concept that success hinges on how well you sell yourself. If you don't sell, you don't succeed. Conceiving the widget is the first step. Convincing others to buy it is the tough part. If it's radically different from anything on the market, you face an uphill battle.

There is comfort in sticking with the status quo. The thinking is: If something works, leave it alone. Charles Schwab faced that hurdle in 1974 when he launched his discount brokerage house, The Charles Schwab Corporation, to provide better and cheaper services than his full-service competitors. Back then, discount brokerage was considered a third-rate, bargain-counter substitute compared to the giant full-service brokerage houses. Discount brokerage was likened to a bare essential cheap motel without luxurious extras. Most discount brokerage houses offered no research facilities or portfolio management, standard accoutrements of the full-service houses.

Schwab, however, gave customers incredible prices and a raft of services. He prided himself on exceptional customer service plus the latest in information technology. Investing heavily in advertising, Schwab got his message across within a few years. His company took off, and Schwab was heralded as a pioneer. Today, his company is the leading discount broker in the United States, controlling 45 percent of the discount market.

It doesn't matter whether you're selling yourself, a product or a service. To achieve success, someone has to buy what you're peddling. Along with tactful aggression, you have to be prepared to sell your heart out and play the political games that make success possible.

10. Strong Political Consciousness

Politics, the business of high-stake schmoozing and winning people over, isn't for everyone. But the measure of success, how far you go on the career scale, is directly correlated to your stomach for politics. Not everyone can play power games.

Don't say you're in a nonpolitical field. That field doesn't exist. Even painters, composers and poets must wage political battles if they want to succeed. Art does not transcend politics. Politics is a part of life. Painters who hope to build a reputation must also suck up to the right financial people. They're playing the same intense political games corporate executives play on a different playing field. They're asking identical questions. Who should I know to get my paintings out there? Who wields power? How do I reach them?

Even the not-for-profit sector is rife with politics. Many experts in the field contend it's more political than the corporate arena because it operates under the guise of do-goodism. The myth is these folks have supposedly transcended political intrigue because they've dedicated their lives to helping people, rather than pursuing the almighty buck. If you believe that one, you'll believe your children could marry aliens. Many of the not-for-profit professionals lust for power as aggressively as their corporate counterparts. The only difference is they're embarrassed to be up-front about it.

Regardless of endeavor, the power brokers of the world learn to be masterful politicians. An organization can be likened to a playing field. The political players check out the other teams for their strengths and weaknesses. Who are the leaders and followers? Where are the conservative, liberal and radical forces? What team do the leaders belong to and who are the influential spokespeople? Who controls the grapevine?

If you're hell-bent on moving up the ladder, being identified with the wrong political faction is the equivalent of being sentenced to organizational purgatory.

Success Takes Luck and Other Half-Myths

Real people win lotteries. A convenient out for not trying to be successful is believing success is based solely on luck. Or if you're not in the right place at the right time, you don't stand a chance.

Balancing these clichés are the sages who preach "You make your own luck." Who's right? They all are.

To a large extent, we create opportunities for ourselves by knowing the right people, working for good companies and hanging out in the right watering holes. Career-long networking doesn't hurt either.

You're going to be very disappointed if you wait for luck to knock on your door. Yet, there are also mysterious, unexplainable things that happen to us in the course of a lifetime. They defy logic or reason. Winning a lottery is a spectacular example. The odds are often a million-to-one that your number will come up. One day, you're agonizing over where you're going to find the money to get credit card bills off your back and the next you're sitting on a $40 million bank account. That's luck.

Yet lucky souls win lotteries every day. Needless to say, the event changes their lives. The important thing to remember is your chances of winning are no better or no worse than anyone else's.

Even on a mundane everyday plane, inexplicable things happen to us. Miraculously, we just happen to be in the right place at the right time to receive a call or meet someone that gives us a job, an account or a major sale that temporarily or significantly changes our lives. You figure it? It defies logic.

Or take kooky gadgets like the Hoola-Hoop, Slinky or Pet Rock that just happened to catch on. These were products of the moment. MBA-toting market researchers couldn't have forecasted that the world was ready for them. Somehow, these off-the-wall products caught on. They were funny, silly and totally useless. Maybe that's precisely why they were successful. Could they have made it if introduced now? Probably not.

No matter how cynical you are, luck exists. Accept it or not, there are people who have the Midas touch. You can't make yourself lucky, but you can open yourself up to it by realizing it can happen to anyone—even you. It's not just the other guy who gets lucky. That other guy could be *you*. The instinctive networkers of the world, for one, are more prone to luck because they're always cultivating new contacts. As we said in Myth 4, networking is not only for when you're looking for a new job, it's for 7 days a week.

Are You Sure You're Up for the Joust?— The Dark Side of Success

Despite the lip service we give the word, earth-moving success isn't everyone's game. Not everyone lusts for fast cars, boats and ocean-front homes—not enough to dedicate their lives to their pursuit.

Money isn't the root of all evil, but money is a measure of success. And, success also has a dark side. The multimillionaire head of a national office supply company put it this way: "People envy me. They think I have it all. All they see is the stuff I've acquired. They don't understand I've sacrificed a social life and short-changed my family to get it."

Others avoid this trap by finding a balance between their personal and business lives. No matter how much you love your career, there are other things in life.

Find Your Own Comfortable Stride

See the playing field clearly. Ask yourself who you're competing against. Is it yourself or others? Don't underestimate either one. They're both formidable foes.

Before we wind down, remember success is relative. There are many ways to play the career game. You can go at it half-heartedly and take your chances or you can put into it everything you have. It's up to you. Take this journalist's advice: Find your own comfortable stride and stick to it. If it works for you, you've achieved career nirvana. Don't try and live anyone's life but your own. Everyone doesn't share the same appetite for the fast lane.

Or take the advice of the world's largest retailer, the late billionaire Sam Walton, founder of Walmart. In his autobiography, *Sam Walton: Made in America,* he passes on many pearls of wisdom. Two of my favorites are to ignore conventional wisdom and celebrate your successes. Walton's message is that no matter how complicated life gets, don't lose sight of what's important. Find your own path and most important, *have fun.* Career building involves stress, frustration, disappointment, failure and rejection, yet the rewards of finding and building something you love makes it all worth while. No matter how rough things get, don't ever lose sight of that fact.

Epilogue: You Got the Job, Now What?

Chapter Snapshot

- [ ] Job Tune-Up
- [ ] Strategies While Employed
- [ ] The Game Isn't Over

✽ ✽ ✽ ✽ ✽ ✽ ✽ ✽

Congratulations! You've arrived. You're hired. You have a job. Now what?

Enjoy the victory for a while, then keep your eyes open. Don't mistakenly think you've found a permanent home. Odds say its only a stopover. For how long is anyone's guess. Getting too comfortable can be dangerous. It can lead to sloppiness, complacency and a loss of control.

Job Tune-Up

Just as you tune up a car after driving it a few thousand miles, you should apply the same principles to your career. Every 6 months find out if you're on course by asking yourself these questions:

1. What do I like about this job?
2. What don't I like about it?
3. What am I learning?
4. Are the skills transferable?
5. How far can I go?
6. Am I challenged?
7. Do I like the people I work with?
8. Is management supportive?
9. Am I earning enough money?

10. Could I earn more elsewhere?

11. Are there better options out there?

Be honest with yourself. Don't try to justify a bad situation. Six months on the job ought to be enough time to give you an honest reading.

Don't expect a rave review. As I said, the perfect job doesn't exist. The big question is: Do the job's pluses overshadow its minuses? If they don't, it's time to think about saddling your horse and moving on down that lonesome highway.

Strategies While Employed

Operate from a Position of Strength

Remember what we said earlier—a job is no security blanket. This may be your fantasy job, and you could be with your current employer for your entire career. Or you could be pounding the pavement next year—even next month. Either way, know what's happening on the street. Never stop monitoring the job market. You never know, there may be a *better* job with your name on it.

Even though you're working for someone else, make sure you, not your employer, is controlling your destiny. Although it's great having that weekly paycheck coming in like clockwork, don't become overly dependent on it. Don't allow yourself to be seduced by the bureaucratic security web many companies spin around their workers. Companies love telling you, "We're all one big family." They don't tell you that it's only as long as profits are rolling in or the company avoids mergers, takeovers or reorganizations.

The conditions of the past two years should have made us all street-wise and taught us two basic maxims about careers and job hunting:

1. Don't believe everything companies tell you.

2. No matter how talented, smart, innovative or creative you are, you are dispensable.

Take the hint and operate from a position of strength by being in control at all times. Keep your antennae up so you know what's happening around you.

Build Your Network

Never stop building your network. Keep it current by adding and subtracting names as you go along. When a potential resource surfaces, follow up and develop it. There is no limit to the size of your network.

Periodically go over your contact list to make sure it's current. Eliminate people who are no longer valuable and replace them with new ones who are.

Keep Track of Accomplishments

Keep track of your accomplishments. You never know when you'll have to jump ship for a better job. The idea is to have your life jacket—your credentials—handy so you can whip up a strong selling letter without having to wrack your brains trying to remember every brilliant thing you accomplished.

More efficient than a job diary is an accomplishment file. As long as your accomplishments are clearly documented, it doesn't matter whether it's a paper or computer file. An accomplishment file ought to include the following information:

1. Date of accomplishment.

2. Description of event. People involved, length, costs, your role, lessons learned.

3. The effect accomplishment had on the company and yourself. Did it save time or money, boost sales? Were you rewarded?

Finally, keep all documentation and correspondence that proves your worth. Letters from clients congratulating you on an excellent job, awards, citations and membership in a select group of employees are valuable when trying to impress prospective employers.

Create an Emergency Fund

It doesn't hurt to have "just-in-case" money handy if the sky should fall and you find yourself pounding the pavement again. It's happening every day, and just because you think you have the job of the century, don't be naive and think the situation can't change overnight.

Put aside a comfortable amount of your earnings each week for an unemployed emergency fund. The more you sock away, the better off you'll be. Rather than let it sit in a bank, consider certificates of deposits or mutual funds for greater appreciation.

The Game Isn't Over

Finally, the game isn't over. More likely than not, the job you're in will be another notch on your experience belt. Make the best of it.

Never forget that career building is one of the best games in town. Yes, it's serious, time consuming and hard work. But like Sam Walton said, it also should be fun. Keep that in mind and the sky is the limit. As I said, money ought not be the sole reason for working. Equally if not more important is personal fulfillment and satisfaction.

Good luck.

Index